D1570928

THE WARREN-FLEW DEBATE

ON THE EXISTENCE OF GOD

A four-night, oral debate held in the Coliseum on the campus of North Texas State University, September 20-23, 1976.

DR. ANTONY G. N. FLEW, Professor of Philosophy, Reading University, England.

DR. THOMAS B. WARREN, Professor of Philosophy of Religion and Apologetics, Harding Graduate School of Religion, Memphis, Tennessee.

NATIONAL CHRISTIAN PRESS

P.O. Box 1001 Jonesboro, Arkansas 72401

THE WARREN-FLEW DEBATE

Printed by McQuiddy Printing Co., Nashville

DEDICATION

To all who love truth and who are willing to make the search to find it.

—The Publishers

You are encouraged to study the following points of interest in the Warren—Flew Debate.

Study Dr. Flew's comments on Loch Ness Monsters, Centaurs, round squares and fairies (pp. 1—4, 23) which he uses in discussing logical and contingent impossibilities. Notice that he takes a bold atheistic position in his first affirmative speech (pp.1 & 5), then in his first negative speech he says he has difficulty with this position (p.143), and then in his fifth negative speech he says "there has got to be someone else for this monkey trial" (p. 222).

Study the questions which Dr. Warren submitted to Dr. Flew and the answers he gave to them. These are found in the appendix. Notice carefully the charts Dr. Warren used, especially the charts on pp. 8—9, 57—62, 113—117, 159, 217.

It is our conviction that if you will carefully and thoughtfully study this debate, you will have no difficulty in deciding which position is logical, consistent and true. If you desire further information on these vital subjects, write the following address.

THE INSTITUTE FOR THE ADVANCEMENT OF CHRISTIAN THEISM
3333 Old Brownsville Road
Memphis, Tennessee 38134

PRELIMINARY STATEMENTS

Publisher's Statement

On the campus of North Texas State University in Denton, Texas, from September 20 through September 23, 1976, a public debate of considerable significance occurred. The two disputants in this discussion were Dr. A. G. N. Flew, Professor of Philosophy in the University of Reading, Reading, England and Dr. Thomas B. Warren, Professor of Philosophy of Religion and Christian Apologetics, in Harding Graduate School of Religion, Memphis, Tennessee.

This debate was of significance because, among other reasons, the propositions affirmed by the respective disputants so plainly stated the real issue which obtains between thorough-going (positive) atheism and thorough-going (Biblical) theism. Professor Flew affirmed, "I know that God does not exist," and Professor Warren affirmed, "I know that God does exist."

The reader of this debate must remember that this was a *spoken* (oral) debate. Therefore, the various speeches of the two disputants will not have the grammatical smoothness which written material would have. The two disputants were allowed to make small changes in the word-for-word manuscripts when these changes would help the readers to follow the basic point being made by the respective disputants. Neither disputant was allowed to make any change which would change the thought or basic thrust of any point made. Neither disputant was allowed to delete any word, phrase, etc. which would remove a significant point. Thus, the reader has in this book a faithful reproduction of the debate.

It is our conviction that this debate can make a considerable contribution to the study of the question as to whether God exists.

According to an agreement signed by the two disputants before the actual debate began, each of them was to have the privilege (not obligation) of asking, in writing, as many as *ten questions* of his opponent.

These questions, if used, were to be given to the respective opponent no later than thirty minutes before the beginning of the speeches each evening. The person being questioned was then to answer the questions in writing and to return them with his answers to the questions no later than ten minutes before the beginning of the speeches. Dr. Warren, exercising this right, submitted questions to Dr. Flew each evening. Dr. Flew chose not to exercise this right.

Both disputants also had the right to use *charts* to illustrate various points being made. Again Dr. Warren exercised this right, and Dr. Flew did not.

The format for the debate was as follows: (1) each disputant had three twenty-minute speeches each evening (delivered alternately, with the affirmative speaker each evening delivering the first speech and (2) the affirmative speaker had a one and one-half minute rejoinder to close the debate each evening.

The debate was well attended. Reliable estimates were that the audiences ranged in number from five thousand to in excess of seven thousand.

The debate was video-taped (in full color). These tapes are available for purchase and/or rental from National Christian Press, Inc.

(The following statements, by various persons, were made on the opening night of the debate, just prior to the first speech of the debate itself.)

Statement by Hollis Adams

Welcome to the first night of the four night "Debate of the Century." My name is Hollis Adams. I represent a student organization here on the campus of North Texas State University called DAWN. We are a Christian student organization both on North Texas and T. W. U. We work under the oversight of the Elders of the University Church of Christ with the Bible Chair Directors. Our Bible Chair Director for North Texas is Rex Dean, the producer of the debate, if he would at this time stand up. (Applause) And the T. W. U. Bible Chair Director, the coordinator for the debate is Gary Ealy. At this time he will come to the microphone. (Applause)

Statement by Gary Ealy

Without taking a lot of time, I feel that it is necessary to say "thank you" to a number of people who have worked very diligently to bring this debate to this point. I would like to say, first of all, "thanks" to the University Church of Christ and the Elders there who have overseen the work that has gone on for this debate. It is by their approval that we are having it.

Secondly, to the staff, to Perry Hall and to Ree Hall—who are our minister and secretary—for the hard work that they have done; and thirdly, to Rex Dean. We appreciate that very much. We want to thank also all the Churches of Christ and individuals who are members of the Church who have sent contributions in order to enable us to have the funds to conduct an event of this magnitude.

The proposition for tonight simply reads "I Know That God Does Not Exist." The affirmative speaker tonight is Dr. A. G. N. Flew. He is Professor of Philosophy at the University of Reading near London, England. He received his Doctor of Letters degree from the University of Keele. His moderator throughout the debate will be Dr. Pete Gunter, Professor of Philosophy here at North Texas State University and is the Chairman of the Philosophy Department. He received his doctorate at Yale University.

Dr. Thomas B. Warren will be the negative speaker the first two nights. He is a Professor of Philosophy at the Harding Graduate School of Religion in Memphis, Tennessee. He received his doctorate in philosophy from Vanderbilt University. The moderator throughout the debate for Dr. Warren will be Dr. James D. Bales, Professor of Christian Doctrine at Harding College. Dr. Bales received his doctorate from the University of California at Berkeley. Our Chairman for this debate is Dr. J. E. Barnhart, Professor of Philosophy here at North Texas State University; he received his doctorate from Boston University. We are thrilled that so many have come to hear this debate.

At this time I want to give the two disputants an opportunity to say whatever they may desire to say before this debate officially begins. Since Dr. Flew is in the affirmative tonight, we are going to give him a minute or so to make any comments he would like to prior to our discussion. Immediately following that, Dr. Warren will make any comments he would like to make, and then we will begin the debate without any further comment.

Dr. Flew's Introductory Statement

I have, I think, only two things to say at this moment. The first is how glad I am to be in Texas again, and the second is to point out a difference, as I see it, between this debate and those presidential debates which will be occurring in the next week or so. I take it that both parties to the presidential debates will be concerned almost exclusively with the possibility of getting people to shift from one side to the other; and their success or failure will certainly in the eyes of the participants be judged by the number of votes that go to the Republican or to the Democratic candidate in November.

My attitude to the debate tonight is that perhaps there will be someone either on Dr. Warren's side of the house or perhaps on mine, who will be led by the debate to change their theological or antitheological position. I do not think there will be many people like that. What I hope, and in my optimistic moments expect, is that most people will go away having got one or two things clearer, having seen for the first time that there is some important distinction that has got to be made in their thinking in this area, or having seen that some old favorite argument will not do. I think it is perfectly possible that Dr. Warren will show some person who is not a member of the Church of Christ something that they have not seen before. And maybe I will do it the other way around. Certainly I look on the thing rather differently from the presidential debates.

Dr. Warren's Introductory Statement

I would just like to express my appreciation for the wonderful opportunity to be a disputant in this debate—and for the presence of so many which indicates an interest in things beyond the ordinary things, matters which transcend the purely physical. I am happy to be involved in this discussion because I have such high regard for the scholarship of the man who is my opponent in this discussion, and I assure you that every word that I shall speak will be from love and concern for *him* as well as for everyone else. I have not the slightest bit of animosity toward him personally. I have great admiration for *him* as a scholar, though, of course, you understand—from the very fact that we are here—that I do not agree with his *position*. He and I will agree, I take it, that every person should study the evidence and draw only the conclusion that is warranted by that evidence. That is in harmony with what it means to be a Christian and it is in harmony with what I will try to do throughout this discussion.

Table of Contents

FLEW'S FIRST AFFIRMATIVE

(Monday Night)

Since I arrived in Texas around noon on Saturday, I have been enjoying, as I am sure all Texans here would both hope and expect, a lot of real Texan hospitality. In the intervals of watching a rodeo, attending a Unitarian church, and having—because the rains stopped the proposed cook-out—an indoor barbecue, there has been talk both about the presidential election and about this four-day debate here in Denton. It has nothing to the present point. But I think that many of the people I have been meeting with have been a little surprised to discover that my own political and social attitudes are in many ways much more conservative than those of your Eastern intellectual establishment.

What is to the present point is that some people, both those inclining to Dr. Warren's side in this debate and those inclining to my opposite side, have been surprised and even a little shocked to find me proposing a straight atheist resolution—"I know there is no God"—rather than something more cautiously agnostic—"I do not think the thing is proved, or even can be proved, either way; and anyway do not expect me to stand up to be counted." It seems that the best way for me to fill this first Flew slot is to begin to try to explain why I now take this atheist stand; and, incidentally why I think that many other people who live much as I live, and believe and disbelieve pretty much what I believe and disbelieve, ought similarily to describe themselves not as agnostics, as they mostly do, but as atheists. My father, who was a Methodist minister of religion, always used to argue that the word "atheist" was the more correct description. I now agree that on this he was right and I am hopeful that this is the first of many points on which Dr. Warren and I will be happily seeing eye to eye.

So let us begin the business of trying to explain and to justify the bold atheist rather than the more respectably cautious "agnostic." Consider four sorts of case in which people might want to say that some particular thing or some sort of thing does not exist—that there ain't no such thing. I shall take these four possible cases in order of increasing difficulty. The first and easiest I think of as the Loch Ness monster or the Abominable Snowman case. Here there is no problem, or not much problem, about what is in question. Some people believe, or even claim to know, that there are large denizens of the deep in Loch Ness in Scotland, or, in the other case, that there are still some unrecognized and unclassified creatures, two-legged and about human size but not actually human, in the high Himalayas. Other people of course believe, or even incautiously claim to know, that this is all rubbish, that there is no such thing as a Loch Ness monster or an Abominable Snowman. And in this case there is a third group inclined to say that there is not yet enough evidence, or that what evidence there is is conflicting, and that the only sensible position at this time is to be agnostic about the existence of a Loch Ness monster or Abominable Snowman. But in this first and simplest case no one is saying that it is in any sense impossible that there should be such creatures. And we all know perfectly well the sort of thing that is being affirmed. Another perhaps rather less memorable example of this first kind would be: "Are there, or are there still, any wolves in Manitoba?" There is nothing unfamiliar or impossible about wolves. But there may be ignorance or disagreement as to whether there are, or are still, any in Manitoba.

Now, that is the first and easiest case. I do not believe that that has any direct relevance to our present and much more difficult discussion. But it has to be mentioned in order to distinguish it from two other cases which are directly relevant.

The second of my four is again similar to the first in not being directly relevant. But I have to mention it in order to distinguish it from the third and the fourth. This second case differs from the first in that it provides an occasion to make one of those fundamental distinctions which I mentioned earlier, a distinction of which much more will surely be heard as our discussion proceeds. Now, the first case, as you will remember, was that in which it is suggested that there are creatures of such and such a kind here, or there, or everywhere; and where there is no problem about understanding this suggestion; and where the only question is whether or not there are in fact such creatures. The second case is the same as the first, except that now the suggestion is that it is in fact impossible that there should be creatures of the sort in question. Take for example the suggestion that there are centaurs. Everyone knows that the centaur is a fabulous beast, the head and shoulders being the head and shoulders of a man or a woman, and the rest of the body being the body of a horse or a mare. We can of course say that no one has ever met a centaur; or, at least, no one has ever been sober when he did. We may also say that we know perfectly well how we could recognize such creatures if they did exist. But we also know that it is as a matter of fact impossible that they should. Of course we've got pictures of what centaurs would be like and, given the description I have given, we would not even need pictures. Because we have all seen people and horses and we could recognize a centaur if we met one.

What makes this second case of mine useful is that it provides occason to begin to distinguish two sorts of impossibility, two senses of the word "impossible." If we claim, as I think we all would, ·that centaurs are or would be impossible the point we would be making is that the known biological laws—or what we believe to be known biological laws—rule them out. This sort of mixture of the top parts of a man or a woman and the body and back legs of a horse just could not have evolved, the two elements just could not be put together so that they would go on living as one. The crux here, what one means by saying that these things are impossible, is that, the world and the laws of nature being what they in fact are, there could not be centaurs. Centaurs are in a word impossible. In this case there is no problem about what centaurs would be if there were any. There is no contradiction in the description of a creature which would be half horse and half person. But things being as we think we know they are centaurs just can not be.

Now, we begin to come on to the other sense of the word "impossible." Certainly it is perfectly clear that there would be no difficulty for an omnipotent being in making centaurs, since such a God would decide what the laws of nature are to be. He could —if He so chose—choose to have a system of nature in which centaurs were not only as a matter of fact possible but actually existed. Thus we here have a case where what is in fact impossible to man, and to all other creatures, is not by the same token impossible to God.

We have had the first two cases, and the first sense of "impossible." The second sort of impossibility, the second sense of the word "impossible," is best explained in connection with a third sort of issue of existence or non-existence. Consider such claims as that there is no such thing as a round square. Or—perhaps a more suitable local example—consider the claim that you cannot have an automobile which is smaller outside than inside; handy though that would be for traffic. We know there ain't no such things, and there could not be, as either round squares or automobiles which are smaller outside than inside. We know this, not of course because we or other people have searched the world and drawn a blank, nor yet because our physicists have found that some law of nature which in fact obtains in the universe as it actually is rules them out—though of course God might, had he so chosen, to have arranged things differently. No, the reason for saying that these things are impossible is that the very idea of something with smaller external dimensions than its internal dimensions, or of a round square, is a contradiction. The reason why these things are impossible, the nature of the impossibility, is the reason why you will never find an unmarried husband or a 90 year old teen-ager, and so on.

This is a fundamental and very important distinction between what one may call logical impossibility—the sort of thing where a contradiction is involved; and contingent impossibility—impossibility as a matter of fact. It is important for us because one sort of attack on a system of belief about God and about His arrangements according to that system, is to urge that there is in fact some contradiction between the statements made within that system. Of course it would be absurd to say that it is as a matter of fact impossible for a God to exist, or, if He existed, impossible for Him to do this, that, or the other. But it is not absurd to urge that some system of beliefs may have a contradiction in it, and hence that to say that there might be a God who did this and this and this would be contradictory and hence impossible.

One sort of argument that I am going to offer about a system of belief about God is that the system that we are going to have presented to us contains that sort of contradiction. If this is right, then it would be ridiculous for someone who thinks he has shown that it is so to say that he is agnostic in this case. It would be like being agnostic about whether there are any unmarried husbands or round squares. If one can make out an argument of this sort, then one has shown that the thing is logically impossible. Then there is no question of being agnostic.

Well, I think before actually going on to the fourth case, it would be wise—especially because of the technical breakdown*—to recapitulate.

I have started by trying to show why I am going to take a boldly atheist rather than a modestly agnostic line. To do that I undertook to distinguish four sorts of case in which there could be a dispute about existence. The first was the Loch Ness monster case. Here the suggestion being made about the existence of something is intelligible. It is not known to be impossible. There is just a question whether, as a matter of fact, there really are these creatures in Loch Ness. The second was the centaur case. Here again the suggestion is intelligible. But we have, or can have, scientific reason for saying that the existence of centaurs is impossible. This impossibility is a matter of what is as a matter of fact, impossible; though, of course, it would not be impossible for God. The third was the round square case. Here the suggestion may look intelligible but if it really does involve a contradiction, as the idea of a round square or of an unmarried husband does, then it is basically incoherent. But if you can show that a system of beliefs about religion is in this way incoherent, then the correct thing for you to say is that you know that, whatever else is true this system is not true. Here it is wrong to be agnostic and right to be positive.

I think I will not go on to the fourth case in this slot. I will simply say a little more about the idea of logical impossibility. There have been many theologians, including St. Thomas Aquinas, who have made—in connection with the problem of evil and other such problems—the point that "nothing which involves contradiction falls under the omnipotence of God." I think they would have done better to reformulate what they were after by saying that if you utter nonsense and make God the grammatical subject of a sentence, the rest of which is nonsense, or if you make the word "God" the grammatical subject of a sentence which is contradictory, then you do not show that there is a limi-

*Publishers Note: Dr. Flew is referring here to a slight delay caused by technical problems in connection with the TV equipment being used to videotape the debate.

tation in God's power, because He can not realize that contradiction in the world. You simply show that you have been contradicting yourself and it is that sort of thing which is one of the sorts of things I hope to show as the evening goes on.

WARREN'S FIRST NEGATIVE

(Monday Night)

Dr. Flew, Gentlemen Moderators, Ladies and Gentlemen. I am very happy to come before you to reply to the speech to which you have just listened, and I should like, by way of helping you see what I plan to do in my negative response, to call your attention to my chart on the overhead projector, Chart No. 9. (See Page 8.) Now, on this chart you will see a series of rooms. I want you to envision these rooms as being made of steel and concrete with no windows or doors. There are no holes in either the floors or the windows, and Dr. Flew is in the innermost room and the only way he can arrive at atheism is to come through all of these walls. And I submit to you that he is in the midst of a *prison* and that he not only cannot come through all of the walls but that he cannot come through *any* of the walls.

Basic to his contention that he *knows* that there is *no* God, there are certain things that he must know before he can know that his proposition is true. You will understand that he has affirmed a universal negative. Now we will be talking about that —the universal negative—more in this speech and in the succeeding ones tonight and tomorrow evening, but I want to get the point before you at the very beginning.

Next, I want you to see Chart No. 1. (See Page 9.) I had intended to look at the screen itself while the chart was on it, but since I will not be able to do it due to the television arrangement —I will have to be looking at a notebook here at the lectern. But now, please note Chart No. 1. The basic issue in this discussion is this. I myself am an empirical fact. I am a human being, and so is each and every one of you. There are only two possible explanations. One explanation is to go back to *dead matter*, which Dr. Flew holds is eternal, but which he cannot prove to be such. However, he *must* prove such in order to prove his case. But, even if he could prove that matter is eternal he cannot prove that *dead matter* has ever produced anything *living*. You are then to decide that the ultimate source of you yourself, of all of your loved ones, of every human being who has ever lived on this earth, is *rocks and dirt* and—if Dr. Flew wishes—gas and water (though he has a tremendous problem there also). But he has

"FLEW'S PRISON"—FROM WHICH HE CANNOT ESCAPE (TO ATHEISM) 9

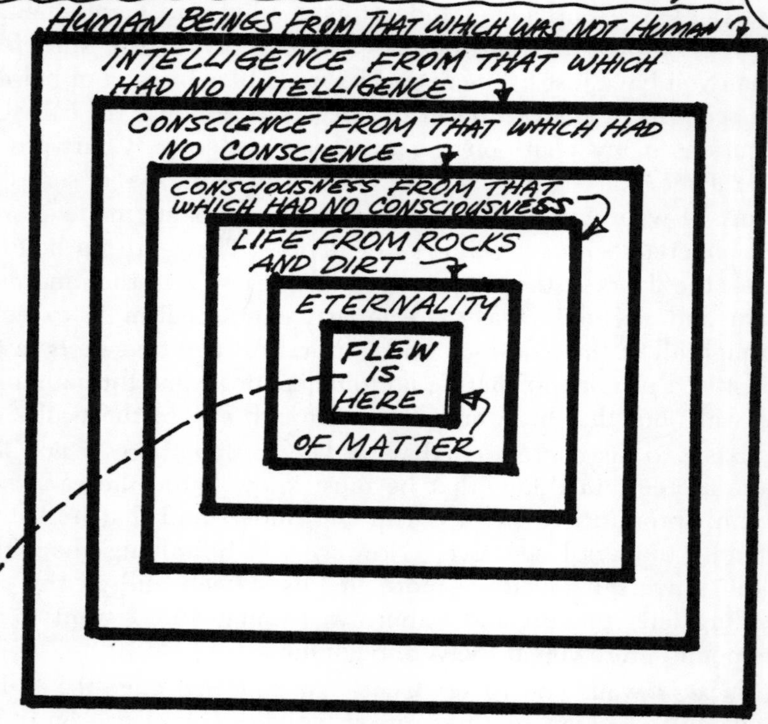

THE PATH WHICH FLEW MUST FOLLOW IF HE IS PROVE HIS PROPOSITION (MAKE HIS WAY TO THE POINT THAT HE KNOWS THAT GOD DOES NOT EXIST)—BUT HE CANNOT GET THROUGH ANY OF THESE "PRISON WALLS." UNLESS HE CAN FIND A "DOOR" THROUGH EVERY ONE OF THESE ROOMS, HE WILL BE MANIFESTLY DEFEATED!!!

A CRUCIAL MATTER—

THE REAL ISSUE IN THIS DEBATE:

1.

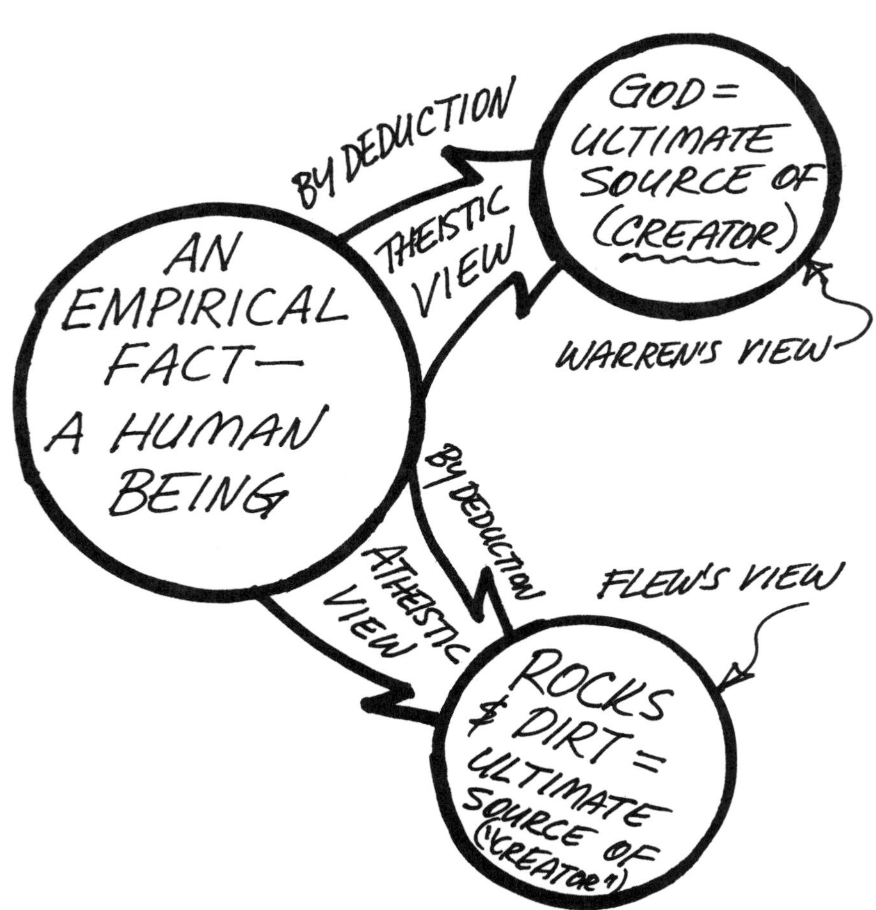

absolutely no proof of that! It is purely and simply a matter of *assumption* upon his part.

On the other hand, there is the alternative of the personal living God, the supreme personal being who is the creator of the universe and yet transcendent of the universe.

Let us look now at Chart No. 4 (See Page 11) on the overhead projector and I would like for Dr. Flew to be sure to note these matters and call for the chart and they will be shown on the screen for his consideration. This debate is vitally important. It is not merely an intellectual enterprise: it is not merely that we have gathered here to discuss things and leave them "up in the air." If the atheistic view is true, then during our lives here on this earth we are nothing but organized matter. Our alleged "creator" has been *rocks and dirt*, or *dead matter* to say the best. If such is the case, then everything we are and do is the result of dead, non-intelligent, non-purposive matter. Given *atheism,* there is no real *objective* right or wrong, though Dr. Flew and his fellow atheists do not wish to admit that. Given atheism and its implications no one has any *real obligation* to do anything or not to do anything. Also physical death would be the absolute end of each and every one of us. At death our total being will go into the dust of the earth and no matter how we may have acted or what we may have done (murder on the level of the Nazis, rape, lying and stealing and so forth) there will be absolutely no accounting or judgment or punishment.

On the other hand, if the *theistic* view is true, then our Creator is *God*, there is real objective right and wrong, there is real objective moral good and evil. If God is, if the *theistic* view is true, then we do have real obligation to recognize it, to recognize the evidence for God and to obey God. And each and every one of us will live on as a unique center of personality after this life on earth is over. And each one of us will give an account to God for how he has lived.

Dr. Flew is on record as contending that the law of rationality (that we should draw *only* such conclusions as are *warranted* by the *evidence*) should be accepted by all men. Now I want to look at Chart No. 17A(1) (See Page 12). Dr. Flew has this to say in his book, *God and Philosophy*, page 11: "To be irrational precisely is to refuse to consider relevant evidence although knowing

IMPORTANCE OF THIS DEBATE ④

1. IF THE ATHEISTIC VIEW IS TRUE, THEN:

(1) During our lives here on earth:

a. We are nothing but organized matter.
b. Our "creator" has been rocks & dirt.
c. Everything we are and do is the result of dead, non-intelligent, non-purposive matter.
d. There is no real (obj.) right or wrong, good or evil.
e. No one has any real obligation to do anything or not to do anything.

(2) Physical death is the absolute end to each and every one of us.

a. Our total being will go into the dust of the earth.
b. No matter how we may have acted (what we may have done [murder on the level of the Nazis, rape, lying, stealing, etc.]) there will be absolutely no accounting, no judgment, and no punishment.

2. IF THE THEISTIC VIEW IS TRUE:

(1) Our Creator is God.
(2) There is real (objective) right and wrong, good and evil.
(3) We have real obligation to obey the will of God.
(4) Each and every one of us will live on (as a unique center of personality) after this life (on earth) is over.
(5) Each of us must give an account to God for how he has lived.

FLEW ACCEPTS THE LAW OF RATIONALITY

17A(1)

"TO BE IRRATIONAL PRECISELY IS TO REFUSE TO CONSIDER RELEVANT EVIDENCE ALTHOUGH KNOWING IT TO BE RELEVANT, TO ACCEPT ONE POSITION WHILE REFUSING TO ACCEPT ITS PLAIN LOGICAL CONSEQUENCES, OR WHILE INSISTING ALSO ON HOLDING SOMETHING ELSE FLAT INCONSISTENT WITH IT, AND SO ON." (GOD AND PHIL., p. 11) it to be relevant. To accept one position while refusing to accept its plain logical consequences or while insisting also on holding something else flat inconsistent with it and so on." I agree with that, but I believe that Dr. Flew has already demonstrated the fact that he *has* not and, as a matter of fact, *cannot* be consistent with what he has affirmed here in his book.

I have submitted, in accordance with the agreement which we had prior to the debate, a series of ten questions. I shall note some of them in this speech and some of them later. One of the crucial things you should always look for in a debate of this kind is to see how well each disputant handles the questions that are involved, because an erroneous position cannot maintain consistency, it will cross itself; and I want you to see how Dr. Flew has already been guilty of that.

QUESTIONS FOR DR. FLEW, MONDAY NIGHT, SEPTEMBER 20, 1976

1. ☐ True ☐ False
   Value did not exist before the first human being.
2. ☐ True ☐ False
   In murdering six million Jewish men, women, and children the Nazis were guilty of real (objective) moral wrong.
3. In torturing and/or murdering six million Jews, the Nazis were guilty of violating (check all appropriate boxes):
   ☐ Law of Germany
   ☐ Law of England
   ☐ Law of U.S.A.
   ☐ Law of God
   ☐ Some other law (explain): ____________________
   ____
   ☐ No law at all
4. Of the following statements, check the box in front of each true statement. (If a statement is false, leave the box blank.)
   ☐ A woman was on earth before any human baby;
   ☐ A human baby was on earth before any woman.
5. It is at least possible that a *sound argument* (i.e., one the conclusion of which must be true) may involve deduction

from some *observation* (i.e., empirical fact) to (check all appropriate boxes of the following):

- ☐ The *non-existence* of some alleged existent event, state of affairs, or set of things *within* the universe;
- ☐ The *existence* of some alleged existent event, state of affairs, or set of things *within* the universe;
- ☐ The *non-existence* of some alleged existent event, state of affairs, or set of things *transcendent* of the universe;
- ☐ The *existence* of some alleged existent event, state of affairs, or set of things transcendent of the *universe.*

6. Of the following statements check the box in front of each correct answer. (If the statement is false leave the box blank.)
   - ☐ At least one human being *now living* on earth formerly was an ape (or some other non-human being) and that ape was *transformed* into that human being;
   - ☐ At least one human being who lived in *the past* (but who is now dead) was at one time an ape (or some other non-human being) and that ape was *transformed* into that human being.
7. Of the following statements check the box in front of each correct answer.
   - ☐ At least one human being now living on earth was begotten of a male ape (or some other non-human male) and born of a female ape (or some other non-human female);
   - ☐ At least one human being who lived in the past (but who is now dead) was begotten by a male ape (or some other non-human male) and born of a female ape (or some other non-human female).
8. ☐ True ☐ False

   Each one of us has a real (objective) moral obligation to become an atheist, so that if he does not become such he becomes guilty of real (objective) moral wrong.
9. ☐ True ☐ False

   Real objective evil does exist.
10. ☐ True ☐ False

    From the *concept of God* and the actual existence of *subjective evil* one can soundly deduce the *non-existence of God.*

Let us begin with noting question number 1. True or False, "Value did not exist before the first human being." He answers that as *true.* Now that means, according to Dr. Flew, that before there was a human being on earth—and he recognizes that human beings came into being at a certain point in time—there was absolutely no value. Therefore, if value *began*—or at least it did not exist before human beings—then value could be nothing else than a function of the human mind. It can be nothing more than what one *likes* or dislikes (such as liking or not liking spinach), his approvals or disapprovals, and, that means that even the horrors of the Nazis in Germany—where they took even little children and put them in boxcars with quicklime so that they not only would die but would die excruciatingly—are nothing more than one's individual approval or disapproval. In just a moment I want to go into more detail than that, but at this moment I wanted you to see how he has answered this question.

Question number 2: "In murdering six million Jewish men and women and children, the Nazis were guilty of real objective moral wrong." It has long been a contention of the atheists that we should reject theism because it entails self-contradiction. But notice: in his answer to my first question, Dr. Flew, in a move which involves him in a rejection of the basic argument he made in his first speech, has pitched morality purely on the *subjective* basis, that is, that morality is solely and completely a function of the human mind, for according to Flew, there was no value before there were human beings. But now he says the Nazis were guilty of real, *objective* moral wrong. That means real moral wrong, which entails an *objective standard*! My friends, an atheist simply cannot fit together these first two questions.

Then in question number 3: "In torturing and/or murdering six million Jews, the Nazis were guilty of violating (I asked him to check all appropriate boxes, and the boxes which I gave him were these): The law of Germany; The law of England; The law of the United States; The law of God; Some other law; or, No law at all." He checked the box, "Some other law;" and said this, "International (Nuremberg trials). Moral."

In that connection, I want you to note these charts. First, Chart 43W. (See Page 16.) My friends this is a fantastic thing for human beings to allow themselves to get caught in this kind

UNDER WHAT LAW WERE THE NAZIS PROSECUTED, CONDEMNED?

43-W

(2)

THE ACCUSED – THE NAZIS	THE ACCUSERS – THE ALLIES
THEIR DEFENSE	THEIR PROSECUTION

THEIR DEFENSE

1. Our society had its own needs & desires.
2. Our society made its own laws, based on those needs and desires.
3. Our society commanded us to exterminate the Jews.
4. It would have been WRONG for us not to have obeyed.
5. Now you try to condemn us by the law of an alien society – a value system which had nothing to do with the Nazis (claimed an ex post facto law).

THEIR PROSECUTION

They appealed to a higher law which "rises above the provincial and transient ..." — (R.H. Jackson, Closing Address in the Nuremberg Trial.)

[see also: Chart 43-A23]

of thinking. Let us note, in Chart 43W, the *accused* were the Nazis. Dr. Flew was a member of the British Army, and I was a member of the American Air Force in World War II. Our nations accused, tried and condemned and in some cases even executed the Nazis. They were accused of heinous crimes.

Now here was the *defense* of the Nazis, as you will notice on Chart No. 43W. They said, "Our society had its own needs and desires." If I have understood Dr. Flew, this is his basis for morality. He holds if an individual or society meets its own needs and/or desires, then it is acting morally. The Nazis also said, "Our society had its own needs and desires. Our society made its own laws based on those needs and desires. Our society commanded us to exterminate the Jews. It would have been wrong for us not to have obeyed. But now you try to condemn us with a law of an alien society, a value system which had absolutely nothing to do with us. You are therefore condemning us by the use of an ex post facto law which you force upon us."

But note: there is the *conscience* within man that will simply not allow Dr. Flew to accept that kind of ungodly doctrine, that the German nation had the right to invent a law, which because of the alleged needs and desires of their own society allowed them to seek to exterminate this nation of people—not only to exterminate them but to do so in the most agonizing ways; e.g., to build roads to the East in such fashion that none of them could survive the ordeal. Robert Jackson, one of the Supreme Court Justices of the United States, who was the prosecutor, in his closing address during the Nuremberg trials, had this to say, "These men should be tried on this basis, on a higher law, a higher law which rises above the provincial"—(the provincial is the area of Germany, the geographical area)—"and the transient" (the period of *time* in which the Nazis had charge of Germany). In other words he (Jackson) contended that the Nazis did not have the right to invent a law within their own nation and say, "This is right for us even if it is wrong for you."

Now let us note, if there is no higher law, if there is no law which rises above the provincial and the transient (above what is involved in a certain *locality* during a certain period of *time*) by which the conduct of individuals and/or societies may be correctly judged as either morally right or morally wrong, then it is false to say that the Nazis actually did *real wrong* in murdering six million Jewish men, women and children! But Dr. Flew insists they *did* do wrong! Therefore he has *admitted* that there is a *higher* law that transcends the provincial and the transient.

I want you to note further the Chart 43-A10. (See Page 19.) I want you to note on this Chart, we have the law of England on one side of the chart and the law of Germany on the other. You will note that the law of *England* is authoritative to the people of *England.* The law of *Germany* is authoritative to the people of *Germany.* But notice I have an arrow pointing from England to Germany, but England's law is not authoritative over Germany. We could have put America on there as well; our law is not authoritative over the people of Germany. They are not amenable to *our* law. Neither were they either then nor now amenable to the law of England. So, it could not have been the law of *England.* It could not have been the law of *America* by which they were guilty, and they were not tried on that basis. There was and is a *higher* law which rises above the provincial and the transient, and we will have more to say about that.

My friends, the very fact that there can be *moral degeneration*—as there was in Germany—and *moral progress* makes clear that the attack made by the prosecutor at Nuremberg was exactly right. There is a higher law which transcends the provincial and the transient.

Just for a moment let us look at Dr. Flew's attack. He has said there are various ways of holding that you *know* that a thing does not exist. He considers such matters as the Loch Ness monster, centaurs and the logical impossibilities such as round squares or the old question—he did not actually *say* this—"Can God make a rock so large that he cannot lift it?" And he proposes to say that God is involved in this kind of situation. In other words, that he implies that it is simply impossible for God to exist. He said that: It is an *assertion;* he made no *argument* for it! But I will not make Dr. Flew's argument for him. I am sure that he has an argument to make to try to show you that the very concept of God itself is meaningless or self-contradictory—such as a round square. I do not know for certain that he proposes to do that, but it seems to be the kind of thing that he has

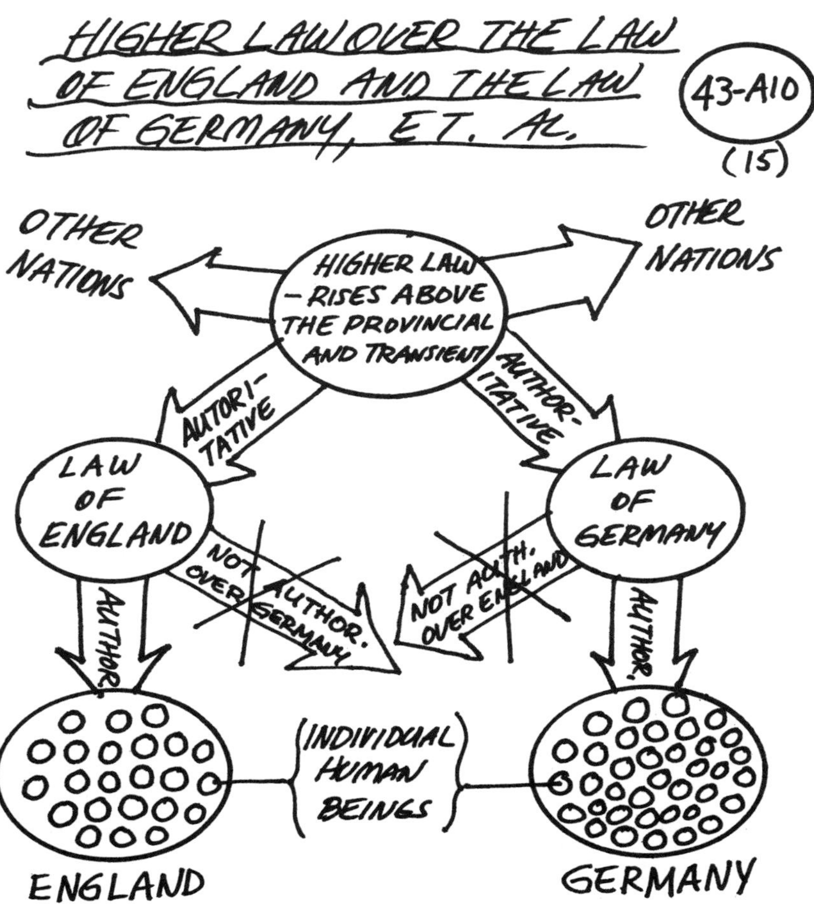
HIGHER LAW OVER THE LAW OF ENGLAND AND THE LAW OF GERMANY, ET. AL.
43-A10
(15)
OTHER NATIONS
HIGHER LAW - RISES ABOVE THE PROVINCIAL AND TRANSIENT
OTHER NATIONS
AUTORI-TATIVE
AUTHOR-ITATIVE
LAW OF ENGLAND
LAW OF GERMANY
NOT AUTHOR. OVER GERMANY
NOT AUTH. OVER ENGLAND
AUTHOR.
AUTHOR.
INDIVIDUAL HUMAN BEINGS
ENGLAND
GERMANY

done in the past, and I suppose that he will do it in the future. And so, I have replied to all that Dr. Flew has done in his speech. I have shown you the self-contradiction that is involved in his answering of my questions.

Now let us note something further about his answers. Question number 4: "Of the following statements, check the box in front of each true statement. (If a statement is false, leave the box blank.) A woman was on earth before any human baby." He left that box blank. "A human baby was on earth before any woman." He left that box blank. So, according, to Flew, it is simply not the case that either a woman or baby was here before the other. If so, then somehow or other they must have gotten here at exactly the same time. Dr. Flew, I am certainly going to be listening for you to explain how that happened.

Further, let us notice in question number 6: "Of the following statements check the box in front of each correct answer." (If the statement is false leave the box blank): Box No. 1: "At least one human being *now living* on earth formerly was an ape (or some other non-human being) and that ape was *transform*ed into a human being." He left that box blank. Box No. 2: "At least one human being who lived in *the past* (but who is now dead) was at one time an ape (or some other non-human being) and that ape was *transformed* into that human being." He also left that box blank. So, he is saying there is no human now living or who ever did live that was *transformed* after it once had existence as some *non-human* being into a *human* being.

Question number 7: "Of the following statements check the box in front of each correct answer." Box No. 1: "At least one human being now living on earth was *begotten* of a male ape (or some other non-human male) and *born* of a female ape (or some other non-human female)." He left that box blank, and therefore counts it false. Box No. 2: "At least one human being who lived in the past (but who is now dead) was *begotten* by a male ape (or some other non-human male) and was *born* of a female ape (or some other non-human female)." And he holds that is *false*. So, now note according to Dr. Flew, no non-human thing was ever *changed* after once having existence as a *non-human*, was ever changed into a *human*, and no non-human male and female were ever the ancesters of a human being. I submit to you that there is no other way of even conceiving of the origin of human beings, and I therefore submit to you this is why Dr. Flew would not, cannot, and will not answer the question, "Which was on earth first—a woman or a baby?" He has therefore given up completely the theory of evolution and since there are no other theories or alternatives other than *creation* or *evolution,* he has therefore *admitted* that *creation* is the one and only possibility. He therefore, admits that his own proposition is false.

Question number 8: "Each one of us has a real (objective) moral obligation to become an atheist, so that if he does not become such he becomes guilty of real (objective) moral wrong." And he left that box blank, thereby taking the position that the statement is false. Well, Dr. Flew, what on earth is the purpose of our being here in this debate? If you should give us the evidence that would prove that atheism is right and that we then would have no obligation to become atheists, you are saying that we have absolutely no obligation to accept the truth. Then why debate the subject? If we have no obligation to accept the *truth,* how could there be real *objective* moral right and wrong—which you have said is the case?

You see, friends, how utterly self-contradictory this doctrine (atheism) is. And please remember that Dr. Flew has already said tonight—as he has said over and over in his books (and *I* agree)—that any position which involves self-contradiction is false. I do not know how a man could have admitted any more clearly than Dr. Flew has admitted already tonight that his position is false. And I plead kindly and lovingly that he recognize the evidence and the conclusion which it warrants—just as he has urged others to do. Anyone who sees the evidence and rejects its implication is being irrational. I call upon him to be rational, to accept the only conclusion which follows from the evidence (as we shall see in the following nights when I present the case for the affirmative). By his admissions, he has eliminated one of the only two possibilities and therefore admits creation which could be only by God.

Question number 9: "Real objective evil exists." I asked him to answer true or false. He did not answer either one. Now, Dr. Flew, I want you to answer that question, number 9! You did not check either true or false. There is no way you can answer that without contradicting one of the answers you have already given.

Question number 10: "From the *concept of God* and the actual existence of *subjective evil,* one can soundly deduce the *non-existence of God.*" I do not have the time to go into a discussion of this particular point to show that it simply is not the case. I will show you in succeeding speeches by the charts that there are no two attributes of God which contradict one another. Dr. Flew may try to show that there are. Please listen carefully to see whether he will try to discuss the concept of God and prove it to be self-contradictory without applying or referring it to some empirical fact of evil. I predict that he will not confine himself to the concept itself. Thank you very much.

FLEW'S SECOND AFFIRMATIVE

(Monday Night)

I think I will begin by continuing with my fourth case. Then I will proceed to try to take up some of the points raised by Dr. Warren. Remember the three different cases, ending with the one where existence is denied on the grounds that a contradiction is involved. (Of course I have not begun to try to show that any contradiction is involved here, I just wanted to first review those three cases.) My fourth case is a rather queer one. I suppose the best example I can give of this is the example of someone who said that there are fairies. They might begin by saying, "Yes, of course there are fairies and if you go and look on the appropriate occasion, or perhaps use special devices for detecting these creatures you will find them." Well and fine; if that is what the suggestion is, then it is not my fourth case. But it could happen that someone who was very keen on this belief in fairies, very committed in some way, when he was confronted with the negative reports of the witnesses, the blank photographs, and so on, said: "Well, yes, but fairies are rather peculiar things you know, they do not show themselves to skeptical people, to scientists and the like."

I will not go on about this, I think it is enough to indicate that it is possible to start with some assertions about the existence of something, but then to put in various qualifications which make your assertion less and less one that could be tested at all. It is my belief, which I have argued in other places, and which I shall be arguing in the course of these next four evenings, that this often happens with religious beliefs. For instance, people affirm confidently that prayer is always answered. But then they say, "Yes, but sometimes the answer is no." Well, when one has done that, and unless one has got some method of determining that the answer is no, provides a distinction between a no answer —you know, say "No, you shan't have that" and no answer at all, one has qualified one's original assertion in such a way that it is no longer possible to test whether it is true or not.

Confronted by this sort of performance, it seems to me that what we all do, and rightly, is to say, not "I am agnostic about fairies" but, "There are no such things." When it has been qualified and qualified beyond the point of testing, and of course I think that is what one does with that sort of assertion—I think that it is appropriate to say that anyone who does not believe or rejects some assertion that has been qualified in that way, should say that he knows there are no such things, rather than that he is agnostic about it because he is not in the situation where he is waiting for more evidence, the whole thing has been so qualified that evidence can not ever circle it whatever one had. So, that was the last of my four cases.

I distinguished these mainly because I wanted to contrast factual and logical impossibility, but partly because I wanted to give some sort of explanation of the reasons why I am adopting the bold atheist rather than the modest agnostic line.

Now I must begin to say something about the points which Dr. Warren has raised. I think I will deal with the last one first, partly because it is certainly freshest in my mind, and probably freshest in everyone else's mind, but also because I think I can about that say something useful very briefly. It is the one about my saying that I did not think that there was an obligation on everyone to become an atheist. The reason I do not think there is an obligation on everyone to become an atheist is this: It seems to me that the obligation is to pursue the truth as you see it and as best you can. That is the obligation which rests on all of us. But then it is perfectly possible, and indeed very common for people, after the best and most honest and thorough investigation they can make to be in a position where the only thing that they honestly and conscientiously can decide in the light of the material they have considered and the way it seems to them is a quite different conclusion. For them, the only honest thing to do is to be theists. So, the reason I do not want to say that everyone has an obligation to agree with me is that while I do think everyone does have an obligation here, that obligation is an obligation to honest inquiry. But I know that honest inquiry may lead different people in very different directions.

Next, moving backwards, I come to Dr. Warren's points about whether there was a baby or a woman first, or a woman or a baby. I think this is an important one. The difficulty as I see it arises, and the reason why I had some trouble about answering Dr. Warren's set question is, because the distinction between the human and the not human is not in all cases absolutely sharp. Here, as I believe elsewhere in the world of evolutionary biology, there must have been a continuous process of development. You can not always draw a sharp line and say: "Well, that is the last so and so and this is the first something else." The position is that there are of course lots of cases where you can say without hesitation: "It is a lion, it is a horse, it is a man or it is not a man." But it is, it seems to me a consequence of evolutionary theory that species shade off into one another. Hence when you are confronted by marginal cases, you can not say this is definitely human or this is not definitely human.

Perhaps it would help if I used a somewhat light hearted and unfortunately all too personally appropriate example, the distinction between people who are bald and people who are not bald. These are both vague terms—you know, it shades off into it. You go from the case of someone at one extreme, who is, Afro and fuzzy wuzzy, no one would say they were to the case at the other extreme, of my much respected supervisor, Gilbert Ryle—positively egg-like and no doubt but that everyone must call that bald. Here we have a case, where we can go from one extreme, which is unequivocally one thing to another extreme, which is unequivocally the other. We can go by possible stages of one more hair at a time. The whole idea of drawing a sharp line by saying that—say—if the population density of the hairs is 100 per square inch then the man is not bald, but if it is 99 or less then he is bald just does not work at all. And the same applies wherever one has a difference of degree.

Perhaps it would be helpful for me to say two things about differences of degree. One, what I take a difference of degree to be. I take it that a difference of degree is a difference such that, between the two extremes which we say that the difference of degree is a difference between, there is a spectrum of actual or possible cases shading from one into the other. The second thing enormously worth saying about differences of degree is that a difference of degree can be crucially important. Most of my students when they hear someone say, for instance that the difference between human and non-human is a difference of degree, will go away and report the speaker said it was a mere difference of degree, and so it is not really important; and really human and non-human are the same thing. If I say nothing else of any use this evening, I think that it is very worth saying that differences of degree are *not* all *mere* differences of degree. All the humanly most important differences are in fact in this sense differences of degree. There may not actually be the intermediate cases in all these examples but they are of the sort where there could be. For instance, the differences between riches and poverty, between age and youth, between sanity and insanity, and I think the difference between the unequivocally human and the highest non-human animal are all differences of degree. But now insofar as this is right, there just can not be any answer about which in the evolutionary series was the last non-human being and which was the first fully human being. If any evolutionary theory is true, then there must always be marginal cases; just as there must also be clear cut paradigm cases for the marginal cases to be marginal and borderline between.

I move next to Dr. Warren's fundamental questions about the objectivity of value. I begin with a slightly adapted quotation from one of Plato's dialogues. The word that Plato actually used was "piety." But I change that to "goodness, because "piety" would be confusing here. The question that was raised in the dialogue, *Euthyphro* is: "Are the things which are good good because God approves of those things, or is it the case that God approves of those things which are good because they are good?" If you react to this question by saying "My goodness, that's a typical philosopher's question," then you are absolutely right. It is and it is one I have often used with boys and girls wondering if they want to study philosophy. I try it now on Denton! For if after a moment of explanation of what it is about, you find this interests you, then philosophy would interest you. If, even after a moment of explanation, you think it is all pointless and silly, then the subject will not interest you.

Let me explain what the point is. The point is this. If you answer this question by saying: "Oh the things that are good are good because God approves of them," then you are committing yourself to saying that in effect it is God who not merely makes good things but brings it about that they are good. You are in effect defining goodness in terms of God's will. Now, the snag about doing this is that by this definition you commit yourself to approving of absolutely anything that might be done by the being in question.

It may seem that that is alright if it is God. Think of another case though. Suppose that you define "right" and "wrong" in terms of the prescriptions of a legal system. So this or that is good because the law prescribes it; and it would be bad if the law forbade this and prescribed something else. Now, if you live in a society where what the laws tells you to do are on the whole things that ought to be done, and what the laws tell you not to do are on the whole things that ought not to be done, then it may seem to you that it would be alright to say that things are good because the law tells us to do them. But of course that would commit you to saying, if you once accepted this, that whenever, and in whatever way, the law was changed, then necessarily it would still be right to do whatever the law commanded; simply because it was the law. So, are the things that are good good because God approves of them, or does God approve of the things which are good because they are good? If you take the first of these two options, you become committed to approving and commending as good absolutely anything that an all powerful being might say should be done. If, on the other hand, you take the other line and say that God approves of the things which are good because they are good, then the implication is that goodness can be defined without reference to God's will. You could know that these things are good even without knowing that God approves of them. If that's the line you take then the news that God favors these things is indeed good news. You are now assured—and how excellent this is—that the creator of the universe favors these admirable things.

So, where are we? Are things that are good good because God approves of them, or does God approve of the things that are good because they are good? This is an important question. If you give the first of the two answers then you are committed to approving absolutely anything that an all powerful being might say or do. If you take the second line, then you take it that things are good, and can presumably be known to be good, independent of any theological knowledge.

How does this all bear on these questions of whether you could know that things were good independent of your knowledge of God—whether things could be good independent of your knowledge of God. Well, in this way. It is only insofar as there is an idea of goodness which does not have to be defined in terms of what God actually wills, that it is even going to have to be possible for you to recognize your God as being good. For if you are not defining the word in some way independent of God, then to say that your God is good is—roughly speaking—to say that what He does is what He approves of. That may be news.

But it is scarcely good news at all. It becomes good news if you can be assured that what He does is good. It is not just what He happens to be in favor of, but that this really is good. It is no basis for praising a God to say that what He wills is the things that He does in fact will. It is only a basis for praising Him if you can say that He does certain things which you know to be good and how splendid this is because you can know these things to be good without knowing this definition of the word God. So, the point that I want to conclude from this sort of investigation of Plato's *Euthyphro* is that, so far is it from being the case that if we do not know of the existence of God, we can not know anything is good; it seems to me that we can not be in a position to recognize that God is good unless we have some meaning for the word good, some knowledge of good and evil, independent of our knowledge of God.

WARREN'S SECOND NEGATIVE

(Monday Night)

Dr. Flew, Gentlemen Moderators, Ladies and Gentlemen. It certainly affords me a great deal of pleasure to come before you for my second speech of the evening to reply to the speech which Professor Flew has just delivered in your presence. I shall follow this format in this speech. I will go through his speech, as I did last time, and I think you will find—if you listen carefully—that I will reply to my opponent's speech item by item, statement by statement, and argument by argument. Then, I propose to present further *negative material,* to which he has the obligation to reply, that will constitute further proof of the fact that the proposition which Dr. Flew has affirmed, namely that he *knows* that God does not exist, is false! You must understand that Dr. Flew is not merely saying that someone else has failed to prove that God exists, but that he himself *knows* that God does *not* exist.

In his first speech, Dr. Flew said that men *ought* to be atheists. He made that a part of his speech. I do not know that he really meant it. Later he seemed to reverse himself and indicate that he thought only that we *ought* to be *honest* and to try to pursue truth. But I wonder where he obtained that information. *Why ought we to be honest, Dr. Flew? Why ought we to pursue truth?* From where does this obligation come? I ask for an explanation, and I know that everyone in this audience is asking. Remember Dr. Flew's answer to one of my questions: namely, that before there was a human being on this earth, there was no value. Therefore, he has made clear that according to his viewpoint—and it is consistent, it is an implication of the atheistic viewpoint—value is nothing but a function of the human mind, that it is merely the approval or disapproval of the individual or of a society. Now, friends, that simply means that according to Dr. Flew, that Nazis were right because they were convinced that it was the right thing for them to do. In fact, I have here photostatic copies of statements in which the Nazis said they thought it was their *moral obligation* to try to exterminate those people. Now then, Dr. Flew, you have the obligation to try to explain that in harmony with your position.

He comes back and talks about another possibility of a group of things that we might know do not exist, differentiating between factual impossibility and logical impossibility. He talks about fairies and so forth, and I anticipated at that point that he was going into the question of *falsification,* which is a big thing with Dr. Flew. I anticipate his getting into it. In fact, if he does not hurry up and get into it I am going to get into it before he does.

Now he says, "As a reply to Dr. Warren we have no obligation to become an atheist, but an obligation to pursue truth." On what basis does Dr. Flew conclude that we have an obligation to pursue truth? But now notice carefully in this question, he has admitted obligation—real (objective) obligation. You see on the one hand, atheists want to claim objective obligation and, on the other hand, they want to deny it. They do not want to be out here in the bold position of saying that any and everything that any person wishes to do so long as it pleases him even if it is the rape and murder of a 5 or 6 year old girl or the putting of Jewish children into boxcars coated with quicklime so that not only they will die but that they will die agonizingly over a period of several days, and to work people to death as they build a road from Germany toward Russia, and to work them so hard and so agonizingly and to so degrade them that not a single one of them would survive it to form the core of a nucleus of the Jewish nation—is merely *subjective* wrong. He does not want to say that is merely subjectively wrong. He, in fact, says that it is a monstrous thing; but, on the other hand given his position he has absolutely no ground for saying that such is "monstrous." Notice carefully, everytime he speaks, he speaks about moral obligation, but then he *denies* real, objective moral obligation even though he has, in answering these questions, admitted that there is such a thing as real, objective moral obligation.

Then he raises the question of my talking about the question of a baby first or a woman first, and he goes into the question of the distinction between human and non-human, contending that there is a "shade" of difference involved that cannot be clearly differentiated. What he was doing, in saying there were creatures which were really neither human nor non-human, was imply an effort to provide a basis by which he would appear to be under no obligation to answer my question, "Which was first, a woman or a baby?" The truth of the matter is, no atheist can answer that question because every atheist—to establish his case—must *know* that every human being owes his ultimate origin to *evolution* from dead matter (rocks and dirt)—back to that which had no intelligence, no life, no purpose, no power to accomplish anything requiring intelligence.

He *cannot* consistently answer the question, "Which was first, a woman or a baby?" So, he invents a *period of time* in which he alleges that there were beings that were neither human nor non-human. I deny this position with every ounce of my being! Everything in this auditorium is either a human being or it is not. This watch [holding up a watch] is either human or it is not human. This ring on my finger is either human or it is not human. Every object in the world is either a rock or it is not a rock. Every object in the world either has the property of being red or it does not have the property of being red. I am astonished to have to speak to this man, one of the most learned men in the field of philosophy, regarding *the law of excluded middle*! Regarding *things*, the law of excluded middle means that everything either has a certain property or it does not have it. Regarding *propositions*, the law means that every proposition is either true or false. *I submit to you that there never has existed even one thing that was neither human nor non-human!* Stop and think about it. Think of the ridiculous idea—for which Flew has contended—that there were once things on earth which were neither human nor non-human.

Now, this is the best that atheists can do. It is not the weakness of the *man*. If atheists could bring in someone else, he would have no better answer. I assure you the best man, as good as any in the world, is attempting to deal with this question, but he *cannot* tell you which was first—a woman or a human baby—because he *knows* he cannot make it fit with evolution either way. Was there once a woman that was not ever a baby? Was there suddenly a woman who just popped out of a log somewhere? Was there once a human baby that was not born of a woman? If so, where did it come from? Dr. Flew has already said that no non-human thing *transformed* into being a human being and that no non-human thing ever *gave birth* to a human being.

Dr. Flew, since you are under obligation to prove evolution, and since it was not by transformation and it was not by birth, let us hear you explain the way it was. I tell you friends, if ever a man has given up on a proposition, Dr. Flew has given up on this one. The whole idea, he says, of a *sharp line* (between human and non-human) is not helpful. That is simply not true. Human beings and non-human beings *do* have a *sharp line* between them. You do not have to know all about human beings and non-human beings to know that is true. You have no proof of "shades" of things of the kind you allege, Dr. Flew. Your claim that there have been beings which were neither human nor non-human has absolutely no basis in fact.

Then he talks about objectivity of value and refers to Plato's dialogues. He gives us the old medieval problem which raises the question as to whether an action is good because God approves of it or does God approve of the action because it is good? Now, you see, this "problem" is supposed to put us into the dilemma, "If God approves of it because it is good," then there is some law that is above God. Here is God [using one hand above another to illustrate] but above God is a law. Well, that will not do because then there would be something greater than God. But if you say, "It is right simply because God approves of it," then you have something under God that was *arbitrarily* given by God, so that if He had wished, He could just as well have said that lying is good and that fornication and adultery, and murder and rape and all such is just as good as purity and truth-telling. Now neither one of those alternatives will do, and they do not constitute a proper dilemma because goodness flows from the Ultimate Good, who is God. Goodness flows from the very nature of God. It is neither that God is *under* the good nor that God is *above* the good but that good flows from God. The will of God is the very essence, as it were, of the nature of God; that is, the will of God is not *under,* a law and it is not *above* an arbitrary law. Dr. Flew's alleged dilemma is not really a dilemma.

Then, in his discussion, Dr. Flew indicated that something *ought* to be done. He made reference several times to something, or some things that *ought* to be done. Well, Dr. Flew, I would like to know what these things are. Let us hear a list of some things that *ought* to be done and how you decided on the elements of that list.

Then he talks as if God's goodness could be defined without reference to the will of God. Well, the way you have defined it by the answering of my questions, and also in your writings, value is purely a function of a human mind. You remember the question. At one time, according to Dr. Flew, there was nothing in existence except *dead matter*! I asked the question, "Before there was a human being was there anything of value?" He said, "No." That means that value had to depend upon the human mind. Therefore, Dr. Flew is taking the emotive theory of ethics. If he holds that such is not the case, I would like to hear him explain how it is not as I have explained it.

Thus, I have covered his entire speech.

Alright, let us now look at Chart No. 6. (See Page 34.) On Chart No. 6, which I am introducing as *negative* material, I want to show that I have only to establish one of these things to show that Dr. Flew's proposition is false. I have to establish *only one* of them! As a matter of fact I have already established one of them in that I have shown that he has been guilty of self-contradiction. I have already established that his proposition is false by showing that he has given up on the only way by which it could possibly be established: one thing that is absolutely necessary to his case is to *know* that man has *evolved* and has *not* been *created*! But since *creation* and *evolution* are the only two possibilities, by his admission (by implication) that evolution is false, then he has admitted *creation* and, in admitting creation, he has admitted *God*.

Now notice, on Chart No. 6, that I am showing that Dr. Flew's proposition is false. To do so, I have only to do even *one* of these things but I propose, before the close of the last negative speech tomorrow evening, to have accomplished *all* of them. I have already accomplished some, as I have indicated.

But *first*, his proposition and the total position which it involves is self-contradictory. It is a very frequent activity of *atheists* to charge *theists* with holding to self-contradictory positions. Such a view cannot be sustained and when that argument is introduced by Dr. Flew, the affirmative speaker, then we shall reply to it. But, I have already shown that the atheistic position involves self-contradiction, and I shall do more along that line.

Secondly, there are some things which Dr. Flew *must know*

TO PROVE FLEW'S PROP. FALSE, I HAVE ONLY TO DO AT LEAST ONE OF THE FOLLOWING:

1. Show that his prop. obligates him to do what he cannot do.

2. Show that there are some things which he must know—but which he cannot know.

3. Show that his prop. involves self-contradiction.

4. Show that his proposition implies that which is false.

5. Show that his prop. involves absurdities.

6. Show that his prop. involves the use of incoherent concepts.

7. Show that his prop. involves meaningless statements.

8. Show that his prop. involves the denial of major undisputed facts.

9. Show that his efforts to defend his basic position have involved him in admissions of defeat.

(in order to *know* that God does *not exist*) but which he *cannot* know. Does he *know* that matter is eternal? Does he *know* that at one time not one living cell, not one living thing was anywhere in all the universe? Does Dr. Flew *know* that? If he does, then let him tell us *how* he knows it. That is just one of many, many, many (and I am sure could be listed into the thousands) things he *must know* but which he *cannot know*.

Third, Dr. Flew's position involves *absurdities*. When you can reduce a proposition to an *absurdity* or when you can show that a proposition *implies* a false doctrine, then that shows that that doctrine itself is *false*! The argument in logic called Modus Tollens indicates an "if-then" proposition—*if* that is the case, *then* this follows. If you can show that what follows is false, then you have shown that what precedes is false. Now what I am saying is this. If such and such is the case, then this is the case. I can show that atheism involves *absurdities* which proves atheism itself is false.

Fourth, Dr. Flew's proposition involves a denial of major undisputed facts. We will be talking about that in detail.

Fifth, I can show that his proposition involves the use of at least one incoherent concept. Dr. Flew has touched on this tonight in hinting at the idea that the concept of God is incoherent. I am anxious for him to really deal with the concept of God. And then, we have something ready for him on the idea that atheism involves incoherent concepts.

Sixth, if I can show that Dr. Flew's efforts to defend his basic proposition have involved him in *admissions of defeat* then I will have shown his proposition to be false. I do not mean that he must explicitly say "I give up; I admit defeat." But I am saying that implications of his position are admissions of defeat.

Now, I want to go back over the material which I pointed out earlier in the first speech just briefly and then introduce some more material in connection with that. Let us look at Chart No. 10T. (See Page 36.) If Dr. Flew will write these chart numbers down; they will be given to him on the screen at any time he likes. Now, on the screen you will see the German Nazis. By means such as gas, labor, quicklime, shooting and so forth, the Nazis exterminated thousands of Jews. The Nazis said, "It was morally right for us to try to exterminate the Jews." However, the

ETHICAL RELATIVITY AFFIRMS LOG. CONTRAD.

THE GERMANS (NAZIS)

GAS, LABOR QUICKLIME, SHOOTING ETC

THE JEWS

A NAZI: "IT WAS MORALLY RIGHT FOR THE GERMANS TO TRY TO EXTERMINATE THE JEWS."

A JEW: "IT WAS MORALLY WRONG FOR THE GERMANS TO TRY TO EXTERMINATE THE JEWS."

THUS, GIVEN FLEW'S BASIC POSITION, IT FOLLOWS BOTH (1) THAT IT WAS MORALLY RIGHT, AND (2) THAT IT WAS MORALLY WRONG FOR THE NAZIS TO TRY TO EXTERMINATE THE JEWS.

Jews said "It was morally wrong for the Germans to try to exterminate us." Here you have two classes of people in the same nation, the Nazis saying "We are meeting our needs and desires" (if I have understood Dr. Flew, this is the basic way he goes about trying to establish some sort of moral obligation) while the Jews take a rather "dim view" of that and they say that such does not exactly meet *their* needs and desires. And so, given Dr. Flew's basic position, it follows that the Nazis were right in saying that it was morally right to destroy the Jews and the Jews were also right in saying that it was morally wrong to destroy the Jews. So, you have a *logical contradiction* in Flew's position.

Now let us note further in Chart No. 10-U. (See Page 38.) In regard to the intended extermination of the Jews, Nazi Heinrich Himmler said, "We had the moral right, we had the moral duty to our people to destroy this people which wanted to destroy us." (The Nuremberg Document 1,919-PS quoted by Bullock in *Hitler, A Study in Tyranny.*) Therefore, according to the *Nazis* it was morally *right,* but according to the *Jews,* it was morally *wrong,* and Dr. Flew cannot consistently say that either one of them was wrong!

Now let us look at Chart No. 10-M. (See Page 39.) "Flew's Self-Contradications." Dr. Flew wants to affirm *oughtness* i.e., that human beings *ought* to act in certain ways, but by implication he *denies it,* as I have already shown. He wants to affirm that there is real objective *right* and real objective *wrong,* but by implication he has already denied *both* of these. Dr. Flew *wants* to say that Hitler and the Nazis really did *objective* moral wrong in the torture and murder of six million Jews, but his basic position implies that as long as a majority of the Nazis approved of what they did, the action against the Jews was not really objectively wrong!

Now let us turn to Chart No. 43-A 11. (See Page 40.) Let us look at the Nazi solutions to what they called "the Jewish problem." Dr. Flew, I would like for you to deal with this matter. Which of these things are right and which are wrong? To work the Jews to death under unbearable conditions or to subject them to inhuman indignities and then kill them? Here is a nation of people under the direction of their Fuehrer, their leader, who passed laws that actually made it the "right" thing to do in their

ETHICAL RELATIVITY AFFIRMS LOGICAL CONTRADICTION.

☒ Morally right
☐ Morally wrong
(Implication of Flew's Basic position)

IN REGARD TO THE INTENDED EXTERMINATION OF THE JEWS, NAZI HEINRICH HIMMLER SAID, "WE HAD THE MORAL RIGHT, WE HAD THE MORAL DUTY TO OUR PEOPLE TO DESTROY THIS PEOPLE [THE JEWS] WHICH WANTED TO DESTROY US." (N.D. 1,919-PS., QUOTED IN A. BULLOCK, HITLER, A STUDY IN TYRANNY.)

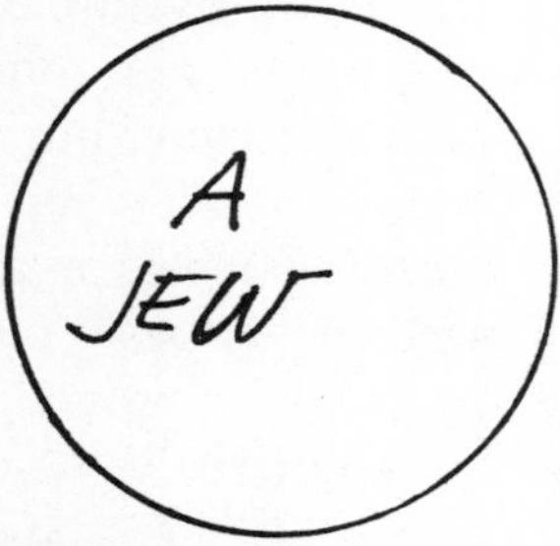

☐ Morally right
☒ Morally wrong
(Implication of Flew's basic position).

THE NAZIS WERE WRONG—REALLY, OBJECTIVELY, MORALLY WRONG—TO TRY TO EXTERMINATE THE JEWS.

ON MORALITY

FLEW'S SELF CONTRADICTIONS

1. O•~O. FLEW WANTS TO AFFIRM "OUGHTNESS" (HUMAN BEINGS OUGHT TO ACT IN CERTAIN WAYS)—BUT BY IMPLICATION, HE DENIES IT.
2. R•~R. HE WANTS TO AFFIRM THAT THERE IS REAL (OBJECTIVE) RIGHT—BUT, BY IMPLICATION, HE DENIES IT.
3. W•~W. HE WANTS TO SAY THAT ONE CAN BE GUILTY OF REAL (OBJECTIVE) WRONG—BUT, BY IMPLICATION, HE DENIES THAT SUCH IS OR CAN BE THE CASE
   (1) HE WANTS TO SAY THAT HITLER & THE NAZIS REALLY DID OBJECTIVE WRONG IN THE TORTURE-MURDER OF SIX MILLION JEWS.
   (2) BUT HIS BASIC POSITION IMPLIES THAT—AS LONG AS THE NAZIS EMOTIONALLY APPROVED OR IF A MAJORITY APPROVED—WHAT THEY DID WAS NOT REALLY (OBJECTIVELY) WRONG.

(MORAL ARG.)

NAZI "SOLUTIONS" TO WHAT THEY CALLED "THE JEWISH PROBLEM" (43-All)

1. DR. FLEW, CHECK THE BOXES OF THE THINGS (16) THAT ARE REALLY MORALLY WRONG:

(1) ☐ - WORK THEM TO DEATH, UNDER UNBEARABLE CONDITIONS.

(2) ☐ - SUBJECT THEM TO INHUMAN INDIGNITIES AND THEN KILL THEM (MEN, WOMEN, CHILDREN) IN GAS CHAMBERS.

(3) ☐ - NOT ONLY TO MAKE THEM DIE, BUT TO MAKE THEM DIE IN AGONY - E.G., TO PUT THEM IN FREIGHT CARS COATED WITH QUICKLIME, WHICH (PRODUCING EXCRUCIATING BURNS) REQUIRED ABOUT FOUR DAYS TO KILL THE VICTIMS.

-(Rob't. Payne, THE LIFE & DEATH OF ADOLF HITLER, pp. 468-71).

2. DR. FLEW, IF YOU CHECKED ANY OF THE ABOVE, CHECK WHICH LAW THEY VIOLATED:

☐ LAW OF GOD.	☐ LAW OF GOD.
☐ LAW OF ENGLAND.	☐ NATURAL LAW.
☐ LAW OF GERMANY.	☐ SOME OTHER LAW.

sight. Not only did they work them to death, they subjected them to inhuman indignities and then killed them—men, women and children—in gas chambers. They did this not only to make them die, but to make them die in agony, that is, to put them into freight cars coated with quicklime which produced excruciating burns requiring about four days to kill the victims. (Robert Payne, in *The Life and Death of Adolph Hitler.*)

Now, Dr. Flew, if you had checked any of these boxes as being really wrong, what *law* did they violate?

You said, "*International law.*" But, my friends, International law, the simple invention of another *human* law, is nothing more than the mere function of a human mind. To be sure, international law is comprised of the views of human beings from several nations, but that is not the basis upon which the Nazis were tried and convicted, and it *ought not* to have been the basis upon which they were. Robert Jackson, prosecutor, said, "There is a higher law which transcends the provincial" (the mere geographical area of a country) "and the transient" (a particular *time* in which it was involved).

Let us look at Chart No. 43-A12. (See Page 42.) Over there to the left of the chart you will see "the law of Germany prior to 1933." The people of Germany are under it. There is moral *degeneration.* Follow the dotted line to the people of Germany under the law of Germany in 1933 with the rise of Adolph Hitler to 1945 and his demise. There has been moral *progress* among the people of Germany under the law of Germany from 1945 to the present. Now, I say there was real moral *degeneration* among the German people during the time of the rise of the Nazis at which time they did the horrible things they did. After that there was moral *progress.* But now notice, the law of Germany was judged by a *higher law,* by a standard which transcends the provincial (the geographical area) and the transient (mere time). Now friends, there is absolutely no way you can hold that the accusations, the trials, the condemnations and the punishments, even the executions of those men could be justified on the basis of a mere human *emotion,* a mere human *approval.* There can be neither moral progress nor moral degeneration if there is no ultimate standard. My time is up and I thank you very much.

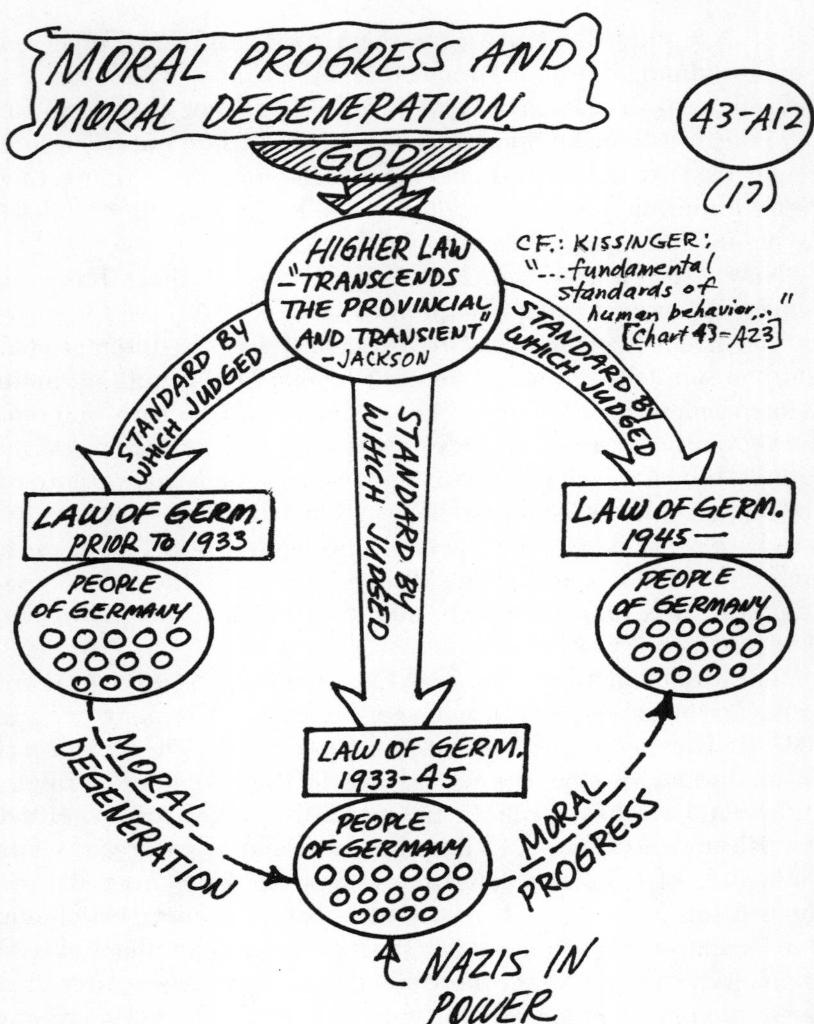
MORAL PROGRESS AND MORAL DEGENERATION
43-A12
(17)
GOD
HIGHER LAW
-"TRANSCENDS THE PROVINCIAL AND TRANSIENT"
-JACKSON
CF.: KISSINGER;
"...fundamental standards of human behavior..."
[Chart 43-A23]
STANDARD BY WHICH JUDGED
STANDARD BY WHICH JUDGED
STANDARD BY WHICH JUDGED
LAW OF GERM.
PRIOR TO 1933
PEOPLE OF GERMANY
LAW OF GERM.
1945—
PEOPLE OF GERMANY
LAW OF GERM.
1933-45
PEOPLE OF GERMANY
MORAL DEGENERATION
MORAL PROGRESS
NAZIS IN POWER

FLEW'S THIRD AFFIRMATIVE

(Monday Night)

It is high time, or over time, for me to offer some positive reason for taking the line I do, and to get past the preparation. But before proceeding to that, I think that it would be appropriate to try to say something more about two issues which Dr. Warren has been pursuing.

The first, and more difficult, concerns the nature of value. I can not give a complete account of the nature of value and particularly of moral value, which I regard as even halfway satisfactory. All that I think I can do is to make one fundamental point, and one suggestion which I think constitutes a certain amount of progress. The general line I want to take, as I think all humanists do, is that value is somehow—somehow—a function of human desires, human wishes, and so on. This carries the implication that there would be something absurd about saying that there was value in a world where there were no (not perhaps human beings but) no conscious rational beings at all. However, it is also pretty clear to me that one cannot from this statement immediately infer that therefore value is just a matter, merely a matter; either of individual tastes, desires and so on, or of group tastes, desires, and so on, of a collective taste.

The most helpful thing I can suggest to bring out why one can not immediately infer this is to think of another sort of value —not of moral value but of market value. Now, surely, the going price—say—a 1974 Volkswagen Beetle in Northern Texas is a matter of fact independent of the desires or wishes of any particular buyers or would be buyers of Volkswagen Beetles, and of any particular sellers or would be sellers of the same. If you are either a buyer or seller, you will recognize this, with very understandable regret. For you can not fix the price just where you would like to have it. It is determined by something independent of you. And yet, and yet, it would clearly be absurd to say that there could be a going price for this or any other marketable product if there were just no people around at all. The idea of, you know, the going price for a Volkswagen Beetle in North Texas if after some unhappy natural disaster there was no one left in North Texas would be an absurdity. We have here an example of a sort of value which is in a way objective. It is, that is to say, independent of any particular tastes, desires of any particular people. On the other hand, it is not objective in the sense that it is somehow written into the structure of the universe and would be there regardless of any human desires at all. So, seeing things in this way, it seems to me, though I can not give a full and adequate account of the nature of moral value, that it is at least possible to maintain without contradiction that value is somehow a function of human purposes, desires and so on. That is to say it would be absurd to suggest that there were values of any sort without human beings or other conscious beings, we can nevertheless, so it seems to me, without contradiction, say that it is not just and always and only a matter of "well I like it and you do not" or even "my group, my peer group likes this and your peer group likes that and that is that." Well, I know that is not enough but that is the best I can do and it seems to me it is the best anyone can do at the moment in that I know of no other philosophical writing in this area which seems to me to constitute clear progress on that.

The second of the things which Dr. Warren is keen to pursue and which I think I ought to take up—again—is this business about the first woman or the first baby and so on. I found this a bit difficult because it does seem to me that I have already provided a reply that is within evolutionary assumptions satisfactory. Of course, I appreciate that Dr. Warren will not agree with me that the theory of evolution by natural selection constitutes a true account of the origin of species. I do not at this moment ask him to believe that it does. But it does seem to me that, if once you allow that it is a true account, then it would seem to be that the obviously right thing to say, consistent with this account, is that there will not be sharp and absolute lines between the population of one species and the population of another; lines such that you can have a set of labels for different species and be absolutely certain beyond the possibility of doubt, if you've seen the whole creature, that this is where lions stop and that is where something else begins. You are bound to have cases shading from one into the other.

About the law of the excluded middle: in general surely it can only be applied to terms and contrasts which are adequately sharp. You can not just say: "Well, either he is bald or he is not"; do not beat about the bush, I want to have a straight answer to this is he, or is he not? There just are people whom you can not describe as being either categorically or decisively bald or categorically and decisively not bald. To allow for this we invent an intermediate term for these people "getting a bit thin on top," perhaps. In a parallel fashion there is no absolutely sharp line between human beings and non-humans. So much for those two things.

It is now high time and over time for me to offer some positive reasons. The first of these positive reasons will be a version of an old favorite, very familiar I am sure to an apologist as experienced as Dr. Warren. It is the contention that the things that are said in his religious system about evil are just inconsistent with the things that are said about the power and the goodness of God.

Now, I am going to try to put my point here in a way which leaves a bit of the argument which I imagine that he and I would agree about behind. I hope, as it were, to come in at the point where I think we are going to disagree. There is a standard reply (which I think would be the line that Dr. Warren would take) to the objection that it is just inconsistent: first to say that God is all powerful, and that God is good without limit; and then to say as a third thing that there is a dreadful amount of evil in the world, and above all human sin. The comeback to this objection is always: "Ah, but you could not have free, responsible human beings without there being a live possibility that these free, responsible human beings would be delinquent and would [as alas all too many of us do] commit lamentable sins."

Here we need to look a bit carefully at what is involved in freedom. Perhaps we will come back to that later. But as a quick objection here, without going into all that, it is surely part of the system shared by Dr. Warren and by many many other Christians, that it says that on earth we are living through a period of probation. It is then said that, for it to make sense to talk about human responsibility and choice and so on, there has got to be this live possibility (which is unfortunately realized) that people will make the wrong choices.

Okay, so let us allow this. I think that this is substantially right, but now how, if you are going to say this, are you able to offer a guarantee that some of these responsible creatures, creatures for whom the live possibility of going both right and wrong—and in particular the live possibility of going wrong—is an essential, will eventually be, and permanently stay saved? How are you going to be able to say, as constantly is said that if they are among the saved then for all eternity they are going to continue as both saved and presumably free responsible human beings, children of God and so on; and there is no danger thereafter of them lapsing again? If the live possibility of disastrous evil is a necessary condition of human freedom and responsibility in this life, why does it cease to be a necessary precondition of responsible life in a world to come?

Of course one can apply the same argument to God Himself. Presumably God has a power to choose. So on the usual assumptions about freedom, there must be the same sort of live possibility of even God making the wrong choice if God is to be a free responsible agent. But I do not want to press that one in particular. Instead the thing which it seems to me must be pressed must be pressed most urgently. I can see how one can say: "Ah, well, it is too late for the damned." Even allowing that they might change their minds, perhaps their new choice would not be recognized. Perhaps they would be told: "It is too late for you to apply for heaven, though you have now changed your mind." But what I can not see is how you can consistently insist that this live freedom, involving a real live possibility (constantly realized in this life) of deplorable sinfulness, is essential to human responsibility under the sun; but it somehow suddenly becomes not essential once you are well and truly saved. This does seem to me to be a contradiction. And it is a very important one. For supposing it is admitted that it is not essential to have this live possibility of error, however we define this live possibility of error, then we are back again at the beginning. "If God could (as it must now be admitted that He could) have created people so that we would all always have done the right thing, why, if He is infinitely good did not He do so?"

The upshot is that the old familiar dilemma of the problem of evil which is a challenge to the consistency of Christian fundamentals. I do not think this dilemma can be met. And in particular it does not seem to me it is met by any system that says the reason the two things are compatible is that it is a necessary condition of freedom that there should be a live possibility of delinquency. I may go on to say but of course, these free beings when they are saved after death are guaranteed for all eternity not to lapse again. After all, in some systems at any rate, apparently even the angels in heaven existing with God presumably from a stage earlier than the creaion of the world were not apparently truly guaranteed secure. Lucifer and others sinned and fell before. But now how is it possible for Lucifer to have had this live possibility again of delinquency which he then realized but for human beings after death to be safe?

I think I will go on to another objection of a different sort. I think I may have more difficulty making this one clear but still all one can do is try.

Someone says that they believe that there is a Supreme Being: all-powerful, and so on: personal and so on: and of course this being is immeasurably greater than human beings, and of course it is incorporeal. How do we point out, how do we pick out as a subject of discourse, the object that we are saying has these characteristics? One way of meeting this challenge would be to say "Oh, well, these characteristics, of infinite power and so on, do not belong to any particular thing in the universe—you know, we are not saying that something over there has all these." This would be ridiculous. Of course we are not saying that. We are really saying these things about the whole universe. This move has been made by some. But it is clearly unacceptable to Christians, because this is a pantheist move.

So try again: "Oh, well, we are not saying these things either about any particular being in the universe or about the universe as a whole. We are saying them about something outside the universe." Certainly, I can see what is being said. My difficulty is to see to what I have got as the subject of these remarks. What are these things being said about? It will not here do simply to say: "They are being said about God." For the crucial question is: "How are we to identify this putative subject, how are we to indicate what it is about which we are wanting to say the various things said?" Maybe this is not clear, maybe it is not satisfactory. Yet it seems to me that there is a difficulty here, and that it is one of the several difficulties of my second sort. The first positive objection which I gave fell into my Group three—the round square, contradiction group. This second, less familiar, more difficult objection belongs rather to the unfindable fairies group. For I am suggesting now that though it looks as if a substantial assertion is being made, an assertion that might be tested, really one is not making that substantial suggestion, one has got a doctrine that just can not be tested or even applied at all.

WARREN'S THIRD NEGATIVE

(Monday Night)

Dr. Flew, Gentlemen Moderators, Ladies and Gentlemen. I am happy to be before you for my closing speech this evening. Dr. Flew will have a very brief rejoinder to close the session tonight.

I should like to begin with a question that was raised in my last speech. In fact, I have raised it in two speeches and it has not been referred to by Dr. Flew as yet. He has indicated that the Nazis, who were tried at Nuremberg, were tried by international law and I have indicated that this was not really the basis upon which they were tried. It was not the *final ultimate* basis. There was a recognition that there was a higher law.

If it were the case that only various men from various nations got together and decided on it, I would like to raise this question for Dr. Flew—I would like for him to write it in his notes and be sure to deal with it—"Would it have been possible for those in the prosecution at Nuremberg to have decided that the Nazis actually did *no wrong* in murdering the Jews as they did, and to have decided to set free such men as Adolph Eichmann, and, had Adolph Hitler survived the war and had been on trial, to have set him free simply because those in the prosecution had decided on the basis of human needs and desires that everything he did was right?" I want you to be sure to be listening to see if he will deal with this. The truth of the matter is, the basic implication of the atheistic system does not allow objective moral right or objective moral wrong and, therefore, Dr. Flew cannot deal with this problem on an adequate basis.

Dr. Flew then promised to give us positive reasons as to how he *knows* that God does not exist, but he suggested that perhaps it would be better if he first dealt a little more with the nature of value. He hastened to tell us that he *could not* give us a satisfactory explanation of it. For once, I am in agreement with Dr. Flew: he did *not* give a satisfactory explanation. Value is somehow, he says, a function of human needs and desires, which really is a way of saying that it depends on nothing more than your likes and dislikes, your approvals and disapprovals. But, Dr. Flew says you cannot infer that value is merely a matter of *taste*.

It is a very crucial word for him to say "merely." While he holds that morality is *subjective*, he hastens to add, "It is not *merely* subjective." Now what this amounts to is this. He wants to say, in harmony with the *implications* of his *atheistic* doctrine that morality is *subjective*, but there is something in him that will not let him be consistent with this implication. That thing is *conscience*! He cannot tolerate the actions of the Nazis, or many things that happen all around us every day, and simply dismiss it and say "Well, those people *believed* it was right." Dr. Flew, value is a fact of life and if you cannot give empirical evidence of its nature and origin, then you cannot prove atheism, because a fundamental doctrine of atheism is that *matter is the sole reality*! In fact, an absurd quotation, which Dr. Flew has endorsed, is "Everything there is, is a product of nature." But, if *everything* that exists is a *product of nature*, then nature is a product of itself. That would mean that at one time neither nature nor anything else existed. And, if such had ever been the case, nothing could now exist. It is therefore clear that Dr. Flew simply cannot deal with the matter of value. His position is absurd.

He then comes to the question of the first woman or the first baby. He says that he feels very satisfied with the answer which he has given, *provided* we will allow him the evolutionary assumption. But, Dr. Flew, that is the very thing that we will *not* allow you! It is not merely your responsibility to tell us what you might *assume* or what might be concluded from your various assumptions. It is your responsibility, when you put your signature to the proposition, "I know that God does not exist," to *prove* that *matter* is all that exists, that matter is *eternal*, that *dead rocks and dirt* are the ultimate source of human beings, by what he alleges to be the various stages of evolution.

The truth of the matter is, in these questions which I read before—I will not take the time to reread them—he first said that no human being now living or who has ever lived came into being from something that already existed that was *not human* but was *transformed* into a human being. He has also said that no human being now living or that ever has lived was *born* of some non-human thing—begotten by some non-human thing and born of some non-human thing. These are the only conceivable ways evolution could have occurred, and he has given up (rejected) both of them. Now, Dr. Flew, you have not dealt adequately with this matter at all. To simply say, "If you will grant me the evolutionary *assumption*, then it is alright for me to say I can not tell you which was first, a woman or a baby," is not sufficient. The truth of the matter is, the theist, who believes in Almighty God, has absolutely no trouble with the question of which was first—a woman or a baby. Dr. Flew must deny the major undisputed fact that human beings come only from human beings. He has no proof, absolutely no proof, to the contrary. The human race had to begin by miraculous power, something out of the ordinary of the physical law by which all of us now living came to be. The record that the first man and woman owe their existence to the miraculous, creative power of Almighty God fits the facts as we know them. Dr. Flew's contention does not fit the facts. He has already denied it in your presence here tonight.

Next, he comes to the *law of excluded middle*—and again I am amazed at this man, whom I assure you is among the most learned men in the world—and seeks to rid himself of the law of excluded middle by asking us to accept his explanation which involves that it simply will not do to say that either a man is bald or he is not bald. Now, Dr. Flew, that depends up the definition of "bald." If two men have agreed that we will talk about "bald" without *knowing* what we are talking about, then that statement could be an illustration. But if by "bald" you mean a man who has less than 100 hairs on his head and a man has 99, if you say he is bald, then that statement is true; but, if he has 101 then it is false. The law of excluded middle applies only to *precisely stated* propositions. It does not apply to *ambiguous* propositions. But, every precisely stated proposition is either true or false. You can not "get off the ground" with the enterprise of human thought without recognizing the truth of the law of excluded middle and the law of contradiction.

I reiterate that every thing in this world is either human or non-human, and it has *always* been that way. *There never has been anything on this earth that was neither human nor non-human!* Now, Dr. Flew, since your doctrine is based upon empirical evidence—observation—I ask you, "Have you *ever* seen something that was neither human nor non-human?" I plead with him to write this in his notes and to give us the answer in his rejoinder which he will have in just a moment. *Have you ever seen anything that was neither human nor non-human?* Have you ever heard of anyone else who did? Is there any kind of scientific, historical record of any thing that was neither human nor non-human? My friends, that is simply a dodge and an evasion of the very obvious truth that God Almighty has given to us, that everyone of us can see: "I am fearfully and wonderfully made." Every human being constitutes evidence for God. If evolution is true, then Dr. Flew must have these "shades" which he talks about, but he does not have them. He does not have the evidence which he alleges.

Now he turns to evil. Dr. Flew, I am not going to make your argument. I am not going to make your arguments for you. If you have an argument involving *evil*, if you want to say that there is something about the *concept of God*, that along with evil constitutes some kind of problem, then *you* are going to have to *make the argument* that shows it! Are you willing to say that the concept of God itself, without reference to any empirical fact, is incoherent, meaningless, self-contradictory? Pin this down in your mind and listen to see if he deals with it. Or, is it the case that in order to allege that the concept of God is incoherent—that somehow or other it is logically imcompatible with itself—that Dr. Flew must refer to some empirical fact(s). You see, he is not merely talking about the concept of God, but he is talking about some sort of incompatibility between *God* and some alleged *fact* in the universe, which is an entirely different argument from merely saying that the *concept of God* itself is *incoherent*. Now, Dr. Flew, it is not enough to say there are some very *interesting, puzzling,* or *difficult* questions for us in regard to the fact that evil and suffering—even such monstrosities as occurred in Hitler's Germany. You have not shown this is true, this is true, this is true, therefore God could not exist, and I await the time until you do it. I assure you that there is no problem. There will be no reason for us to be afraid of it at all. But, I will not make your argument ahead of you. I demand that you make the *argument* on evil, if you have it.

Next, he considers freedom. He asks, "If freedom is necessary in this life (in other words for there to be moral beings, for there to be moral accountability), why is it not necessary in the world to come?" Now, again, this is merely a *question*. It is *not* an *argument*! He has not said, "This is true, and this is true, and therefore there can be no God." All he is doing at this point is raising what he at least assumes to be rather *puzzling* questions. Now, Dr. Flew, I insist that you make an *argument*! His responsibility is to come up with the information that says, "I, therefore, *know* that God does *not* exist." To merely ask a question, "Why must we be free in this life and not free in the life to come?" does not warrant the deduction: "therefore, God does not exist."

Of course, it is the case that in the infinite wisdom of God, this world was formed to be inhabited as an environment of soul-making, a place for us to make our decision, during the one and only probationary period of man. And we have been informed (by God's omniscience) that when this life is over, we will not fall from that place in heaven. We will have already seen the destiny of evil men and be eternally reminded by the existence of the lost. What Dr. Flew *must* do is to show that he knows that it is the case and that the concept of God involves the logical contradiction which demands the conclusion that God does not exist. But he has not done so. He says he is going to show us a dilemma which obtains between God and evil, but he has not done so. I even started writing, in brackets underneath, what I was going to say about it, but he did not go on and make the argument. Dr. Flew, we await your making of the *argument* instead of simply raising an interesting *question*!

He says we have the problem of knowing what these things are being said *about*. But again he has not made any *argument* on it. He has not shown why there is any *problem* at all. Do men know what "God" means? Let us have Chart No. 22-B. (See Page 54.) Atheists *cannot* determine the non-existence of God from the *concept* alone. If Dr. Flew thinks he can, I invite him to the task. Let him set forth merely the *concept* of God without reference to anything in this world, that is, the problem of evil, and show us that God does not exist. The truth of the matter is his argument will, when he finally makes it, involve both the concept of God and the empirical fact of, evil, which will be a *combination* of a *concept* and a *fact* (God and the ob-

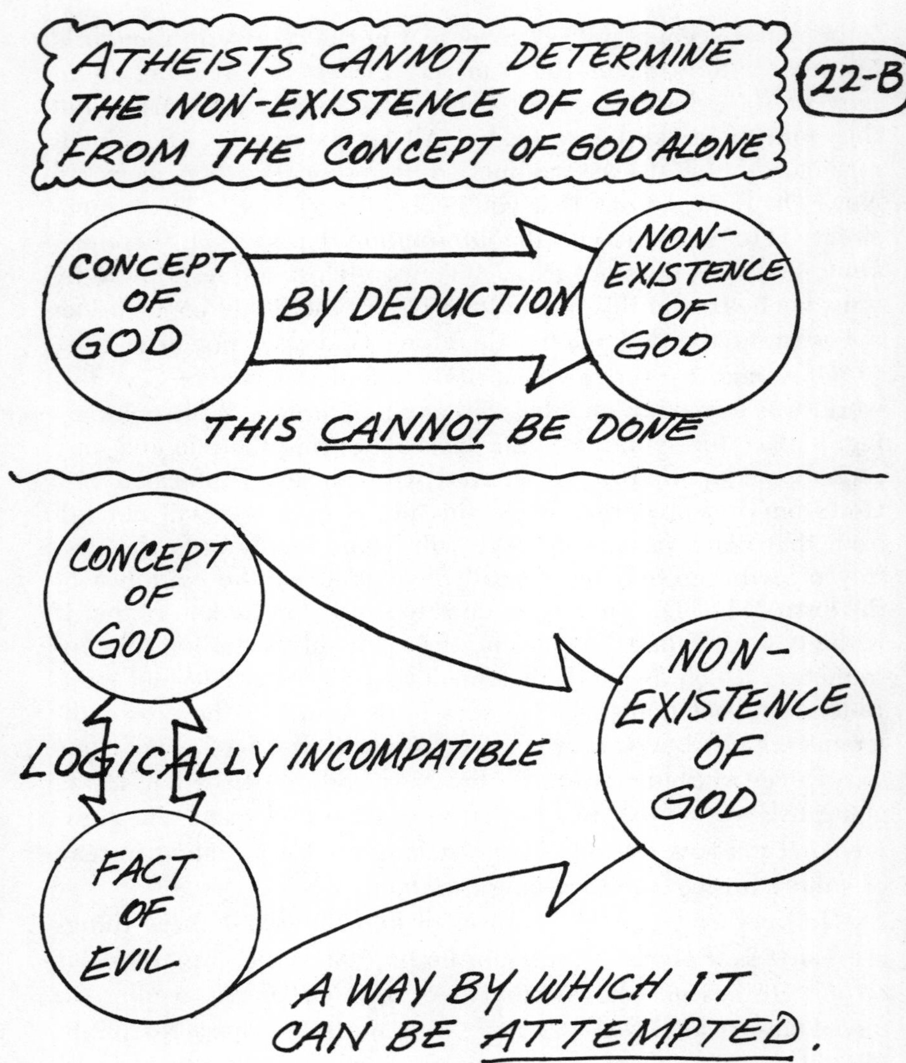
ATHEISTS CANNOT DETERMINE THE NON-EXISTENCE OF GOD FROM THE CONCEPT OF GOD ALONE
22-B
CONCEPT OF GOD
BY DEDUCTION
NON-EXISTENCE OF GOD
THIS CANNOT BE DONE
CONCEPT OF GOD
LOGICALLY INCOMPATIBLE
FACT OF EVIL
NON-EXISTENCE OF GOD
A WAY BY WHICH IT CAN BE ATTEMPTED.

jectivity of evil), and from that he will seek to deduce the non-existence of God.

Now let us see Chart No. 22-C. (See Page 56.) "When only God existed." We have here a circle indicating that God is infinite in all his attributes—power, knowledge, wisdom, presence, goodness, love, justice, righteousness, holiness and so forth. Next note: "No evil anywhere in the world, thus no empirical facts with which to allege incompatability with God." I challenge Dr. Flew to take this chart, and to show the incompatibility which allows the conclusion, "Therefore, God does not exist," which he alleges.

I have covered everything that Dr. Flew has said, so I want to go to some more negative material. I call attention to Chart No. 9-A(1). (See Page 57.) I have introduced a chart earlier (Chart No. 9) in which I have shown a "prison" which Dr. Flew is in because it involves a number of things which he *must know* before he can know that God does not exist. My experience with atheists, no matter how honestly they may allege the atheistic position, is that you will find them not wishing to talk about these matters—as if they had absolutely no responsibility whatever in regard to them.

But, he cannot prove that God does not exist unless he can *first* prove that matter really does exist *non-contingently,* that is, that it is eternal, that it does not have a beginning.

He must prove *secondly* that matter is all that exists. Note in the chart, however, that Dr. Flew is on the left side of the chart. These matters (matters listed in the middle of the chart) constitute a barrier between his going from that side to the other side of the chart where he can say "I know that God does not eixst."

In the *third* place, a great barrier to his doing so, is the obligation of proving that matter has always existed.

Fourth, that no one piece of matter is worth any more than any other piece of matter. Now if everything that exists is matter, simply molecules in motion, there really can be no ultimate or significant difference in any piece of matter. There can only be different *arrangements* of matter.

Fifth, he must prove that by sheer chance, rocks and dirt, that is, *dead* matter, possibly including gases and water, became *living*

WHEN ONLY GOD EXISTED

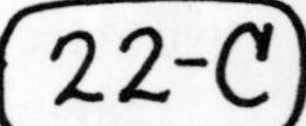

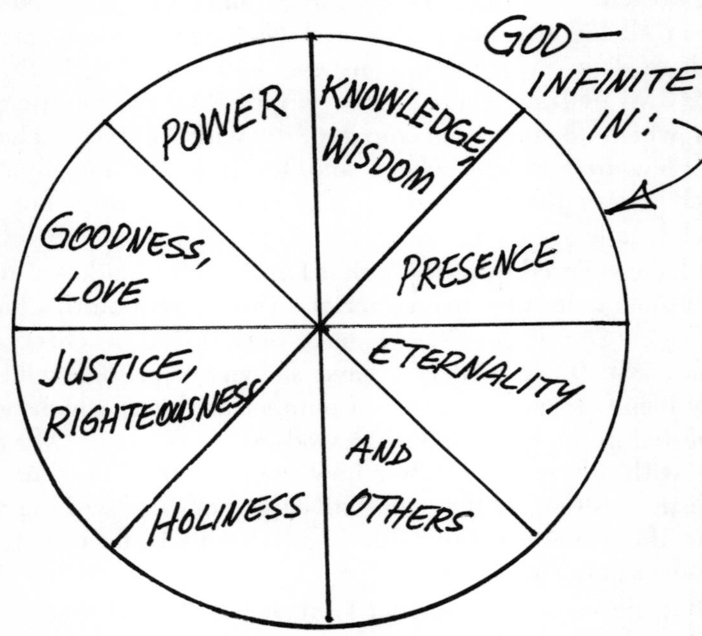

NO EVIL ANYWHERE—THUS NO EMPIRICAL FACTS WITH WHICH TO ALLEGE INCOMPATIBILITY WITH GOD!!!

THE INSURMOUNTABLE BARRIERS TO DR. FLEW'S SUCCESS 9-A(1)

(1)

DR. FLEW MUST KNOW

1. THAT MATTER REALLY DOES EXIST NON-CONTINGENTLY
2. THAT MATTER IS ALL THAT EXISTS.
3. THAT MATTER HAS ALWAYS EXISTED.
4. THAT NO ONE PIECE OF MATTER IS WORTH ANY MORE THAN ANY OTHER PIECE OF MATTER
5. THAT BY SHEER CHANCE ROCKS AND DIRT (I.E., DEAD MATTER, POSSIBLY INCLUDING GASES AND WATER) BECAME LIVING MATTER.
6. THAT BY SHEER CHANCE ROCKS AND DIRT BECAME CONSCIOUS MATTER.
7. THAT BY SHEER CHANCE ROCKS AND DIRT BECAME A HUMAN BEING.

BEFORE HE CAN KNOW THAT THIS PROPOSITION

"I KNOW THAT GOD DOES NOT EXIST"

IS TRUE

DR. FLEW

matter. He has never seen this occur. He has absolutely *no proof* for it. Yet his whole case depends upon it.

Sixth, that by sheer chance rocks and dirt ultimately, by various changes which he alleges, became conscious matter.

Seventh, that by sheer chance rocks and dirt, by a series of changes, became human matter, became human beings. On the next chart, 9-A(2), (See Page 59.) I note, eighth, that by sheer chance rocks and dirt developed in such a way that a *woman* was first on earth before any *human baby*. Ninth, that by sheer chance rocks and dirt developed in such a way that a baby was first on earth before any woman. I want to reiterate that he has not dealt with this matter at all. He *cannot* do so. He cannot tell you which was first—a woman or a baby. His reference to things which he alleges were neither human nor non-human does not deal adequately with this matter.

Tenth, he must know that by sheer chance, rocks and dirt developed human female breasts so they could change blood into milk.

Eleventh, he must know that there is no law higher than the civil and/or criminal law of a society or nation.

Twelfth, that when a human being dies, his or her death is the absolute end of him or her, the totality of his or her being goes to dust. He has no way of knowing this. If it is not the case that Dr. Flew *knows* this, then atheism is not true.

Thirteenth, that by sheer chance rocks and dirt developed conscience.

Fourteenth, that by sheer chance rocks and dirt developed spiritual capacity (the need for salvation from sin, right relationship with God, and the hope of eternal life, etc.).

Fifteenth, that by sheer chance rocks and dirt developed intelligence.

Sixteenth, that by sheer chance rocks and dirt developed a respiratory system in human beings. Now friends, none of us can live more than 5 minutes without oxygen. Chart No. 42-A1* (See Page 62.) There must occur in the human lungs, in the alveoli, the air passage and the blood passage, an osmosis of oxygen into

*Even though there was no specific oral call for this chart at this particular point, under prior instructions by Dr. Warren, the operator of the chart projector, when Dr. Warren began to discuss a particular chart, flashed that chart on the screen.

[INSURMOUNTABLE BARRIERS, CONT'D.]

9-A(2)

DR FLEW MUST KNOW

8. THAT BY SHEER CHANCE ROCKS AND DIRT DEVELOPED IN SUCH A WAY THAT A WOMAN WAS FIRST ON EARTH BEFORE ANY HUMAN BABY;-OR-

9. THAT BY SHEER CHANCE ROCKS AND DIRT DEVELOPED IN SUCH A WAY THAT A BABY WAS FIRST ON EARTH BEFORE ANY WOMAN.

DR. FLEW

10. THAT BY SHEER CHANCE ROCKS AND DIRT DEVELOPED THE HUMAN FEMALE BREAST SO THAT IT COULD CHANGE BLOOD INTO MILK.

11. THAT THERE IS NO LAW HIGHER THAN THE CIVIL AND/OR CRIMINAL LAW OF A SOCIETY OR NATION

(2) BEFORE HE CAN KNOW THAT THIS PROPOSITION

"I KNOW THAT GOD DOES NOT EXIST"

IS TRUE

[INSURMOUNTABLE BARRIERS, CONT'D.]

DR. FLEW MUST KNOW

12. THAT WHEN A HUMAN BEING DIES, HIS (OR HER) DEATH IS THE ABSOLUTE END OF HIM (OR HER)—THE TOTALITY OF HIS (OR HER) BEING GOES TO DUST.

13. THAT BY SHEER CHANCE ROCKS AND DIRT DEVELOPED CONSCIENCE.

14. THAT BY SHEER CHANCE ROCKS AND DIRT DEVELOPED SPIRITUAL CAPACITY (NEED FOR SALVATION FROM SIN, RIGHT RELATIONSHIP WITH GOD, HOPE OF ETERNAL LIFE, ETC.).

15. THAT BY SHEER CHANCE ROCKS AND DIRT DEVELOPED INTELLIGENCE.

DR. FLEW

9-A(3)

(3)

BEFORE HE CAN KNOW THAT THIS PROPOSITION

"I KNOW THAT GOD DOES NOT EXIST"

IS TRUE

[INSURMOUNTABLE BARRIERS, CONT'D.]

DR. FLEW MUST KNOW

16. THAT BY SHEER CHANCE ROCKS AND DIRT DEVELOPED A RESPIRATORY SYSTEM (AS IN HUMAN BEINGS).

17. THAT BY SHEER CHANCE ROCKS AND DIRT DEVELOPED A CIRCULATORY SYSTEM (AS IN HUMAN BEINGS).

DR. FLEW

18. THAT BY SHEER CHANCE ROCKS AND DIRT DEVELOPED A DIGESTIVE SYSTEM (AS IN HUMAN BEINGS).

19. THAT BY SHEER CHANCE, ROCKS AND DIRT DEVELOPED A REPRODUCTIVE SYSTEM (BOTH MALE AND FEMALE).

20. THAT BY SHEER CHANCE ROCKS AND DIRT DEVELOPED THE ENDOCRINE GLAND SYSTEM.

9-A (4)

(4)

BEFORE HE CAN KNOW THAT THIS PROPOSITION

"I KNOW THAT GOD DOES NOT EXIST"

IS TRUE

[USE WITH 41-D]

[RESPIRATORY SYSTEM— CONT'D]

✿ THE MARVELOUS INTERCHANGE OF OXYGEN (IN AIR) AND CARBON DIOXIDE (IN BLOOD):

42-A1

(1)

1. WITHOUT THIS AMAZING INTERCHANGE, NO HUMAN BEING COULD LIVE MORE THAN A FEW MOMENTS.
2. YET, THE ATHEISTIC POSITION DEPENDS UPON ITS EVOLVING OVER A PERIOD OF TIME AS LONG, PERHAPS, AS A MILLION YEARS
3. EVOLUTION COULD NOT HAVE OCCURRED—
4. —SO— ATHEISM IS FALSE!

*cf. CHART 41-D

the blood from the air and carbon dioxide from the blood into the air passage. This occurs because of a difference of pressure tension in the air passage of the oxygen particles as over against what is in the oxygen of the blood. So the oxygen in the air passes through the capillary wall into the blood but the carbon dioxide, because of a difference of pressure in the carbon dioxide in the blood and in the air, passes through the capillary wall into the air; and therefore, it could not have evolved since all atheists recognize that it demands millions of years to bring about changes which involve such complexity. My time is up, thank you very much.

FLEW'S REJOINDER

(Monday Night)

I'm glad that Dr. Warren and I are, I think, coming closer together about the law of the excluded middle. He was putting the point in a way which emphasized exactly what I had wanted to emphasize, that *every precisely stated* proposition is either true or false. Yes, indeed. If, instead of using the word "bald" in its vague everyday meaning we define it in terms of either total numbers of hairs or populousness per square inch, then certainly it becomes a straight matter of fact whether there are 99 per square inch or not. So, we're obviously moving together on that.

About whether I have met anyone who was not unequivocally either human or non-human: yes, I am afraid I have. I have met people who were very senile. I have also met people who were mad. Both cases raise very serious and bitter problems. Can we say that these former people are people any longer?

Third point: about the things that I am supposed to show: that matter must exist non-contingently, that is to say be eternal; and that matter must be all, but matter must never have begun. I do not see why that is necessary at all. It seems to me that someone could perfectly consistently be an atheist and believe that the universe is going as a matter of fact to have an end, or believe that it had had a beginning but was not going to have an end. However, I am myself inclined to believe that matter is without end and without beginning. But I do not see why as an atheist I have got to.

FLEW'S FOURTH AFFIRMATIVE

(Tuesday Night)

It is high time, indeed perhaps over time—for me to say more, more directly to the central questions: how I come to my atheist position; and what reasons there are for thinking that that position is correct.

Nevertheless, before returning again to the treatment direct, which I began in my third slot on Monday night, I want to try yet once more to satisfy Dr. Warren about the objectivity of value. Certainly I do not regret the time we have already spent on this and on the evolutionary theory, and on differences of degree. For these are relevant matters even if their relevance may seem a little indirect; and they are certainly important as well as, I think, relevant. Now, Dr. Warren believes that one cannot consistently hold that anything is categorically wrong or right, bad or good, while at the same time denying that these values are sustained by a Creator. Without that support by a Creator, it is suggested, we should be left only with arbitrary individual or group preferences. The imperatives of duty would be without authority, without any standing in the universe.

I want to say right away that I fully sympathize with, and share the concerns behind, this line of thought. People feel, and I sympathize with their feeling, that the decencies of good families and good communities must be threatened if there are no solid standards to live by. In this, though I do not draw the same theological conclusions that they do, I am sure that these people are right. Believe it or not, I have myself been married for twenty-three years to my first and only wife and I am a doting father of two daughters so the sort of concern for the values of a decent family and a decent community are something which I share.

Again, I fully share Dr. Warren's outrage against the monstrosities of the Nazi era. And I am much the happier to go along with him about this since I know that he is not one of those all too common in my own doomed country—who find the same frightful cruelties entirely acceptable when they are the work of a Socialist or Communist government in Russia, or Cambodia or wherever else. Dr. Warren, I know, is not in this like the labor union leaders in Britian who recently entertained as an honored guest the former head of the Russian secret police and sometime director of *The Gulag Archipelago* (all this, I may say, at just about the same time as their American opposite numbers were similarly but more honorably honoring Alexander Solzhenitsyn). But now, while I fully share these concerns about values, values which are not an arbitrary matter of individual or group preference, still I do not agree that an appeal to divine support can do what Dr. Warren and so many others are sure that it can do. We need, I think, to distinguish two sorts of support which a god might be believed to provide for a system of values. The first of these sorts of support, which is not the one which Dr. Warren has been asking for, I believe could in principle be provided. The second sort of support which, as I understand it, is what Dr. Warren has been asking for, I think could not even in principle be provided.

We can deal with the first, and here irrelevant, sort of support in short order. Certainly, a god could lay on rewards and punishments for those who satisfied or failed to satisfy the practical requirements of whatever system of values that God might choose to support. And of course any offender against the requirements of any system thus supported by an all-powerful all-knowing being will most certainly be detected and convicted. Here I think of the poster issued by the Christian Democratic Party in Italy during the 1948 elections. It showed an elector in the privacy of the polling booth, and the caption read: "Stalin can not see you, but God can. Vote Christian Democrat." On that occasion apparently there were enough Catholic believers in Italy who took their religion seriously to insure a very satisfactory Christian Democrat vote.

However, it is not that sort of support which is in question, at any rate not here and now. The idea here, as I understand it, is that standards of justice, compassion and so on, can only be genuinely authoritative insofar as these standards are endorsed and given their authority by a creator and if this is right then anyone who allows that any such standards do have an authority transcending any individual or group preferences is thereby committed to recognizing the existence of God. Certainly, it is a perfectly sound argument but I think the premise of this sound argument is false. For, to recognize standards as being correct and authoritative does not in fact assume either that these standards are supported by a creator or that it is precisely and only that supreme endorsement which makes them the authoritative correct standards.

To make this point clear. Consider again a slightly different version of that old question first formulated in Plato's dialogue *Euthyphro*. Are any arrangements which are just, just because God supports them, or does God support any arrangements which are just because they are just? Apply this to the question of whether the arrangements under which it is said God provides for the saved eternal bliss and for the damned, eternal torment. Suppose now that, considering those alleged arrangements, someone says, as I would say, that it would be absolutely wrong to keep any conscious being, man or animal, in such torment forever; and, furthermore that it would be to the last degree monstrously unjust for a Creator Himself to punish His own creatures in that way.

Is the correct reply to that sort of challenge the reply that, since these are the divine arrangements, and since arrangements are just precisely and only because God supports them, therefore these arrangements must be just by definition; and that is that? Certainly, some Christians and perhaps most Moslems have taken this first option. I do not think it would be unfair to Calvin, and to such leading Calvinists as Jonathan Edwards in what later was to become this country, to say that this was the option which they took, or took at least half of the time. Certainly anyone who does take that option very clearly makes his religion a worship of absolute infinite power as such. On the lips of such a person, the claim that his God is always just amounts to no more than the rather unedifying assertion that his God always does what his God wants, and likes it. While that may be very true, it is scarcely what anyone ordinarily means by talking about justice; or, incidentally, by praising a God as just.

The alternative option is to say that the objector has somehow misperceived, misunderstood the situation. The divine arrangements for creation salvation and damnation are, the reply might be, when properly understood, perfectly just. And to say that they are indeed just is to say something more than, and something different from that saying God supports these arrangements. But this second option, which I believe is the one taken by Dr. Warren, and which I believe is common to the whole Church of Christ, takes it for granted that there is some proper standard of what is just and unjust; and that this standard is not an arbitrary function of the Creator's will. Surely, it is precisely and only by reference to this logically independent standard of what is just and unjust that Dr. Warren himself—and, if I am right, the whole Church of Christ too—affirm that God is just, and praise God for his justice.

The upshot of this argument is that, while I agree with Dr. Warren that certain things are categorically right or wrong, when I do this I am appealing to the same perhaps mysterious, I suppose objective standards to which he himself appeals when he labors to justify the ways of God to man. Where we disagree is: first, that I am maintaining that these standards do not and cannot derive their authority from any fiat or command, divine or otherwise; and, second, and not immediately to the present purpose, I am maintaining that the arrangements which Dr. Warren and others attribute to their God are to the last degree monstrous, unjust and, if I may use the word, satanic.

Well, as perhaps too often in these performances, I seem to have spent most of my time responding to an important point made by Dr. Warren, and to have left rather too little for an apology for my own atheism. Still, I doubt whether the situation is really as bad as that may have made it seem. For we are in fact between us covering subjects which obviously do need to be covered, even if we are not doing it in the most systematic possible way. What I will do now is to begin to outline what I think the systematic order would be. I do not think I shall be able to finish in the first slot. But I will start. The object of the exercise will be to provide people with a framework. If they agree with me that this is the right framework, then it will be within this framework that they think of all my various arguments—and, of course, of all those of Dr. Warren too.

Surely any systematic inquiry into the truth of some or any system of religious belief must begin from a completely this-worldly naturalistic position. That is to say we have to start from and with our common sense and our scientific knowledge of the universe around us. This is the undisputed knowledge available to people of all religions and of none. This starting point, you might describe as atheist but in a negative sense. For at this first stage we are not going to assert, or to deny, or even to entertain any religious beliefs at all. I call this negative atheism to distinguish it from the positive denial which I am defending these evenings here in Denton.

(Perhaps I should add some adjective to remind us that there have been and are innumerable notions of God: God with a big "G", or god with a small "g" and soon. Of course we are here confining our attention to one of these nations. Yet perhaps it is just worth saying to bring this out a little more clearly that the early Christians were in a sense rightly called atheists, as they were by many of their contemporaries. These contemporaries were quite right in what they said because the early Christians, like all Christians, did deny categorically the existence of various pagan gods; gods no doubt with a small "g". All of us are indeed atheists, positive atheists, in respect of the God or gods of most religions.)

Suppose we start from the position of naturalism and negative atheism. I emphasize *negative*. I am not suggesting that you should all start by agreeing with me as positive atheists. It would make it all much too easy for me if you had to start by agreeing with me from the beginning! What I am suggesting is that every inquirer should start from—take as given—everyday, undisputed, commonsense knowledge of the world as well as our reservoir of scientific knowledge. (That reservoir is available to us even if we do not actually know much of it ourselves.) If we do start from this position we become ready to examine any and every proposal that there may be something, some being, some force or what not beyond and behind the universe and the familiar things we take for granted. Now, what someone who then tries to make out a case for any sort of religious belief will be confronted by two tasks. The first task he must try to fulfill is to introduce his own favored notion of God, explain what he means by God, what he wants us to believe. His second task is to provide us with some good reason for believing that this concept does in fact have application. Only when both these tasks have been satisfactorily completed will we have or, for that matter, will he have adequate warrant for his particular proposed belief.

That is how it seems to me, the tasks should be undertaken. Someone who is to maintain the opposite view, that this particular sort of God does not exist, will naturally and properly, if he is being quite systematic, start from this same everyday and undisputed knowledge, shared by people of all religions or of none. He will consider the notion of God that is proposed, and perhaps offer some objections. After that he will consider the argument which might be put forward for saying that a God thus and thus described actually does exist.

This is the framework within which I am operating. If you think that this is a reasonable framework, then you will be able to put various things said by Dr. Warren and me within this framework and see for yourselves how the conclusions work out. Perhaps it is also worth my saying that someone could very well agree, I hope they will agree, that this is the right framework for systematic inquiry even if they do not agree with my actual conclusions. Indeed, I believe that St. Thomas Aquinas accepted that a framework of this sort would be the right framework; although he, of course, believed the two essential tasks could be satisfactorily completed from a theist point of view.

Assuming that this is the framework to go on, I am going, as the evening proceeds—though no doubt beginning on each occasion taking up something that Dr. Warren has said—to make some points first about stage one, the explanation of the notion of God, and then about stage two, the consideration of what if any reasons might be offered for saying that there is a God of that sort. I have of course already said something under the first of these two heads—when I suggested in the third piece last night, not exactly that the concept of God itself is incoherent, but rather that notion, combined with certain assertions about God involves a contradiction. The suggestion then started from a familiar ancient objection, though I was taking it in a particular form to allow for various things that are agreed between me and Dr. Warren. It was a version of the old objection that you can not consistently say that God is all-powerful and all-good and then attribute to Him the sorts of arrangements about salvation and damnation which are attributed to Him within the system.

WARREN'S FOURTH NEGATIVE

(Tuesday Night)

Dr. Flew, gentleman moderators, ladies and gentlemen. I am extremely happy tonight to be before you again to reply to the speech to which you have just listened. I want to say again, in harmony with what Gary Ealy has said, that Dr. Flew is certainly one of the most eminent—so far as *scholarship* is concerned—to defend the position which he has affirmed in this debate. His proposition, "I know that God does not exist," could not be defended better by anyone, so far as I know, in England or America. Any weaknesses, therefore, that you may see manifested in what is being done in this debate, in regard to the atheistic position, cannot be attributed to the *man*. It must be attributed to the *position*.

It is entirely in order for me, as the negative speaker in this discussion, as I follow each night what he has said, and consider it item by item and statement by statement, to present certain other materials which are relative to the undermining of his case. And, since it is certainly pertinent to my reply to what he has said tonight, I want to refer to the ten questions which I have given him according to our agreement, some of which he has answered and some of which he has not.

QUESTIONS FOR DR. FLEW, TUESDAY NIGHT, SEPTEMBER 21, 1976

1. What would have to occur (or to have occurred) to convince you that your proposition is false?
2. What would have to occur (or to have occurred) to convince you that my proposition is true?
3. ☐ True ☐ False

   The following statement is a precisely stated proposition: either a woman was first on earth before any human baby, or a human baby was first on earth before any woman.
4. What known biological law explains the development of the respiratory system?
5. If you met a man with one mechanical hand and one natural hand would you know (please check):

   ☐ That the mechanical hand was designed by an intelligent being?

☐ That the natural hand was ultimately designed by an intelligent being?

6. ☐ True ☐ False

If the Nazis had captured you and your regiment and had given you the choice of joining them in their efforts to exterminate people, you would have had the objective moral obligation to die rather than join them in the murder of men, women, and children.

7. ☐ True ☐ False

Every precisely stated proposition is either true or false.

8. ☐ True ☐ False

The Judges at Nuremberg would have been justified in concluding that, since the Nazis were obeying the law of their own land, the Nazis were *not* guilty of real (objective) moral wrong in torturing and/or murdering six million Jewish men, women, and children.

9. ☐ True ☐ False

If the Mars probe discovered a rock with a king's head carved on it, and with a message of gratitude to the king, then men on earth could know that at some time an intelligent being had been on Mars.

10. "Maximal greatness" is (please check all appropriate boxes):

☐ A coherent term; ☐ Dead matter; ☐ Living matter;

☐ Non-human living matter; ☐ Human living matter;

☐ Something else? (please explain) ______________________

____

Some men who are given questions in such a discussion do not answer because they do not know *how* to answer. But, Dr. Flew is a scholar of the highest rank. When *he* does not answer, I must raise the question, "Has he merely decided that he *will* not or that he cannot?" Is it that he *cannot* answer and remain consistent with the doctrine which he has espoused? For he himself is on record, again and again, that any position which cannot maintain itself without self-contradiction ought to be abandoned, that the law of rationality would demand that one do that, that honesty would demand that one do that. Let me go hurriedly through these questions and I will have occasion to say something more about them because there are some very very important matters in them.

Dr. Flew is a man who has given a great deal of attention to the question of falsification. He holds that in regard to this debate, one must be able to answer this question, "What would have to occur or to have occurred to constitute for you a disproof of the love or the existence of God?" This is a question which he has posed to theists again and again all over the world. Now, that question has been posed to *him* (Dr. Flew) and what do you suppose he has answered?

Question No. 1: "What would have to occur (or to have occurred) to convince you that *your* proposition is *false?*" Dr. Flew did not answer even one word. Why not?

Question No. 2: "What would have to occur (or to have occurred) to convince you that *my* proposition is *true*?" Not one word was written in reply.

Question No. 3: True or false. "The following statement is a precisely stated proposition: Either a woman was first on earth before any human baby, or a human baby was first on earth before any woman." And Dr. Flew says "false." Now, Dr. Flew, surely you are the only one in this audience who holds that that is not a precisely stated proposition. Everybody knows the meaning of the words. There is nothing ambiguous about the words. There is nothing ambiguous about the way it is stated. Now, he has already conceded his position by recognizing that nothing non-human ever *transformed* into a human being and nothing that was non-human gave *birth* to a human being. So, he has given up the possibility of any human being ever being here by virtue of evolution, and if atheism is true that (evolution) is what absolutely must occur. Therefore, he has already given up the debate but still he persists in refusing to deal with this question.

He did not answer the fourth question. I will now skip down to question six because I will refer to the others in just a moment. True or false—"If the Nazis had captured you and your regiment and had given you the choice of joining them in their efforts to exterminate people, you would have had the objective moral obligation to die rather than to join them in the murder of men, women, and children." And Dr. Flew says it is true. Now consider this admission. I indicated to you last night that no atheist will live according to the implications of his own doctrine. The implications of his doctrine are that there is *no objective moral law,* that there is no law higher than what mere human beings simply *invent.* Last night he answered the question which indicated that prior to the existence of the first human being there was no value in the universe; therefore, according to Dr. Flew value must be nothing more than a function of the human mind —i.e., value is nothing more than an invention of men and women. Yet he said he would have been under the *moral obligation to die,* rather than to join with the Nazis. Therefore he admits the point that I made last evening, that the Nuremberg trials were based not upon merely international law that human beings had invented, but a higher law that transcended so called "international law."

Question No. 8: Now this is true or false—"The judges at Nuremberg would have been justified in concluding that, since the Nazis were obeying the law of their own land, the Nazis were *not* guilty of real (objective) moral wrong in torturing and/or murdering six million Jewish men, women or children." And Dr. Flew said "false." In other words, according to Dr. Flew, these men functioning under international law, which last night he said was the basis by which they were judged, could not have decided to have let them go free. Therefore, he is again recognizing a higher law above international law, above any law that mere human beings have invented, and therefore Justice Robert Jackson was right when he said that we condemn these men on the basis of a higher law which transcends the provincial and the transient. My friends, this debate will close without my learned colleague answering that point. The reason why it is true is because he has a *conscience* within his soul. He cannot tolerate the idea of the Nazis putting little children into box cars coated with quicklime so that they will die, not only to die, but to die agonizingly. He simply cannot tolerate it. He must recognize that they were wrong—wrong above any mere human law that has been invented. There is only one explanation which satisfies what is required: that is, the law of God Almighty.

Now I come to his speech. Dr. Flew still has not realized that for these two nights he, not I, is in the affirmative. He still keeps trying to have me prove the existence of God. Dr. Flew, I suggest that you go back and reread the proposition. It says, "I, Antony G. N. Flew, know that God does not eixst." I have pointed out his obligation as an *affirmative* speaker to present an *argument*—a sound argument. Now a sound argument is one in which the argument is valid, which means that if the premises are true then the conclusion *must* be true. But, in a *valid* argument the premisess might be false and even the conclusion false; but, in a *sound* argument the argument must not only be valid, it is also the case that the premises must be true. I have asked, I have pleaded, I have begged for the argument that has premises which warrant the deducation, therefore, "I, A. G. N. Flew know that God does not exist." All of these questions that he raises which tend to put me in the affirmative (which will begin tomorrow evening) have nothing whatever to do with the proposition, for tonight, and I shall show, as I go through his speech, that he has not until this good moment made an argument which he even claims to be a sound argument, the conclusion of which is therefore, "I know that God does not exist."

He says, "I come now to my atheistic position." I have noted recently in Dr. Flew's book, *The Presumption of Atheism,* that he hedges away from thorough-going atheism in which you say, as he did in this debate, "I know that God does not exist" to merely saying that "What I mean by 'atheist' is simply that I am *not a theist.*" But, Dr. Flew, in *this debate* you have affirmed, "I know that God does not exist" and the proof of it *your* responsibility!

He then promises us that he is going to tell us *why* he has espoused the atheistic position and we are still waiting. He promises us that he is going to do it and he promises and promises in every speech, and he still has not given it (the proof). I will give you my word that in my very first speech I will give you an *argument.* It will be *valid,* and the *premises* will be true. I will not merely *promise* to give you an argument in sustaining my proposition.

He says that Warren denies you can hold *objective* values without a Creator, that denying God leaves one with only the subjective view of morality. Yes, I certainly do hold that, and by your answer to the questions tonight, Dr. Flew, *you* agreed to that very position. In your answer to question number 6 you said that there is a higher law above the international law that condemned those men and even sent them to execution. Now, Dr. Flew, what was that law higher than the international law? What was that law that meant that these judges could not change and say these men were innocent after all because they were obeying the law of their own land? Why could not the Nazis have met their own "needs and desires," according to Dr. Flew, and therefore have said that it meets our desires as indeed Heinrich Himmler, Hitler's hatchet man, said, "It is our moral duty to exterminate these people. It meets our needs and our desires." The very basis upon which Dr. Flew argues was the basis upon which the Nazis argued.

And even though he now admits that the law of excluded middle is true (that every precisely stated *proposition* is either true or false), he still refuses to apply it to *objects*. Bear in mind that the law of excluded middle applies to *objects* as well as to *propositions*. This means that every object in the world either has a certain property or it does not. This lectern is either orange or it is not. It either has the property of being orange or it does not. I either have the property of being nine feet tall or I do not.

Now, every object there is in the world either has the property of being human or it does not. Dr. Flew's whole case depends upon some invented idea—talk about incoherent concepts. A concept which is absolutely incoherent is Dr. Flew's concept of beings which were neither human nor non-human. He has admitted that nothing can be *transformed* from a non-human to a human, but last night in his rejoinder—and I am sure it was a great shock to us all—he said that humans can become non-human. Referring to senile people, he said, "I have encountered people and, so far as I know, they are no longer human." In taking this position, he joins the Nazis in holding that since they are no longer human, they could rightly be exterminated! But, note how he again contradicts his position on the law of excluded middle, because he did not say that they become neither human nor non-human. He says they become *non-human*. Go back and check the tape, Dr. Flew, and see if that is not what you said. Now that is the very thing for which I contended. Every object that has ever existed is (was) either human or non-human. There is no way you can fix up the theory of evolution to avoid the dilemma in which Dr. Flew finds himself tonight. It is not because he has not thought about it before. It is not because he is not a scholar. It is because the position is false, and there is nothing he can do to answer it.

Then he expresses outrage at the Nazis and the Communists. And in doing so, he admits this higher law to which I have already referred. And he cries that values are not arbitrarily based upon merely the individual or the society. And if it is not the case that law is merely something of the disapproval or approval of an individual or a society, or a part of a society, then it is not something simply invented. It is something that is eternal in its very nature and is based upon the relationship that it has to God.

There is nothing in anything that he has said in the entire speech that has anything to do with proving that God does *not* exist. If you were listening to him and did not know what proposition he was supposed to be affirming, I am sure you would never conclude from what he has said that that was the proposition he is supposed to be affirming.

He then alleges that Dr. Warren will accept some value system only as endorsed by a Creator. Now, Dr. Flew, I want to insist that you recognize that it is *your* responsibility to show how you *know* that there is no higher law which has God's endorsement. That is *your* responsibility while you are in the affirmative.

You need to say this is true, this is true, therefore here is the law by which men are judged. And, you *must know* this—not merely that you are guessing, not merely that you are pointing out something that is curious to you as a sort of intellectual study. But, that you say: "This is true, this is true, therefore I know that the moral values by which men live have absolutely no connection with any Supreme Being.

Then he refers again to Plato. It did not help him last evening. It did not help him tonight. There is absolutely no argument at all in it which shows that God does not exist. You *must show* that you *know* that God has no such law. Dr. Flew, you must make an argument and you have not done it as yet.

He then brings up Calvinism. He brings up Aquinas. I have absolutely no connection with either one of them. They are entirely beside the point in this discussion.

He says that Dr. Warren takes it for granted that there is

some objective standard—the will of God—and that I agree that certain things are categorically right or wrong. I agree: for there to be objective value, there must be the ultimate standard.

Now, I am going through his speech not because it really is relevant to the proposition but to let this audience know that I am dealing with everything he has said. There is nothing in his speech which warrants, "Therefore there is no God."

Then he says that the arrangements which Dr. Warren attributes to God are really satanic. If this is the case then the teachings of Jesus Christ are satanic, but the *inventions* of *Dr. Antony G. N. Flew* are wonderful, good, righteous, holy, and just! But I ask: upon what basis, Dr. Flew, would you even strive to be righteous, or holy, or good when you hold that at one time nothing of value existed and that nothing of value came into being until human beings did? And if value is not then merely a function of the human mind, then there is no way you can harmonize the various positions you have taken. You are involved in self-contradiction.

By way of summation, I want to give attention to some things that have occurred already in this discussion. It is the responsibility of the negative speaker to help the audience to see what is occurring. Dr. Flew has again and again in his writings chided religious people for not being rational, that is, for not accepting the implications of their basic affirmation(s), of not being willing to draw only those conclusions for which they have conclusive evidence. I am in harmony with that position. Certainly Christian theism is in harmony with it. But, I want you to know—and I am not going to get through with this—Dr. Flew, there is going to be a lot more of this before we are through tonight. Self-contradictions, concessions and admissions of defeat that already have occurred in this discussion will be shown. You have heard some already from Dr. Flew's answering of questions tonight.

In the face of the admission that we ought to honor the law of rationality, I want you to note some of the concessions made by Dr. Flew during the sessions last evening. In regard to question number 2 on last evening, Dr. Flew concedes, first, that it is possible for men to be guilty of *real objective moral wrong*. According to Dr. Flew, an actual case of men being guilty of real moral wrong, namely the Nazis' torturing of the Jews has occurred. Second, there is a *higher law* by which human thoughts and deeds may be judged. Third, that moral wrong is not merely, not only, subjective. Of course there can be subjective wrongs. Somebody may say "Well, I *feel* that it is wrong, I have this *disapproval* of it." But Dr. Flew is admitting there is something else: i.e., that there is moral, *objective* wrong! He has admitted that the basis of the prosecution by Justice Robert Jackson was correct, that is, that the Nazis were guilty of violating a higher moral law that transcends the provincial and the transient. This means that the law of any given nation, during a given period of time, is not decisive in deciding objective right and wrong. Fourth, there is a higher law, even above international law, by which men can rightly be tried, convicted, and even executed. That is what actually happened with the Nazis at Nuremberg.

Also, concession is made by Dr. Flew in regard to question number three. On this question Dr. Flew concedes that there can be no wrong unless you *violate* some *law*! Note that—there can be no wrong unless you violate some law. Then, he admits the Nazis did not violate the law of England. They did not violate the law of the United States. They did not violate their own law—the law of Germany. But, they *did* violate *some* law and it was not merely international (human) law. We find in his answers to the questions tonight that it was some higher law which transcends the provincial and the transient. That can be nothing else than the law of *God*! I challenge Dr. Flew to explain what law there is above this international law by which he has put himself in this predicament in the answering of these questions.

In regard to the fifth question last evening, he concedes that you can deduce from empirical fact a conclusion regarding the state of affairs of the class of things which are transcendent of the universe. Now that is the very thing that all these years he has argued you can *not* do. But now he has said that you *can* argue from empirical fact to the class of things which are transcendent of the universe. Of course, God is the only member of that class. But now he is saying you can reason from empirical fact in this world to the condition, or state, or number of members of that class. To do so, is to admit the basic thrust of the theistic argument that one can reason from observation of empirical facts of various sorts in this world to a consideration of a conclusion so that it constitutes knowledge which he claims of that class which transcends the world.

Thank you very much and I invite you to hear Dr. Flew.

FLEW'S FIFTH AFFIRMATIVE

(Tuesday Night)

About babies and women, I do not think I can usefully say anything more. I am afraid that here we shall just have to leave that subject, or so far as I am concerned, we shall have to leave that subject. For I cannot think of anything more which I can say which will illuminate any further the questions about vague notions and differences of degree.

About value, I had hoped that I had said a lot that would be helpful. Indeed, I still rather think that I said a lot that would be helpful. But there is clearly one distinction that I can usefully make now before going on to something else. And that is a distinction between moral law, and moral obligation, on the one hand, and legal laws.

Consider the Nuremberg trial. It seems to me that the court at Nuremberg was at least claiming (the only basis on which it was justified in acting as a court and in prescribing legal punishments) that there was an already existing system of international law in accordance with which that court was acting that at the end of the day it was prescribing the punishments appropriate to offenses against that system of law. It is entirely possible that the situation might arise there, as it would arise in the case of many other courts, where there is no doubt at all that someone did commit an offense under the system of the law of a particular state, or under international law; but where this legal offense was not in fact also a moral one. Equally well, it is entirely possible that some offense may be a moral offense; but not be against the law in this country, or against international law, and so on. And it is the relations between these two things—questions of right and wrong and if you like the moral law, and systems of positive law—which I think have given rise to some confusion here. It is familiar enough that there are many things which we believe ought not to be done which are not illegal under the laws of either Texas or the United States. And perhaps there are still some sorts of conduct which we believe to be right or even positively mandatory as a matter of morals which are actually against the laws of Texas or the United States.

So much for babies and women and for value. Now, I think I

had better go on trying to be a little systematic. Suppose we do start, as I was arguing a little earlier that we should start, from the position of what I call "negative atheism," accepting the findings of ordinary observation and everyday experience, and also referring to the ever accumulating stock of scientific knowledge of the inner workings of things. That is our starting point. The question is: "Shall we in addition to our beliefs about the things around us, and our knowledge about the things around us and in addition to the things we believe because the scientists tell us, shall we in addition to all this, believe something else about a power additional to and somehow behind the universe?"

Someone comes along and tells us that behind all this, behind all the familiar and undisputed things, there is sustaining and controlling it all, an all-knowing and all-powerful Being. Our someone tells us, furthermore that this Being uses this earth as a vale of soul-making; so that after death the winners are awarded an eternity of bliss and the losers an eternity of suffering—suffering infinitely worse than the worse earthly sufferings. Now are we to begin to test this suggestion? I have already indicated the first obvious move to make. Yet I will go on about this again. The first thing, surely, to say is that there is a flagrant inconsistency: between what is said about the goodness of this all-powerful being; and what is said about his plans and arrangements for his creatures.

There would, it seems to me, also be a pretty flagrant inconsistency: between what is said about His goodness and His power; and the existence of a great deal of what is by anyone's standards, including those of the religious believer himself wrong in this world. There appears to be a contradiction here because, if you are going to say that everything is the work of, is sustained by, an all-powerful Being who is all good, then you are going to say that in the words that Miss Mahalia Jackson sings so well: "He's got the whole world in His hands." But then it is hard indeed to see how this power, this goodness, can be compatible with what is going on.

Worse however than the difficulty of reconciling these claims with the familiar facts of the world is I think the difficulty of reconciling the official account of God's goodness and justice with what is then said about how He planned to create a lot of conscious creatures. He did this in the full awareness that while some of them were going to enjoy eternal bliss and were going to be kept in this condition by His sustaining causality, and others of them—perhaps the majority—were destined for unlimited and eternal torment and were to be sustained in that condition by His power.

I must confess that this subject of the doctrine of hell is one about which I find it very difficult to maintain my supposed national British calm and reserve. But let me, with what restraint I can muster, say that if anything can be known to be monstrously, inordinately wrong and unjust, it is the conduct of which this God is said to assume. If anything can be known to be just quite monstrously, inordinately, unquestionably unjust and evil, it is the conduct of a Being creating conscious creatures, whether human or animal, in the full knowledge, and with the intention, that these creatures should be maintained by His sustaining power eternally in infinite and unlimited torment. I speak of this with what little restraint I can muster because, if anything seems clear to me about good and evil, just and unjust, it is clear to me that this is monstrous.

But of course, to say this is not to show that there is not a Being with the power attributed to the Christian God who will in fact do these things. It is only to say that the conduct attributed to this God, the arrangements which it said that he maintains are totally inconsistent with the flattering descriptions it is proposed to apply to that Being. Yet perhaps it is also just worth saying—especially as we have been talking a lot about the desire to find some sort of authority behind good community standards—and so I think of course we have been saying these true and important things about human decencies I think it is because this is so we ought just to notice that it is rather extraordinary to try to recruit such a nightmare monster as the God so described to serve as some sort of guarantor of decent standards, of compassion and so on. After all, all the sufferings that have been so rightly described by Dr. Warren as outrageous and so on, and the deliberate production of those sufferings which he has quite rightly described as absolutely outrageous and monstrous; these are supposed to be as nothing compared with the sufferings of hell, going on forever. So, it does seem to me to be really rather incongruous to try to recruit a Being that you describe in this way whose conduct and plans and intentions are described as involving all this as some sort of guarantor of good moral standards of notions of justice.

So much for the first point that it seems to me that the moral description applied to the supposed God are quite inconsistent, both with the facts of this world, and with the other things that this God is supposed to arrange and to maintain. Now, let us move on to a second point under this first heading, Stage One. It is here that I hope to say something that bears on Dr. Warren's challenge about falsifiability. What I am going to be saying is that one of the things that is wrong with the whole notion is precisely that assertions about God have been made untestable. This is the reason why I am unable to state what would decisively establish for me the existence of God, or decisively show it to be false; if these arguments about inconsistency do not show it to be false. The reason why I have difficulty in answering these questions is that the proposed notion of God has been made one that is not subject to test. My difficulty is to see how indeed one could test theist claim when these employ a sophisticated notion of God.

In the days of the prophet Elijah and the prophets of Baal, people were prepared to say "I believe in Jehovah" and—though they would not have been hypothetical about it—to say in effect that if Jehovah exists He will act thus and thus. In particular He will produce results which Baal and the prophets of Baal will not be able to produce; and according to the record, He did—thereby decisively falsifying the claims of the worshippers of Baal. But today those days seem to have passed. Nowadays we do not find religious believers, and particularly sophisticated religious believers—who will say: "If I am right about God, as of course I maintain that I am, then in such and such circumstances this or that will happen." This said we might try to produce those circumstances, and discover whether this or that does happen. It is, I fear, not like this nowadays. Here I will quote an Associated Press report which was drawn to my attention by Dr. Barnhart. It is dated March 4, 1960, and comes from Nairobi, Kenya. I quote: "The Reverend Dr. Billy Graham was challenged today to a healing contest to see whether Christianity is more powerful than Islam. On his return to Nairobi from Ruanda Urundi on his African trip, the evangelist was handed a letter from the head of the (I am not sure about the pronunciation of these names) Amedia Moslem Mission in East Africa, Mullanah Sheikh Mavadag, contending that Islam alone is the living religion on earth through which man can attain salvation; and contending that Christianity is utterly devoid of any heavenly blessing or true guidance for man. The letter suggested that thirty incurables be satisfied by the Director of Medical Services of Kenya and be equally divided between you and me by lots. [The experimental group and the control group. Sorry that was my parenthesis!] We may then be joined by six persons of our respective faiths in prayer to God for the recovery of our respective patients, in order to determine as to who is blessed with the Lord's grace and mercy and upon whom his door remains closed."

Apparently Dr. Billy Graham—discreetly perhaps—refused to take the challenge; and his aides reported that it was very unlikely that he would even comment on the challenge. Now, I am sure that many people here will think that I have been a little vulgar and unrefined mentioning something like that. We all know that questions about religion are not to be settled in this experimental way, as apparently they were settled in the days of the priests of Baal—settled in this way in many other circumstances. Again, I read recently the Saga of Burnt Njal, and discovered from that Icelandic saga that when the first Christian missionary arrived in Iceland there happened to be a berserk—madman—at the court of the king. It was suggested they should have a test to see whether the existing priests were able to cure the berserk or whether the Christian ones could. The Christian ones succeeded, and these Icelanders—honorable blonde Icelanders—instantly kept their word to accept the religion of the winner.

To mention this sort of thing is, I know, felt to be a little vulgar nowadays. Vulgar or not, I am afraid it is important to the issue. For if you so specify your suggestion about the existence of God that it is improper and impossible to make any test that would be regarded as relevant, then there is a price to be paid for this. The price to be paid is that you are no longer saying or implying something clear cut and definite, of the sort that is implied by other hypotheses that might be offered. It is for that reason that I find such difficulty in answering Dr. Warren's challenge about what would for me settle the issue. That difficulty arises directly from the fact that the notion under discussion is one that has been so specified that apparently there is not any way of settling the issue, or perhaps there is not any way of settling it in this light.

In the first of the two phases of a systematic rational apologetic I have made two points of very different sorts. The first of these points is a point about apparent inconsistency. The second of these points was the point that, whatever may have been true in the days of Elijah the Prophet what was then perhaps a testable hypothesis has become at least for most people an untestable one. It is in that way, it seems to me, degenerate. What has happened to this is what has happened to the belief in fairies. At one stage, I imagine, people believed in fairies. They believed that in certain conditions they could be observed, perhaps on midsummer morning. They believed that if you put milk out for them the milk would disappear and it would not have been taken by the cat, and things of that sort. But those who want to maintain the belief in fairies—and of course few people in this case do want to maintain that belief, because there is no reason whatever to believe—now say: "Ah, well of course they can never be observed by anyone who is not sympathetic: you know they do not like to be observed by non-believers." So what one ends up with is that all one has is some people who say they have seen these things and there is absolutely no reason to distinguish what they are saying and claiming, no possibility of distinguishing what they are claiming from the claim we have imagined these things. Ah, well, though I have just had the one minute notice, I think that even this time I will stop short and not use the last 59 seconds.

WARREN'S FIFTH NEGATIVE

(Tuesday Night)

Dr. Flew, Gentlemen Moderators, Ladies and Gentlemen. I am before you now for the second speech of this session to reply to what you have just heard from my honorable opponent.

He begins by reference to Nuremberg and holds that this is a recognition only of international law. I have shown, by the way he has answered the questions tonight, that he himself does not believe that, for he said the judges did not have the right to say that the Nazis were not guilty of objective moral wrong. That takes away his point here. It recognizes a *higher law* than that and he has chosen not to try to designate what that law is even though I have spoken at length on it and presented a number of charts on the matter.

He persists in claiming that he is involved in what he calls "negative atheism" which seems to amount to nothing more than *agnosticism*! I warned you in the beginning to see and determine if Dr. Flew would do this. He is in the habit of doing it. He is in the habit of shifting away from a thorough-going atheism in which he affirms, as he has in this debate," I *know* that *God* does *not* exist," to merely saying, "I do not believe in God." But, Dr. Flew, we have no intention of letting you make that kind of shift unless you plainly reject the proposition you signed. It is *your* responsibility to offer an *argument*, the conclusion of which is, "I know that God does not exist"! That argument must be *sound*, it must have *true premises*, and until this good moment that argument has not been made. He has, it is true, tantalized us with some *suggestions* of some sort of inconsistency in regard to the *concept of God* and perhaps some *empirical facts in this world*. He has further tantalized us with the second point that the question of the existence of God is not testable. Is it not strange that he has a sort of an immune position? When I asked him the first two questions tonight regarding what would have to have occurred, or to occur, in order to prove that your proposition is false, he makes no reply whatsoever. You see, his proposition, his position, is immune from "testing." When we ask him the status of his falsifiable principle, that is, what would have to happen or to occur to falsify the principle upon which you build your whole case, he is as silent as the stars. There is absolutely nothing he can say about it. He has invented something that applies only to theism.

Now all that he said in his last speech concerned the matter of the problem of evil and the alleged truth of "the principle of falsification." I want to deal with the problem of evil, and Dr. Flew, I still want to insist that I am not going to make your argument for you. I am going to deal with the problem of evil to a certain point but I am not going to say here is the first premise, here is the second premise and therefore this follows. That is *your* responsibility! You have one more speech and a minute and half rejoinder in which to do it, and if you do *not* do it, then you will have let eight speeches go by without giving one single argument comprised of premises and a conclusion. It is not enough to simply throw out statements. There is a very fine statment found in the book *Critical Thinking* by Professor Max Black, Professor of Logic at Cornell University, in which he quotes Isaiah Stamp to this effect: that 400 pages of crowded fact and argument may deceive the very elect, but when reduced to a three line syllogism, will lay bare the bones of the argument and expose the fallacious reasoning involved in it. Is that the reason why this learned man, who knows logic as well as he does, has not until this good moment given us one single precisely formulated logical argument? I suggest to you that all of us ought to be becoming suspicious that such is the case.

I am going to say this much about the problem of evil.

Dr. Flew is on record in his books concerning the problem of evil. He seems to accept this as a sort of basis of proceeding: that if evil exists then God does not exist. That would constitute a first premise. Evil exists. Therefore, God does not exist. But let us note how easily this argument is refuted. First of all, his first premise is false. If the evil referred to is *real objective* evil and not just a matter of *taste* or *opinion* (subjective evil), then the premise should read, if evil exists, then God exists. Because, you cannot have *objective moral law,* in the way that I have already explained, unless there is the eternal Ultimate Good. This is the case because it involves the admission of a *higher objective law.* If when Dr. Flew says that evil exists, he means nothing more than that somebody has a *feeling of disapproval* of an action, then he has no argument against God. If by "evil" all he means is not *liking* something such as when one says, "What about a drink or a glass of spinach juice," and he says" Ugh, I do not like spinach juice," and somebody says, "Why do you not commit murder," and he says, "Ugh, I do not like murder." "Why do you not commit adultery?" "I do not like adultery." Another fellow says, "Well, I do." And they are both right you see. Now, if the evil in Dr. Flew's discussion is *subjective* evil, then it is like a man says, "I believe it is wrong to wear a red coat on Wednesday morning," and if he sees a man wearing a red coat on Wednesday morning he says "Aha, you see there is evil in God's world, therefore God does not exist." You see how utterly absurd it is. If he admits, on one hand, that the evil in his argument is *objective,* then it demands a higher law and therefore demands Ultimate Good, who is God. If it is merely *subjective,* it is merely a human opinion and amounts to absolutely nothing.

It is true that evil exists, but I will insist that *real objective evil* exists. But, Dr. Flew involves himself in contradiction in connection with it. On the one hand he admits *real objective evil.* He has done this on a number of occasions. He did it last night in answer to questions, and he did it again tonight. To admit real *objective* evil is to put the matter beyond the mere function of a human mind, and yet he threw himself into utter self-contradiction when he admitted last evening that no value existed until human beings were in the world. Now, Dr. Flew, if there was no value until there were human beings, it follows, it absolutely *must* follow, that evil is nothing but a function of a human mind. It is nothing but a *like* or a *dislike* and my friend will never extricate himself from that dilemma.

On the other hand, he has argued that *subjective* evil is adequate. His atheistic position implies *only* subjective evil. Bear in mind that Dr. Flew holds that at one time nothing existed but dead matter—rocks and dirt. That is all there was. There was *nothing* of *value*! But along comes a time when there was a human being, and so, value also came. Dr. Flew, you have not rid yourself of the woman and the baby problem—no, no, not by a "long shot." He has admitted—note this carefully—he has admitted, that there is something non-human. He says certain things have never occurred: no human being now living, no human being that has ever lived in the past, was *transformed* from something that was non-human into being human. That simply has not occurred, and never has occurred according to Dr. Flew. He further said that there is not any person now living who was *born* after being begotten by a male ape or some other non-human being and born of a female ape or some other non-human female—not now living or any person who ever did. I showed him that these are the only two possibilities even conceivable: by transformation or by birth. He now has admitted that neither of them has ever occurred. Therefore he has admitted the existence of humans is dependent on the miraculous, creative act of God. Therefore, the whole doctrine of atheism has been undermined. Now this is the reason why Dr. Flew has avoided this question, though it does him no good because of the way he answered the other question. It actually has become moot to a certain degree. I do not see how any of his atheistic colleagues can now advance or endorse him as a defender of atheism because he has completely given up the atheistic position by admitting that there is absolutely no way that human beings have come into this world by evolution.

Now, let me give a summary of the argument that Dr. Flew has made—not *argument,* that would be giving what he has done too high a status—but the *suggestions* that he has made, the *hints,* the *promises* that he has made in connection with the problem of evil. Taking this from his book, which I tired of waiting for him to give, his first premise is simply false and his second premise is contradictory or inconsistent with his own position, and the argument therefore should read that if evil exists, then God exists. Evil exists, that is, *moral objective, real moral objective evil.* Therefore, God exists. Now if he wants to go further into the problem of evil, I shall be ready for him. I shall be anxious for him to do so.

Now let us consider the matter of falsification. I want to turn to Charts No. 19-I, 19-J, 19-K, 19-L. (See Pages 93-96.) Now you can see this on the board. I would like you to read it with me and Dr. Flew can read along with me. In this debate my proposition is, "I know that God does exist." Now that is not under discussion tonight but it will be tomorrow night and I have asked him a question about it, and his proposition is, "I know that God

WHAT WOULD HAVE TO OCCUR TO CONVINCE DR. FLEW THAT HIS PROPOSITION IS FALSE?

19-I (2)

* IN THIS DEBATE, FLEW'S PROPOSITION IS: "I KNOW THAT GOD DOES NOT EXIST."

* WOULD IT CONVINCE YOU, DR. FLEW, THAT YOUR PROP. IS FALSE IF THE FOLLOWING OCCURRED?

1. YOU HEAR A GREAT VOICE FROM THE SKY.
2. THAT VOICE IDENTIFIES ITSELF: "I AM GOD—CREATOR OF THE WORLD."
3. THE VOICE TELLS YOU THAT AT A CERTAIN SPOT NORTH OF DENTON, TEXAS, WHERE PRESENTLY THERE ARE NO BUILDINGS AT ALL, AT EXACTLY 10¾ SECONDS PAST 2:19 IN THE AFTERNOON ON SEPT. 24, 1976, THE FIRST OF A NUMBER OF HUGE BUILDINGS (BUILT OF CONCRETE, STEEL, BRICKS, ETC.) WOULD SUDDENLY APPEAR (COMPLETE IN EVERY DETAIL—ADEQUATE TO BE AN OFFICE BUILDING, INCLUDING APPROPRIATE FURNITURE IN EVERY ROOM, ELEVATORS, RESTROOMS, RESTAURANTS, ETC.) ON THAT SPOT, AND THAT, FOR THE NEXT TWENTY-FOUR HOURS EXACTLY, AT EXACT FIVE-MINUTE INTERVALS, ANOTHER HUGE BUILDING WOULD SUDDENLY APPEAR VERY NEAR THE FIRST

[What would convince Dr. Flew?]

BUILDING.

19-J (3)

4. THIS WOULD CONTINUE, THE VOICE TELLS YOU, UNTIL 289 BUILDINGS (EACH ONE OF WHICH WOULD REACH AT LEAST ONE MILE INTO THE AIR) APPEAR —ALL IN THE SAME SUDDEN FASHION.

5. THE VOICE GOES ON TO SAY THAT YOU, DR. FLEW, ARE TO GO TO SPOT INDICATED, SHORTLY BEFORE THE TIME INDICATED, AND THAT YOU ARE TO TAKE 288 PEOPLE WITH YOU.

6. THE VOICE THEN TELLS YOU THAT EXACTLY TEN MINUTES AFTER THE 289th BUILDING APPEARS, YOU AND THE OTHER 288 PEOPLE (WHOM YOU ARE TO TAKE WITH YOU TO THE SPOT INDICATED) WILL SUDDENLY SPROUT RED AND PURPLE WINGS OF SUCH SIZE, POWER, AND DESIGN AS WILL ENABLE EACH ONE OF YOU TO EASILY FLY TO THE TOP OF ONE OF THE 289 BUILDINGS.

7. YOU GO TO THE INDICATED SPOT AT 2:00 IN THE AFTERNOON ON SEPT. 24, 1976— AND WAIT—ALONG WITH THE OTHER 288 PEOPLE.

8. THEN—AT EXACTLY 10¾ SECONDS PAST 2:19 IN THE AFTERNOON ON SEPT. 24, 1976, THE FIRST BUILDING (COMPLETE IN ALL DETAILS AS HAD BEEN INDICATED BY THE VOICE) SUDDENLY APPEARED.

[What would convince Dr. Flew?](cont'd.)

9. THEN, FOR THE NEXT TWENTY-FOUR HOURS, AT EXACT FIVE-MINUTE INTERVALS, ANOTHER BUILDING, ~~WHICH~~ REACHES AT LEAST ONE MILE INTO THE AIR, APPEARS (COMPLETE IN ALL DETAILS AS INDICATED BY THE VOICE)

19-K (4)

10. THEN—EXACTLY TEN MINUTES AFTER THE SUDDEN APPEARANCE OF THE 289th BUILDING, YOU, DR. FLEW, AND EACH ONE OF THE OTHER 288 PEOPLE SUDDENLY SPROUT RED AND PURPLE WINGS OF SUCH SIZE, POWER, AND DESIGN AS TO ENABLE EACH ONE OF YOU TO EASILY FLY TO THE TOP OF ONE OF THE 289 BUILDINGS.

11. THEN—EACH ONE OF YOU 289 PEOPLE DOES FLY TO THE TOP OF ONE OF THE 289 BUILDINGS.

12. THEN—AFTER ALL OF THIS IS COMPLETED, THE GREAT VOICE AGAIN SPEAKS AND SAYS, "I, GOD, HAVE ACCOMPLISHED ALL OF THIS."

[What would convince Dr. Flew?]

(14-L)

✱ DR. FLEW, CHECK ANSWER:

☐ Yes, this series of events would convince me that my (AF's) proposition in this debate is false. (5)

☐ No, this series of events would not convince me that my (AF's) proposition in this debate is false.

✱ If your answer is "NO", then would you please explain what would convince you that your proposition is false: ____________________

____

____

____

____

____

____

____

____

____

____

does not exist." I asked him this question tonight, "What would have to occur or to have occurred to convince you that your proposition is false?" For a man who makes as much of the falsification principle as does Dr. Flew, and then to claim the sort of immunity which he has claimed is simply "monstrous," to use a word that seems to be familiar to us tonight.

Would it convince you, Dr. Flew, that your proposition is false if the following occurred? Now, listen carefully. If you were to hear a great voice from the sky and that voice identifies itself "I am God, creator of the world?", that voice tells you that a certain spot north of Denton, Texas, where presently there are no buildings at all, that at exactly ten and three-fourths seconds past 2:19 in the afternoon, on September 24, 1976, the first of a number of huge buildings, built of concrete, steel, bricks and so forth, would suddenly appear complete in every detail, adequate to be an office building, including appropriate furniture in every room, elevators, rest rooms, restaurants, etc. on that very spot and that for the next 24 hours exactly, at exactly 5 minute intervals another huge building would suddenly appear very near the first building. And that this would continue, the voice tells you, until 289 buildings, each one of which would reach at least one mile into the air, appear all of a sudden in the same sudden fashion. The voice goes on to tell you, Dr. Flew, that you are to go to that spot indicated shortly before the time indicated and that you are to take 288 people with you. The voice tells you that exactly 10 minutes after the 289th building appears, you and the other 288 people whom you are to take with you to the spot indicated will suddenly sprout red and purple wings of such size, power and design as will enable each one of you to easily fly to the top of each one of the 289 buildings. You go to the indicated spot at 2:00 o'clock in the afternoon on the designated day, September 24, 1976, and wait along with the other 288 people. Then at exactly ten and three-fourths seconds past 2:19 in the afternoon on September 24, 1976, the first building complete in all details that had been indicated by the voice suddenly appears and then for the next 24 hours at exactly 5 minute intervals another building which reaches at least one mile into the air appears complete in all details as indicated by the voice. Then, exactly 10 minutes after the sudden appearance of the 289th building you, Dr. Flew, and each one of the other 288 people suddenly sprout red and purple wings of such size, power and design as to enable each one of you to easily fly to the top of one of the 289 buildings. Then each one of you 289 people does fly to the top of each of the 289 buildings. Then after all of this is completed the great voice again speaks and says "I, God, have completed all of this." Dr. Flew, I want to know: would that convince *you* that *your proposition* is *false*? Now surely you are not immune to that kind of answer! Surely, that is not imprecisely stated.

Now, to look at this proposition, "I know that God does exist," would it convince you Dr. Flew that my position is true if the following occurred? Chart No. 19-H. (See Page 99.) You hear a great voice from the sky. That voice tells you that at exactly fifteen and one-half seconds past 10:07 a.m. on October 1, 1976, he, the speaker, would raise from the dead every person who had been buried in a certain cemetery, let us say cemetery X, and identifies himself as God. You go to the cemetery at 10:00 a.m. on October 1, 1976, and wait and then at exactly fifteen and one-half seconds past 10:07 a.m. on that date, October 1, 1976, every person who had been buried in that cemetery was raised from the dead. Now surely, Dr. Flew, that is not imprecise. Surely you can understand it. Surely neither your proposition nor your principle of falsification is immune from that. Now you tell me, true or false: "This series of events would convince me of the truthfulness of your proposition and the other series of events would convince me of the falsity of my own." Now, Dr. Flew, when you have handled that, then we will be ready to deal with more of the falsification principle.

My friends, I submit to you that there is evidence of God Almighty in this world and that the material will be dealt with in a positive way in the following two evenings.

Dr. Flew has not given the argument that he has promised us. In all the speeches you have listened to, he only said that there *seems* to be some sort of contradiction. But, Dr. Flew, you did not *show* the contradictions! There are your fellow colleagues who say that the contradiction is not immediately evident, and they invent two quasi-logical rules, which have some problem with them. Dr. Flew, I ask you to come forthrightly before this audience and admit that that contradiction is not immediately ev-

WHAT WOULD HAVE TO OCCUR TO CONVINCE DR. FLEW? —(No.1)

19-H

1. IN THIS DEBATE, WARREN'S PROPOSITION IS, "I KNOW THAT GOD DOES EXIST." (1)

2. WOULD IT CONVINCE YOU, DR. FLEW, THAT MY PROPOSITION IS TRUE IF THE FOLLOWING OCCURRED?
   (1) You hear a great voice from the sky.
   (2) That voice tells you that at exactly 15½ seconds past 10:07 a.m. on Oct. 1, 1976, He (the Speaker) would raise from the dead every person who had been buried in a certain cemetery (say cem. X) — and identifies Himself as God.
   (3) You go to cemetery X at 10:00 a.m. on Oct. 1, 1976 — and wait.
   (4) Then — at exactly 15½ seconds past 10:07 a.m. on that date (Oct. 1, 1976), every person who had been buried in cemetery X was raised from the dead.

3. DR. FLEW — PLEASE CHECK CORRECT ANSWER:
   ☐ Yes, this series of events would convince me.
   ☐ No, this series of events would not convince me.

4. IF "NO" (to #3), WHAT WOULD CONVINCE YOU?

____

(GIVE DETAILS)

ident and then try to give us these quasi-logical rules that will make it evident and then we will have the kind of discussion that these people came here to hear—not merely to hear "Here is a very curious idea" or "It seems to me to be monstrous." It is not enough to make an *assertion*! There is a great deal of difference between an *assertion* and an *argument*. I can say the moon is made out of green cheese and offer no support for it. That is an *assertion*. But if I say, "This is the case, and this is the case, and therefore this follows from it," that is an argument. Dr. Flew, you have not done that.

In the remaining part of my time tonight, I want to continue with the *concessions* and the *admissions of defeat* and the *self-contradictions* which have already been made by my learned colleague. Continuing with the concessions made last evening in regard to the questions, I call your attention to Question No. 5. In regard to his question, Dr. Flew concedes that you can deduce from empirical fact the state of affairs that is transcendent of the universe. I discussed that briefly at the end of my last speech. What I want to re-emphasize now is that this constitutes an admission that one can reason from the empirical facts of this world to the state of affairs that is transcendent of the world. Thus, Dr. Flew has admitted the basic thrust of the *theistic argument*! Such does not constitute on his part an argument to show that God does *not* exist, but it *does* constitute a very fatal admission, a concession so far as my case is concerned that will be before you tomorrow evening and the evening following.

He has already admitted that there has never been a human being that has been *transformed* from a non-human. He has admitted that no human being has ever been *born* of a non-human being, and let me ask the projector operator to put for us on the board Chart No. 41-Z. (See Page 101.) Now this is a logical argument stated in symbolic terms. It really is very simple. I ask you simply in a way to ignore the symbolic terms if you are not familiar with them because they are very easily explained. You will notice the first line. I have indicated what is called "strong disjunction." Now that means that one of the propositions is true and the other is false. The C and the E stand for statements or propositions, and it means men and women are human beings who owe their origin either to creation or to evolution. That

[THE ARGUMENT PUT IN SYMBOLIC TERMS— CONT'D.]

TBW'S PROPOSITION: "I KNOW THAT GOD DOES EXIST"

41-Z

(3)

* THE FOLLOWING ARGUMENT PROVES THAT PROPOSITION:

1. $C \oplus E$. ONLY POSSIBILITIES.
2. $C \supset G$. OBVIOUS, SINCE THERE CAN BE NO CREATION WITHOUT GOD.
3. $E \supset (B \vee T)$. IF EVOLUTION IS TRUE, THEN THESE ARE ONLY POSSIBILITIES.
4. $\sim B$. HUMANS ARE NOT BORN OF APES.
5. $\sim T$. APES ARE NOT TRANSFORMED INTO HUMANS
6. $\sim B \cdot \sim T$ 4, 5, CONJ.
7. $\sim(B \vee T)$ 6, DE M.
8. $\sim E$ 3, 7, M.T.
9. C 1, 8, D.S.
10. G 2, 9, M.P.

* PROOF OF THE EXISTENCE OF GOD IS "RIGHT BEFORE THE EYES" OF EACH AND EVERY HUMAN BEING.

means, if one is false, the other is true, and if one is true, the other is false—if by creation, then by God. Of course that could be the only means by which creation would occur.

The third proposition which I have there in a little sign that looks like a horseshoe and then a B and a wedge and a T inside of a parenthesis means that if evolution is true then it was either by *birth* from some non-human thing or by *transformation* of some non-human thing. Dr. Flew has already admitted, as you look at line 4 that it is not by birth. Therefore that little tilde sign in front of the B means, it is false that any human being was ever *born* of a non-human being. And then the next one, point 5, the T means that no human being ever came into being by being *transformed* from some ape or some other non-human being. Therefore, the sixth line by conjunction—putting those two together—you have, it is false that human beings came into the world by *birth* from non-human things or they were *transformed* by some non-human thing. And, then by what is called DeMorgan's theorem we have the transition into—it is false that human beings are here either by birth from non-human beings or by transformation by non-human beings. Then, by Modus Tollens, the law which indicates that any proposition which implies a false proposition is itself false, and going back up to point 3, where you have E implies B or T, we have: it is false that B or T. Therefore, it follows that E is false. Therefore, by admitting neither by birth or by transformation, Dr. Flew has admitted that evolution is false, and since we have to go back to Number 1 the strong disjunction means that creation is the case, and therefore God is the originator of man. This argument involves Dr. Flew's admissions on premises 4 and 5.

FLEW'S SIXTH AFFIRMATIVE

(Tuesday Night)

Perhaps I had better start with these proposed goings on in North Texas. If it is in someway derivable as a consequence of the assertion that God, as Dr. Warren conceives God, in fact exists, that God will do these things in North Texas at such and such a time; then indeed the claims about his God are and in this way, testable and falsifiable. Part of the difficulty of handling things in this area is that so many different notions of God have been held; and quite often radically different notions are held by people who do not think of themselves as holding different notions. However, if you do so arrange it that you have got a concept of God from which you are able to infer validly that if the Being you have described exists, then in such and such circumstances this or that will happen, then indeed you have got a thoroughly testable notion. But I do not think that really is the sort of notion of God which we have got to deal with.

The second thing which I need to say is I know that many people feel, and not only Dr. Warren, that I have not really been offering any reasons for being an atheist. I am afraid I think that I have. You may well judge they are not good enough, but I think that I have offered reasons. Take the two things that I have been saying about the First Stage in any systematic apologetic. If, after all, the things that are said about this proposed Being are contradictory, then to say that there is the Being thus and thus described is like saying that there is a round square or an unmarried husband; and, if this is so then this is a frightfully good reason for saying there is no such Being. It is exactly the sort of reason we have for saying there is no such thing as a married bachelor or a round square.

Again, with regard to the other sort of objection I was offering under that first heading, the objection that what may have started as some sort of testable hypothesis about a power behind the world has by various sorts of qualification been made untestable. In this case it seems to me the situation is strictly analogous to the situation with regard to fairies. About fairies, none of us say cautiously: "It has not been proved." Or I am agnostic about fairies. There is a bit of evidence for, a bit of evidence against, and I am waiting for more to come in." What we all say (if and so far as we believe that the fairy hypothesis has been so qualified that it is untestable), what we all say in these circumstances is "There ain't no such thing." And that is the reaction that I am having in the case of an untestable hypothesis about the existence of God.

Now I am going to go on to the Second Stage of the sort of systematic examination of a view about God which I think is the proper examination for such claims to have. Allowing, what of course I do not allow, that we have got an adequate notion of God the question then arises; "What sort of reason have we for saying that this notion has application, that there actually is a Being corresponding with this notion?" I think there is no doubt at all that almost every believer who is asked to offer some sort of reason for believing will sooner or later, and usually sooner, offer some version of what is traditionally called the Argument *from* Design, but what I in my factitious and cantakerous way call the Argument *to* Design. I will not, I think, trouble you with my reasons for adopting that little fad. Anyway let us here call it the Argument to Design; unless you badly want to call it the Argument from Design. The sort of move I have in mind is that of someone who says "Good heavens, how can you be in any doubt about the existence of God? Look at the regularity of the seasons; look at the sun and the moon; or, look at the inordinate complexity and integration of the human eye, or just consider yourself. Who made it all?"

Let us have a look at this sort of argument which is certainly the sort of argument which I think has seemed persuasive to most people, and which occupies a major place in thinking about this subject for most people. Let us take some examples. Let us consider the inordinate complexity of the human eye, and then say, "Who made it all?" Well, if you simply look and consider only the most obviously available evidence, then the answer is that no one made it, it just growed. Similarly with human children. All of us who know what are curiously described as the facts of life know how babies begin; and that if they are provided with food and all that, they just grow. Whereas, there are other very complicated things with which, at least with the outsides of which, we are familiar, like commuters and for that matter those complex American automobiles, which we equally have good reason to say did not grow but were made—in the latter case usually in Detroit. This may seem to you cheap and inadequate, and somehow missing the point.

It is not the last thing that I am going to say about this; there is more to be said. But it certainly is a necessary first thing to point out, because it is a thing that people curiously overlook. All of us who have been around a bit know very well that—at least if the words are understood in a fairly straightforward way—eyes are not made at all. It is not that they are made by some invisible being, or at least it is not obvious that they are made by some invisible being. As far as we can see they just grow and are not made. Whereas there are other very complicated things—though not I think as complicated and integrated as the human eye—which we also know were made and which did not grow.

No doubt it will be felt that this is somehow missing the point. Perhaps the claim will be that it is the universe as a whole which must have been designed, which can not just be there, or just always have been there. What I will try to do is expound within the very brief framework of the rest of this third slot about this Argument to Design offered by David Hume, a Scottish philosopher of the eighteenth century. As a matter of fact we celebrate the bicentennial of David Hume's death in the same year as you celebrate the bicentennial of the independence of your republic. Indeed there was a certain connection between the two events, because Hume indicated his support for the American Revolution even before it started. He then in response to the signing of the Declaration of Independence made a remark which some of you may think will have a certain bearing on events in this upcoming November. He said: "I am an American in my principles; and believe that these colonists should be allowed to govern or misgovern themselves as they see fit."

But to come to Hume's argument about the Argument to Design. Hume started from recognizing what everyone would say if they saw something like a half completed building but did not see any building workers around. (This is the normal situation on a British building site, you do not see any work going on.) Everyone here would think themselves entitled: to infer that somewhere there must have been some builders, who have completed the miserable amount of work that has so far been done; and, if it is a certain sort of building, to infer that there will have been an architect. And so, the Argument to Design would go, you would all argue like that; just as if you found a watch on the sand of a desert island, you would all argue, "Hm, this watch must have been made somewhere, it is a mark of human visitation or habitation." Yes, of course, everyone would agree that to proceed in this way is sound argument.

Well, now, the advocate of the Argument to Design will say, surely by parity of reasoning, we must proceed from marks of design in the universe as a whole to the existence of a Designer who made and sustains that universe. This is the challenge that Hume tried to meet; and which I think can be met. The Argument to Design urges that we ought to apply in the case of the universe as a whole exactly the same sort of procedures as we would all agree that it would be proper to apply to this half completed building, or to the watch lying around on the beach. Hume's problem in challenging this argument is to show that the parity of reasoning does not apply; to show that there are relevant differences between the case of the universe as a whole and the case of any of these things which suggest design within the universe.

Hume meets this challenge in two ways, by pointing out that there are indeed two differences between the two cases, two enormous differences. There is a fundamental difference in the suggested cause and there is a fundamental difference in the suggested effect. These are in both cases things that are by definition, if they exist at all, unique. Because it ties us up with the earlier stages of the present debate, let us consider the supposed Creator, the supposed cause of the universe as a whole. How does this differ from the suggested causes in the case of the half finished building? It differs in this way, that the suggested cause is a Being by definition, if it exists, unique. If there is any theist God there is certainly only one. It is a Being whose powers are supposed to pass our understanding. A Being in most thinking not a member of any ordinary species or class. But of course these characteristics, these unique characteristics, have consequences.

Supposing you postulate personal causes of something. Since

there are lots of people around, and our knowledge of people enables us to infer certain things that would happen, certain features that the situation would have, if people were responsible for bringing it about. But, there are not any inferences that we can legitimately make, revelation apart, about how the God of theism can reasonably be expected to behave, if there is such a Being at all. We can not, for instance, infer that if there is a God then there will be a universe or that it will have any particular characteristics. Indeed, many theologians go out of their way to say that the whole creation was in no way necessary, it was a matter of an unnecessary free decision by the Creator. The suggestion that there is a God whose activities explain the existence of the universe cannot therefore be made to work like an ordinary scientific theory.

Next consider the supposed effect. The supposed effect is the universe as a whole and the universe as a whole is everything there is with the possible exception of God. So in the nature of the case there can be only one of them. Now, what is the nature of our argument from the uncompleted building site to the building workers? It is surely not a matter of just looking at a building site and you can simply see that this must be the work of human agents. Rather it is that we have been around a long time—some of us more unfortunately than others, and we know that this sort of thing is not brought about without human agency; we have got a lot of experience of half finished building sites. If you are British, half finished building sites is about the only sort of building site you do have experience of. But we have certainly had a lot of that. The argument is from our experience that these things do not come about except in a certain sort of way.

We cannot, however, argue in this way about the universe. We can not say "Oh, there are lots of remarkable things about the universe; and there are, and these remarkable features about the universe, and for that matter the universe itself, could only come about in this way." Or if we do argue like this, it can not be an argument from experience, because in the nature of the case we are only acquainted with one universe. So, in answer to the challenge that, if you allow that there can be a legitimate argument from things like half finished building sites and so on to the builders, or from watches to watchmakers, why do you not allow an argument from the universe to a universe maker, the answer is that this second sort of argument differs from the first sort in two crucial respects. It differs because the proposed cause is essentially unique and it is a sort of cause about the supposed operation of which we can draw no inferences at all. Second, it differs because the alleged effect of this supposed cause is also by definition unique. Hence, in the nature of the case, we can not say that anything about the universe as a whole is either probable or improbable, likely or unlikely. There just is one universe, and our experience of this is the only experience of universes that we have or can have.

I will now go just a little bit beyond Hume's argument here and say something which is strongly suggested by Hume, and which I believe Hume came to believe in his last years though he did not say it out loud. It seems to me that what one has got to do is to take it that whatever are discovered by our scientists to be the most fundamental laws of nature, the fundamental principles that apply in the universe, just are the fundamental features of reality. There is no requirement for any explanation of these, and certainly not for an argument from the fact that there are regularities to the conclusion that there must be a Designer. There would only be a compulsive argument from the fact that there are general regularities in the universe; my goodness, people discover fundamental laws of nature. If we had some independent knowledge of universes apart from our knowledge of this one, and were hence able to say that universes are only like this when they are made by God. Or, alternatively, if we were able to say that if this universe were left to its own devices it would be irregular, so, we must argue that there must have been a God to impose the actual observed regularity on it. This is the end of my first argument against the main argument for the existence of God. At the end I have also been suggesting how it seems to me we ought to look at the universe and its fundamental features.

WARREN'S SIXTH NEGATIVE

(Tuesday Night)

Dr. Flew, Gentlemen Moderators, Ladies and Gentlemen. I come before you now for the last speech which I shall have this evening and I would like to point out that Dr. Flew has spent this last speech almost entirely in a reply to the argument to design. This of course is a negative stance. It presupposes that I am in the *affirmative* and that I have given the argument to design, which is not the case at all. He has allowed this part of his discussion to close without having made a precisely formulated affirmative argument. He has talked about, hinted at it, indicated that it is a matter of curiosity, that perhaps the punishment of man in eternity is incompatible with God. But he has not really formulated an *argument* on the matter.

But I want to show you now that this man has let his part in the affirmative of his discussion come to a close without meeting his responsibility. I would like to have on the screen Chart No. 9A(1) (See Page 110) and 9A(2) (See Page 111). I have presented much material on these matters, since this man has begun the affirmation of a universal negative, and you must understand the basic difference between affirming, as I have, simply the fact that God exists and his affirming that he knows that God does *not* exist. That means there is practically an unlimited number of things which he absolutely must know in order to know that God does not exist.

How much attention has he given to these matters? I have called his attention again and again, he has paid absolutely no attention whatever. I have shown that he *must know,* he *must absolutely know,* he must give us the *proof* in such matters. I will not take the time to read them all again but I will point out that he must know that matter really does exist non-contingently, that matter is *all* that exists, that matter has *always* existed, that no one piece of matter is *worth* any more than any other piece of matter, that by sheer chance rocks and dirt (dead matter) became *living* matter, that by sheer chance rocks and dirt became *conscious* matter, that by sheer chance rocks and dirt became *human* beings, that by sheer chance rocks and dirt developed in such a way that a woman was on earth before any human baby *or* that

THE INSURMOUNTABLE BARRIERS TO DR. FLEW'S SUCCESS 9-A(1)

(1)

DR. FLEW MUST KNOW

1. THAT MATTER REALLY DOES EXIST NON-CONTINGENTLY
2. THAT MATTER IS ALL THAT EXISTS.
3. THAT MATTER HAS ALWAYS EXISTED.
4. THAT NO ONE PIECE OF MATTER IS WORTH ANY MORE THAN ANY OTHER PIECE OF MATTER
5. THAT BY SHEER CHANCE ROCKS AND DIRT (I.E., DEAD MATTER, POSSIBLY INCLUDING GASES AND WATER) BECAME LIVING MATTER.
6. THAT BY SHEER CHANCE ROCKS AND DIRT BECAME CONSCIOUS MATTER.
7. THAT BY SHEER CHANCE ROCKS AND DIRT BECAME A HUMAN BEING.

BEFORE HE CAN KNOW THAT THIS PROPOSITION

"I KNOW THAT GOD DOES NOT EXIST"

IS TRUE

DR. FLEW

[INSURMOUNTABLE BARRIERS, CONT'D.]

9-A(2)

DR FLEW MUST KNOW

8. THAT BY SHEER CHANCE ROCKS AND DIRT DEVELOPED IN SUCH A WAY THAT A WOMAN WAS FIRST ON EARTH BEFORE ANY HUMAN BABY:-OR

9. THAT BY SHEER CHANCE ROCKS AND DIRT DEVELOPED IN SUCH A WAY THAT A BABY WAS FIRST ON EARTH BEFORE ANY WOMAN.

DR. FLEW

10. THAT BY SHEER CHANCE ROCKS AND DIRT DEVELOPED THE HUMAN FEMALE BREAST SO THAT IT COULD CHANGE BLOOD INTO MILK.

11. THAT THERE IS NO LAW HIGHER THAN THE CIVIL AND/OR CRIMINAL LAW OF A SOCIETY OR NATION

(2) BEFORE HE CAN KNOW THAT THIS PROPOSITION

"I KNOW THAT GOD DOES NOT EXIST"

IS TRUE

by sheer chance rocks and dirt developed in such a way that a baby was first on earth before any woman.

But, Dr. Flew has already admitted that evolution is absolutely impossible even though it is crucial to his case. He now has let two evenings go by without replying to the argument that I have given you which is given as precisely, as logically, as validly as it could be to show that the implication of atheism is that man has accidentally come from some lower (non-human) form of life and yet he has admitted by his answers to my questions that it could *not* have occurred in that way.

Now, friends, let him not deceive you by coming here and spending his time in a role that was entirely out of line with his obligation, by functioning in a *negative* role when he was supposed to be in an *affirmative* role. I have not been in the affirmative either last night or tonight. I have not given the argument to design, and therefore Dr. Flew was out of place in even being involved in such. However, I want to point out to you that he paid no attention to the fact that, in answer to my Question No. 9, he answered true to this: "If the Mars probe discovered a rock with a king's head carved on it and with a message of gratitude to the king, then men on earth could know at some time an intelligent being had been on Mars." Chart No. 42-J. (See Page 113.) You see, he therefore *admits* that by simply seeing this empirical evidence, he could know that some intelligent being had been on Mars. The truth of the matter is that atheists in the world were terribly excited when somebody thought they had seen the single letter B on a rock. Chart No. 42-I. (See Page 114.) You remember that. They were all ready to draw the conclusion; therefore, intelligent life is on Mars—no doubt something as smart or smarter than human beings—from the single letter B. Now he has *admitted* that if you found such a thing as this he would have to admit that there was an intelligent being there.

Now his dodge about the fact that we *grow* as over against a car being *made* simply will not do. I want to see on the screen Chart No. 42-A8. (See Page 115.) Now you will note on this screen we have a *natural* hand and a *mechanical* hand. I have asked the question, "Is it true or false that the *natural* hand, was *planned* and *designed*?" And he answered, "No it is not." On the right, the hand that is *mechanical,* he says, "It was planned

[INTELLIGENT LIFE ON MARS?]

42-J (2)

2. WHAT IF WE FOUND ON MARS —

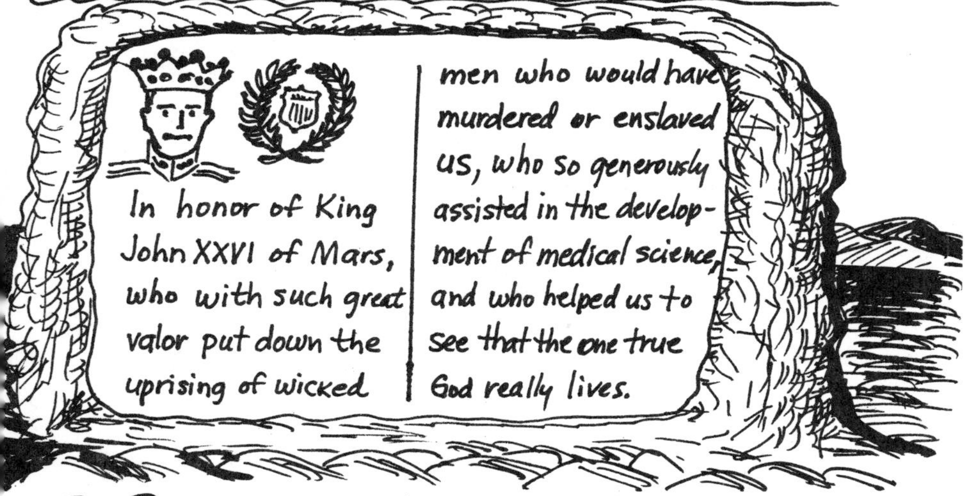

In honor of King John XXVI of Mars, who with such great valor put down the uprising of wicked men who would have murdered or enslaved us, who so generously assisted in the development of medical science, and who helped us to see that the one true God really lives.

3. SHOULD WE CONCLUDE —
(check all correct answers)

- ☐ THAT AT LEAST AT SOME TIME INTELLIGENT LIFE HAD BEEN ON MARS.
- ☐ THAT THE CARVING OF THE FACE AND THE MESSAGE WAS THE RESULT OF THE PURELY ACCIDENTAL (CHANCE) ACTION OF THE ROCKS AND DIRT ON MARS.
- ☐ THAT IT IS IMPOSSIBLE TO COME TO KNOWLEDGE OF THE EXISTENCE OF INTELLIGENT BEINGS WITHOUT ACTUALLY OBSERVING THEM.

INTELLIGENT LIFE ON MARS—& OTHER PLANETS?

42-I (1)

1. WHAT IF WE FOUND ON MARS—

A ROCK WITH THE LETTER "B" CLEARLY CARVED INTO IT?

* WHAT SHOULD WE CONCLUDE?— (CHECK CORRECT ANSWERS):

☐ THAT AT LEAST ONE INTELLIGENT BEING HAD AT SOME TIME BEEN ON MARS?

☐ THAT THE "B" WAS DUE TO THE ACCIDENTAL RESULTS OF THE ACTION OF DIRT, ROCKS, WIND, ETC. (I.E. NON-INTELLIGENT PHYSICAL FORCES)?

☐ SOMETHING ELSE. ______________
EXPLAIN

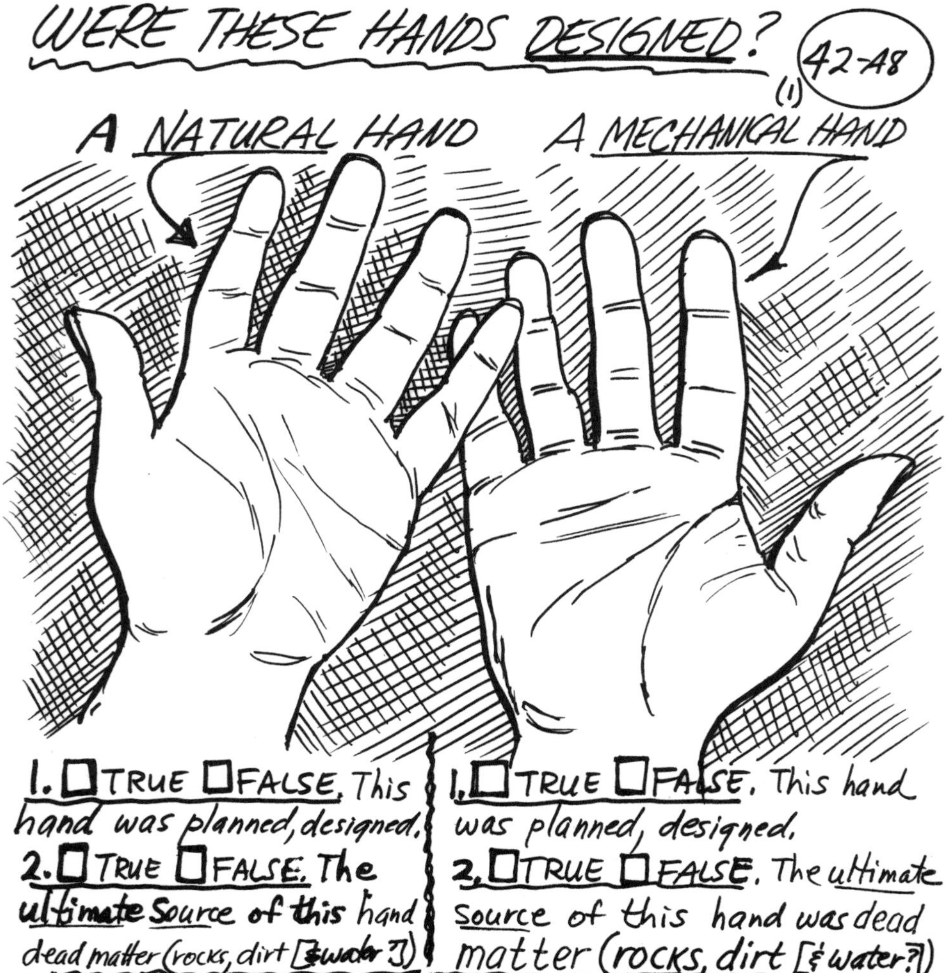
WERE THESE HANDS DESIGNED?
42-48
(1)
A NATURAL HAND
A MECHANICAL HAND
1. ☐ TRUE ☐ FALSE. This hand was planned, designed.
2. ☐ TRUE ☐ FALSE. The ultimate source of this hand dead matter (rocks, dirt [& water?])
1. ☐ TRUE ☐ FALSE. This hand was planned, designed.
2. ☐ TRUE ☐ FALSE. The ultimate source of this hand was dead matter (rocks, dirt [& water?])

and designed." Now, friends, I submit to you that the *natural* hand is tremendously greater than any *mechanical* hand that man has ever made. Dr. Flew would say the same thing if a man had a bone, which reached from his thigh bone socket to his knee, made out of *synthetic* material that has no bone marrow in it. But man cannot live without bone marrow. Dr. Flew would say that the bone made out of synthetic material is great, it is so great that it demands a designer, someone with intelligence, someone to plan it. But now tonight he has alleged that the natural thigh bone, which we must have, which could *not* have evolved according to his admissions, can be accounted for by *sheer chance*—such as from a whirlwind blowing against the mountain side with a human thigh resulting from it.

Now there is further the matter which I have had before him as a *negative* argument. I am not presenting this to say, "Here is design and therefore God." I am presenting it as material which Dr. Flew must know in order to know that God does not exist.

Let us have Chart No. 9-U. (See Page 117.) Now, Dr. Flew, you have about a minute and a half in your next speech and I want you to do the best you can to deal with this matter. Here is an important matter because it shows the utter impossibility of your whole case. If evolution is not true, then atheism is not true. And whatever else you may say about it you will not get over that fact. Further, your admission regarding the fact that human beings could neither have been *transformed* nor *born* from non-human beings really concedes the whole matter. But, let us just pile information on top of information. Notice here, I have shown the significance of the human respiratory system—the bronchial tube, the alveoli, and so forth.

Now, let us look at the next chart, Chart No. 9V, 9W, 9X, 9Y. (See Pages 118-121.) Here we look at a detail of the respiratory system— a part of it, the alveolus, a blood vessel and the air. Now we go quickly on to a description of what happens here. These alveoli are grape-like bunches of very small air sacs. Each person has approximately 750 million of these. All of them together likely have a surface area which is about 25 times that of the skin. Spread out flat they would probably cover as much as 600 square feet. Compare a room of about 30 by 20 feet. Each alveolus is covered with a network of capillaries. These capillaries are so

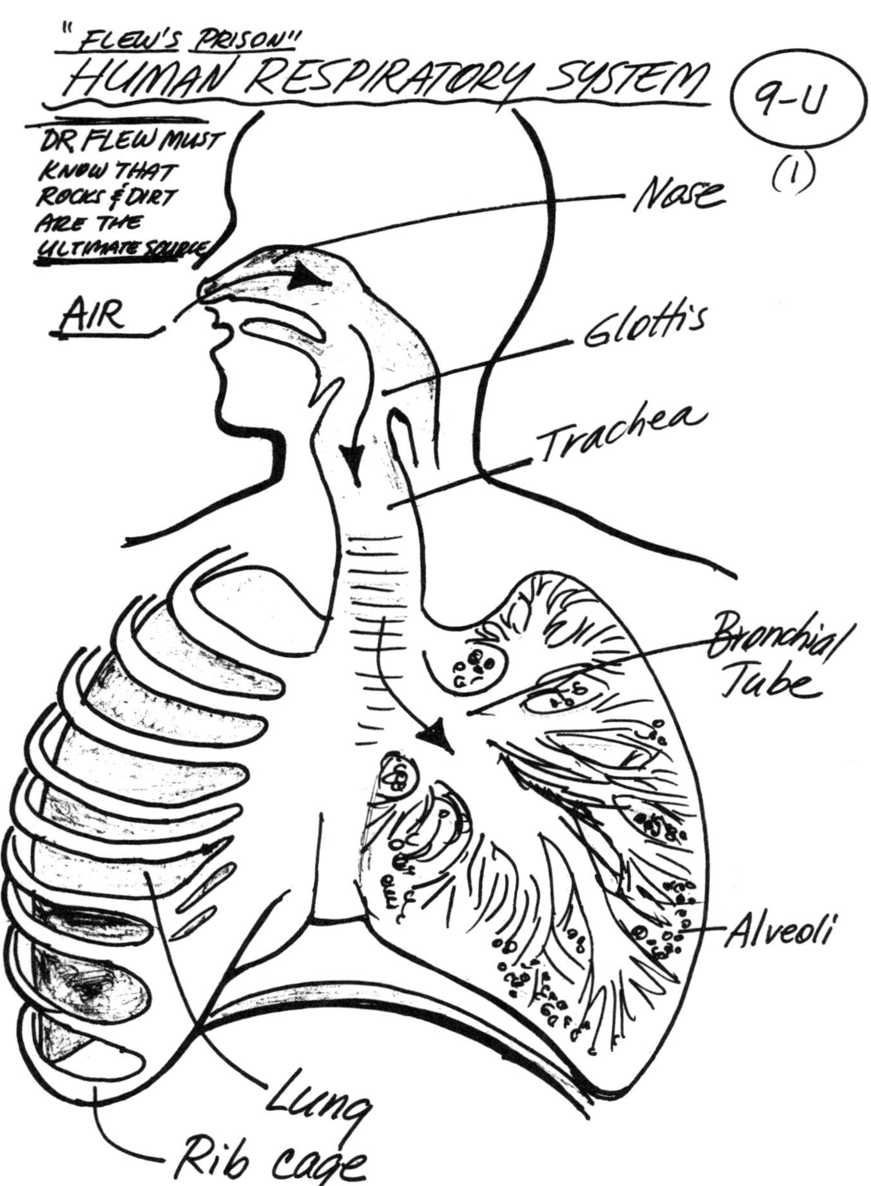
"FLEW'S PRISON"
HUMAN RESPIRATORY SYSTEM
9-U
(1)
DR FLEW MUST
KNOW THAT
ROCKS & DIRT
ARE THE
ULTIMATE SOURCE
AIR
Nose
Glottis
Trachea
Bronchial
Tube
Alveoli
Lung
Rib cage

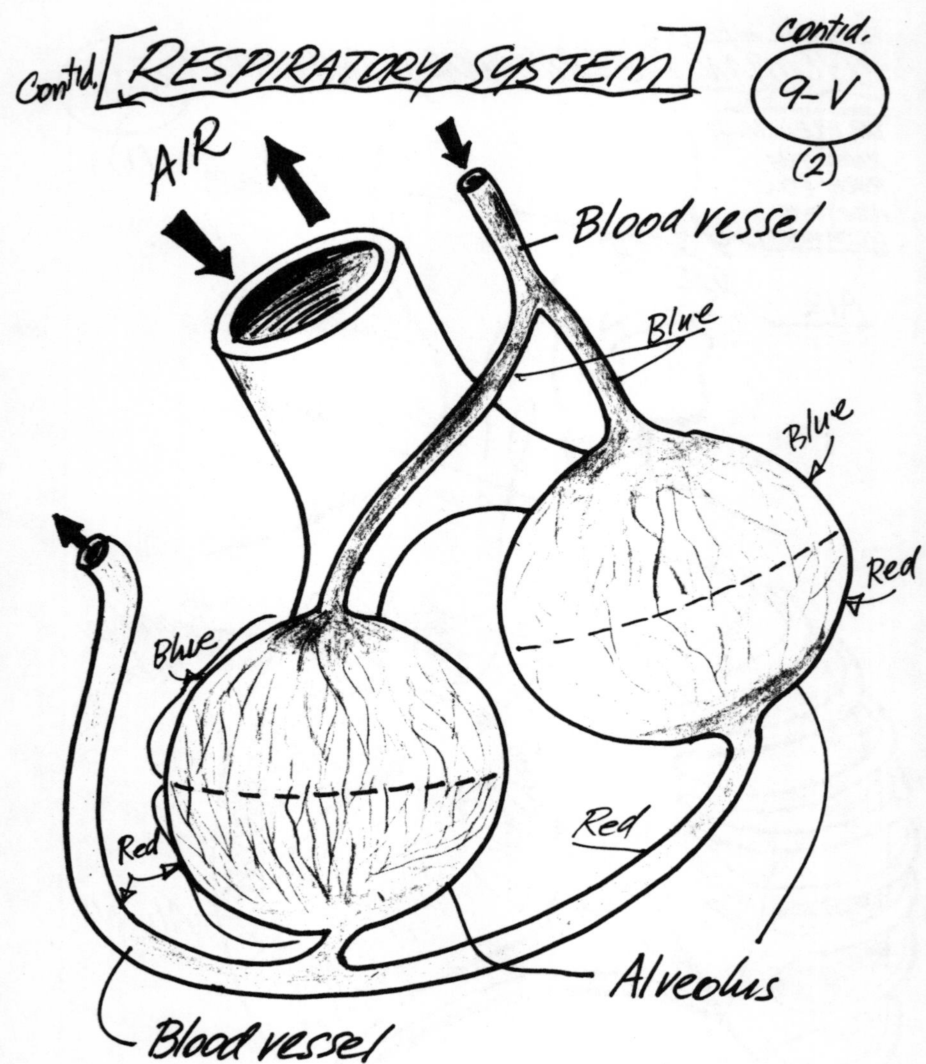
Contd.
RESPIRATORY SYSTEM
Contd.
9-V
(2)
AIR
Blood vessel
Blue
Blue
Red
Blue
Red
Red
Alveolus
Blood vessel

(cont'd.) RESPIRATORY SYSTEM cont'd. 9-W (3)

* THE ALVEOLI

1. Grapelike bunches of very small air sacs.
2. Each person has approximatly 750,000,000 of these.
3. All of them together likely have a surface area which is about 25 times that of the skin. Spread out flat, they would probably cover as much as 600 square feet (compare a room 30' x 20').
4. Each alveolus is covered with a network of capillaries.
5. These capillaries are so small that red blood cells must pass through them one cell at a time.
6. Through the very thin walls of the capillaries, the blood gives up its waste (carbon dioxide) and takes on refreshing, life-giving oxygen. Without this exchange of carbon

dioxide and oxygen, no human being could live more than a few moments.

7. The body's entire blood supply must pass through these small blood vessels every few minutes
   (1) The blood goes IN one end a dark blue-black, and OUT the other a bright cherry-red.
   (2) Day and night this process MUST go on without interruption.

★ IT IS CLEAR FROM THESE FACTS THAT MAN DID NOT EVOLVE BY MERE CHANCE FROM ROCKS AND DIRT (& WATER?) — BUT THAT MAN WAS CREATED BY GOD!

[HUMAN RESPIRATORY SYSTEM— CONT'D.]

* SOME FINAL POINTS:

1. IN ORDER FOR DR. FLEW TO KNOW THAT GOD DOES NOT EXIST, HE MUST FIRST KNOW THAT THE HUMAN RESPIRATORY SYSTEM OWES ITS ORIGIN ULTIMATELY TO DEAD MATTER —ROCKS & DIRT!

2. —BUT— DR. FLEW DOES NOT KNOW THIS.

3. ∴ HE DOES NOT KNOW THAT GOD DOES NOT EXIST!

4. ∴ DR. FLEW'S PROPOSITION IS FALSE!

small that red blood cells must pass through them one cell at a time, through the very thin walls of the capillary. The blood gives up its waste, that is carbon dioxide, and takes on refreshing life-giving oxygen. Now note carefully that without this exchange, this interchange, of carbon dioxide and oxygen no human being could live more than a few moments. The body's entire blood supply must pass through these small blood vessels every few minutes. The blood goes in one end a dark blue-black and out the other a bright cherry red, day and night this process must go on without interruption. It is clear from these facts that man did *not* evolve by mere chance from rocks and dirt and water and gas or whatever he wants to put by way of dead matter.

Now, note carefully, here is the point that I am making. In order for Dr. Flew to know that *God* does *not exist,* he *must know*—he cannot merely give it as an idle guess or a curiosity—he *must know* that the human respiratory system owes its origin ultimately to dead matter, that once there was only dead matter, not a single living cell, not a single living thing, nothing with mind or intelligence, no human being at all and that this marvelous system simply "grew." Oh, he says, "If you find an automobile, or if you find something of that sort, then you have to reason back to some intelligence."

Let us look at Chart No. 42-A1. (See Page 123.) We realize, as we look at this chart, that there *has* to be the interchange (between the air passage and the blood passage) of oxygen and carbon dioxide. Now we all know that one cannot live if that interchange stops longer than five minutes, and yet every evolutionist would say that for such a complexity to develop it would require not only thousands but *millions* of years! You can see the utter absurdity of the claim that Dr. Flew has made in regard to "the argument to design." Dr. Flew, I suggest that you would have done much better if you had gotten into the affirmative role and stayed out of the negative role. For a person to conclude that an automobile manifests such qualities, such characteristics, as to *demand* the conclusion that it was *designed* and *planned* by an *intelligent* being and then to say that the human respiratory system, without which one cannot live longer than five minutes, "just happened," is about as great a monstrosity as I can imagine!

In the last speech Dr. Flew said nothing more about the prob-

[USE WITH 41-D]

[RESPIRATORY SYSTEM—CONT'D]

✽ THE MARVELOUS INTERCHANGE OF OXYGEN (IN AIR) AND CARBON DIOXIDE (IN BLOOD):

42-A1 (1)

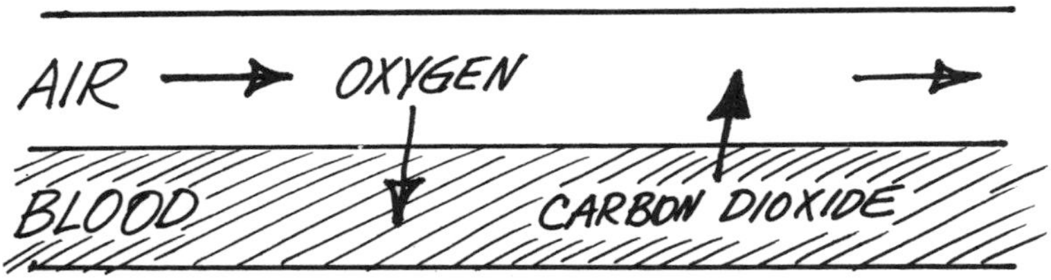

AIR → OXYGEN ↓ ↑ →

BLOOD CARBON DIOXIDE

1. WITHOUT THIS AMAZING INTERCHANGE, NO HUMAN BEING COULD LIVE MORE THAN A FEW MOMENTS.
2. YET, THE ATHEISTIC POSITION DEPENDS UPON ITS EVOLVING OVER A PERIOD OF TIME AS LONG, PERHAPS, AS A MILLION YEARS
3. EVOLUTION COULD NOT HAVE OCCURRED—
4. —SO— ATHEISM IS FALSE!

*cf. CHART 41-D

lem of evil. He has made allegations but again he has not really made an *argument*. It is not *my* responsibility to make *his* argument! He has said in effect, "Look, here is God, and God is supposedly infinite in love, power, etc., but there is something in the world (evil) that conflicts with that concept. I have pointed out to him that even his own colleagues admit that the so-called contradiction is *not immediately evident,* that it requires at least some quasi-logical rules. What attention did he pay to that? Absolutely none! He has said it is simply "monstrous" for one to conclude that the God who provides an explanation for this world could punish anyone forever.

The trouble with Dr. Flew is: *sin* does not really mean much —if anything—to him. He projects himself to the outside of the universe, somewhat in the position of God, and then he judges God and concludes what God can do and cannot do. He does all this from merely concepts—in *his own mind*—of both God and evil. But, I have already pointed out to you that he cannot prove his case merely from the *concept* of God, and he has not replied to that at all. He must depend—to have an argument—upon some empirical fact which he must bring in with some additional "rules." But he has not set forth the precise argument which involves all of this. Now friends, if God is infinite in love and goodness, and He is, as is clear from the fact that he sent His Son to die for every person in this world. He sent Jesus Christ to die even for Dr. Flew, even though he rejects Him. God is infinite in love, he loves every person in this world—even the most wicked man. He wants him to be saved from his sin. Dr. Flew cannot escape his own *conscience,* which is God-given. That is why *he rejects* the monstrosities of the Nazis—because of his God-given *conscience*! If God is infinite in *love* and *goodness,* why would we expect that God would *not* be infinite in *justice*? How could we even follow a God who would tolerate evil, who would tolerate sin? If one should spend his probationary time here on this earth in wicked rebellion to God and then to come into the judgment, should God say, "I see that you do not love me, you care nothing for truth and righteousness, but then truth and righteousness mean nothing to me, I am as wicked as you are." My friends, we must understand that God is *infinite* in *all* of his attributes. I wish Dr. Flew had come on earlier and presented his "argument from evil." It is, as a matter of fact, the only argument atheists have. Why did he not in his first speech come up and give you a logical, precise argument? I have pages and pages to answer that argument but he has not given it. My friends, Dr. Flew has said that, basic to the Christian case, you cannot explain the various elements and the total situation without involving yourself in logical contradiction. But he has not shown that—has only *asserted* it. But I am going to show you anyway that the propositions which are basic to Christian theism *do not* involve logical contradiction. The doctrine of Hell is included. The punishment of people in this world, the suffering, the tribulation, are all constituent elements to make this world the perfect place for men to live and make their decision to either love and serve God or to reject Him. Oh, you may laugh and say "You mean to say that this world is perfect?" It is perfect for the *purpose* God had in creating it. He did not, as Dr. Flew's apparent favorite philosopher, David Hume, would allege that it should be some sort of hedonistic paradise. God did not *intend* for this world to be our eternal home. It is here for us to make our decision either for or against God. The evidence for God is everywhere. As has been indicated, the everlasting power and divinity of God are *made known* by the things that are *seen*. And we must understand, that in this world we have a chance to make a free decision. Dr. Flew, in self-contradiction, demands that we be free but that God make us so that we would be guaranteed to always freely make the right decision. This involves a self-contradiction: that man is *free* and man is *not free*. You cannot have guaranteed freedom, Dr. Flew. That is one of the most absurd ideas that I ever heard of. Now atheists remind us that in this world there is suffering. I am indicating that Dr. Flew is *not*—as he hints at—simply saying the very concept of God is self-contradictory. He does not really do that. What he does is say, "Here is God. There is something about God that contradicts with this empirical fact in this world or with this punishment out there in eternity." You see he is *not* really dealing *only* with the *concept* of God. Do not let him deceive you into thinking that he is. I put a chart on the screen which showed the various attributes of God. I challenged him to deal with it. He has not said one word about it. You see, he has got to try to bring in empirical fact in order to try to make his case, but he has not done it. He has not formulated a logical argument to do it.

Involved in this matter of eternal punishment is the infinite justice of God. As a matter of fact, I could not serve a God who was deficient in any one of His attributes. To say that God is not omniscient, or that He is not omnipotent, or that He is not omnipresent or that He is not completely just, infinite in His justice, His holiness and His righteousness, and therefore that He dare not punish men, is to simply say that He is not God. I have sat in philosophy classes for weeks on end and heard men talk about God, God, God, and all they mean is some kind of force in nature. When you take away from God His infinite justice He is no longer God, Dr. Flew. That is just as much a part of His nature as His infinite love. And because He loves you, He gave His Son Jesus Christ to die, and made clear in the sacred Scriptures, that someday all of us will stand before Him in judgment to give an account of how we have used our intelligence, for how we have used our opportunities in this life. There is something more to a human being, even as you yourself have recognized, than mere matter, mere molecules in motion. *If* all there is to a man is molecules in motion, *there is no such thing as freedom*—there is only physical reaction to physical stimuli. If so, Dr. Flew, you are nothing but a blob of matter. When that dog ate that baby in New York City a few days ago, would there have been any greater loss of value in the eating of that human baby or if there had been a baby pig in that room and he had eaten both of them? Would there have been a bigger loss? They are both just matter in motion according to Dr. Flew. But, friends, to understand Christian theism, as I had hoped that Dr. Flew would, one must understand that God is omnipotent, that God is perfect in goodness, that God is omniscient, that God is perfect in justice. This is the very point he has completely overlooked. To listen to him, you would think he had never heard of the concepts of holiness, of righteousness, of infinity, and justice, and therefore that it is absolutely wrong to punish men in hell. Dr. Flew projects himself outside the universe, and stands on some sort of platform which he invents, and stands in judgment of God on the whole process. I ask him from what platform he stood to make that kind of judgment.

Sin, that which contradicts man's sonship to God and his brotherhood to man—and even Dr. Flew, as you have heard him, as he has talked about the monstrosities committed by not only the Nazis but the Communists shows that he rcognizes his brotherhood to man—is crucial to this matter. Sin is that which contradicts man's sonship to God and his brotherhood to man, that which contradicts the will of God. Sin is the only instrinsic evil. It is not evil that there is evil in this world. God made the world to be inhabited. He put free men here, and, by their own decision, they have decided to go against the will of God. Evil results in every case from an abuse of free moral agency. It is not the case that good is opposed to evil in such a way that a good thing always eliminates evil as far as it can. Now these are matters that Dr. Flew *should* have taken up, *should* have given you an *argument* in a precise logical way, dealt with them, argued against them. But he has not done so. It is not the case that there are no limits to what an omnipotent thing or being can do. It is not the case that a good omnipotent thing always eliminates evil completely. A good omnipotent thing exists, that is, *God*. It is not the case that there is a logical contradiction in the conjunction of the propositions which say that God exists and that evil exists. There is no logical contradiction in that conjunction. He has merely *hinted* at it. He has not given the *argument* and you will leave this building tonight with his case in the affirmative closed without his having done so! Thank you very much.

FLEW'S REJOINDER

(Tuesday Night)

Guaranteed freedom is self-contradictory? If that is so then those who are saved are either not free or not actually safe; are they? Second thing, about this automobile and the respiratory system, my argument is when we proceed from looking at the automobile to the conclusion that it must have been designed, it is not that it is a remarkable thing so it must have been designed but that it is the sort of thing that we know is an artifact. Whereas with the respiratory system it is a sort of thing which is indeed even more remarkable. But it is also a sort of thing which we know from all our experience does grow and is not made. Of course this leaves open the question about whether the whole universe was made. But the first move is surely the one that I have just made. A third thing while we are about it, it is a mistake to think that someone who is, shall we say, less than enthusiastic about the moral characteristics of a God thus and thus described is *judging God* whereas someone who is more enthusiastic is not. Both of them are, if you like, judging—saying that this term or that is appropriate. It is just that they have different views as to which is appropriate.

WARREN'S FIRST AFFIRMATIVE

(Wednesday Night)

Dr. Flew, Gentlemen Moderators, Ladies and Gentlemen. I assure you that it is a pleasure for me to stand before you this evening in affirmation of the proposition which has been read in your hearing, "I Know That God Does Exist." I have a very definite obligation to that proposition, to set out an *argument*, to set set out a *valid* argument which has true premises (which constitutes a *sound* argument) and, therefore, will constitute *proof* of that proposition.

But first just a few introductory words. It has been suggested that perhaps in a point or two I might have been *unphilosophical* and—since this is basically a contention between two philosophers—I just want to make clear that being philosophical does not mean that one does not sound as if he really means what he says. And it does not mean that he does not recognize and honor the law of rationality. In fact most philosophers—including Dr. Flew—hold that recognizing and honoring the law of rationality is indeed the mark of a philosopher. I make no apologies whatever for being both a philosopher and a preacher, a preacher of the Gospel of Jesus Christ. But I have wondered why Dr. Flew failed, while he was in the affirmative, to present a sound argument for his contention in a precise logical way.

It has been suggested that his failure is due to the fact that he is in a foreign country, but such could have little or nothing to do with this proposition. That he is out of his own country has nothing to do with how he handles intellectual material. Neither is his failure due to his not being accustomed to this style of debating. I have heard him in discussion before, and he seemed not to be bothered at all by the kind of format that was involved. Perhaps he did not know the responsibility of an affirmative speaker? But that cannot be so because, in his writings, he constantly chides a man who does not recognize his responsibility as an affirmant. Perhaps because he does not know the arguments? I deny that emphatically. In reading the works of Dr. Flew, I am convinced that he knows the arguments that are involved as well as anybody in the world. Perhaps because he does not understand or accept the law of rationality? The truth of the matter is:

he has written very strongly and frequently in *defense* of it! But he has not acted in harmony with it in *this* discussion. Ordinarily, when he is writing in the affirmative, and he writes almost constantly of matters that are concerned with God or very closely related to God—at least subjects that are peripheral to the subject of God. In fact, it is the case that he is almost *God-intoxicated. He constantly emphasizes in his books that the onus of proof is on the affirmative writer or speaker!* But I am afraid that he has not recognized that truth in this discussion.

I want you to note carefully that I am *not* attacking Dr. Flew as a person at all. If there is anything in this world that I knew to do to help him, I assure you that I would be glad to do it lovingly and with compassion. But I make no excuse for attacking his *doctrine*. That is what I came here to do, and he came here to attack the doctrine which I am teaching. That is our purpose in this discussion. But each of us has a responsibility to the proposition which we are affirming. I have a suggestion perhaps that might explain it, that perhaps for the first time in his life the real burden of proof for showing proof that God does *not* exist has been on his shoulders—that he was not in the role of simply sitting back and saying to the theist, "Now the burden of proof is on *your* shoulders, you have not convinced me yet." But he has had that responsibility and it seems clear to me, and I say it as kindly as I know how to say it, that he has *failed* to meet it. But his failure is due, not to the *man*, but to the *doctrine*. There are no men in this nation, there are no men in his own native country, who can prove the proposition which he set himself out to prove. And, to devastate a *doctrine* is not to devastate a *man*.

I want you to notice further, by way of introductory remarks, that it seems hard for my learned colleague to decide whether he wants to be an atheist or an agnositc. In his debate with Dr. Plantinga in California, which I heard and enjoyed a great deal, he made clear that he had great disdain for agnostics, indicating that they seemed to be willing, if they were with theists, to lean in that direction, or, if they were with atheists, to lean in that direction. He pleaded for the audience to come out clearly and strongly for *atheism*. But in *this* discussion he seems to want to be merely one who says "I am just not a theist." He has therefore not really presented the argument that would show that God does *not* exist.

Further, it seems to be hard for him to decide whether he wants to remain a rationalist—in the usual sense of one who honors, recognizes and abides by the law of rationality—or to become an existential philosopher; that is, one who would uphold the "leap into the dark" approach. I wonder, Dr. Flew, do you wish to decide to become an existentialist atheist so that those who would join you as an atheist will make that decision, not upon the basis of a rational presentation, but simply by a "leap into the dark"? Now, surely Dr. Flew will not want to stay with that. He will want to straighten up what has already gone on in this discussion that would indicate he has gone in that direction.

There is one point which Dr. Flew made in his rejoinder last evening, to which I have not had opportunity to reply, which merits attention. In reply to what I said about "guaranteed freedom" in this life—that we live in this life in a probationary period where we have freedom either to love and serve God or to reject him—Dr. Flew suggested that God should have made man so that he would *always freely* make the right decision. I suggested this was the affirmation of a logical contradiction. But, he raised the question, if it is a logical contradiction here on *earth* for *guaranteed freedom* it would also be the same in *heaven*.

But now I want to make clear that I have said that guaranteed freedom here on this earth does involve a logical contradiction but I have not said what Dr. Flew has assigned to me. You must be very careful to listen to what has been said. It seems clear to me that he misunderstands the whole matter. Let me make clear the truth on the matter. As we go back to the beginning of the scriptural record, Adam's fall was not guaranteed. Adam was a *free* man, but it was *foreknown* by God. Now God can as easily foreknow what will be a *free* act as he could know what would be an act that was determined. A rock falling down a mountain is simply an "act" of something that has no intelligence. God could foreknow that—and he did—and he foreknew the act of Adam falling into sin. And man's not falling from heaven—that is, once he goes into eternal life that he will not come out of it—is not guaranteed, certainly not in the sense that man is not free that he is not one with a free mind in heaven, but that he *will* not do so is *foreknown* by God and revealed to us. So that takes care of Professor Flew's point on that matter.

My fellow disputant's point on hell can amount to nothing more than, "You, Thomas B. Warren, have an incorrect concept of God." That is, that God might exist, but if he did, he could not punish anyone, and Dr. Flew is the one to decide just what attributes God must have. He admitted at one point that it *may* be the case that matter is not eternal. If so, then, since he claims that matter is the only thing that exists, then by implication he holds that at one time nothing existed. But, my friends, if at one time nothing existed, then nothing would exist today. So, since something does now exist, it is clear that he is wrong about this.

He also mentioned miracles, as in the days of Elijah, and says this as a testable situation, but he does not understand the Biblical teaching that miracles served the purpose of the confirmation of the Word during the days of the New Testament, through the apostles and prophets. With the completing of the writing of the New Testament Scriptures, those miracles have ceased.

As to *falsifiability,* he has admitted that his proposition could be falsified, that the situation which I presented to him would, if it occurred, constitute a falsification of his proposition. He, therefore, has admitted that it is *possible* that God *does* exist, and therefore, he has admitted that *his proposition* is *false!*

He also admitted that the situation which I proposed would make clear that *my* propositon *could* be *verified!* He therefore admits that my proposition is possibly true. Thus, he has admitted that *I may* be *right* and that *he may* be *wrong.* For an agnostic that would not be so great an admission, but for Dr. Flew it is indeed a great admission *because an atheist claims that he knows* that God does *not* exist!

As to the *law of excluded middle,* at first Dr. Flew, by implication, seemed to deny it. Then he admitted it when it involved precisely stated propositions. Of course, that is all I have ever contended for. But, he must remember that the law of excluded middle applies to *objects* as well as to *propositions,* so that every object is either human or non-human. There is simply no way that Dr. Flew will be able to escape that. The law of rationality means that we should draw conclusions that are warranted, only conclusions that are warranted by the evidence.

I want you to note, as I begin the presentation of the first argument that I shall give in the defense of my proposition, in Question No. 9 of the second night he *admitted* the validity of the move from empirical observation in this world to the knowledge of the class of things which is transcendent of the universe. Now it so happens that the class of things which are transcendent of the universe is a class of one member. But, Dr. Flew claims that he is able to reason from empirical fact in this world to the state of affairs in that class of things which are transcendent of the universe. He therefore admits the validity of the move. Now note this very carefully, he admits the validity of the move of reasoning from empirical fact—here in the world, which is subject to our observation—to knowledge of things beyond, which are transcendent of the universe. He claims to *know*—by such procedure—that this is a *null* or *empty* class, but he has given absolutely no argument to prove that it is so.

Now then, to the actual presentation of the argument. For two nights we have been looking for an affirmative argument, and now we have one. I have not been asking for anything unusual in asking him to give us an affirmative argument. I have simply been asking for what is ordinarily done in every philosophical paper and what Professor Flew himself does when he seems to be in different situations from this one. Here is the argument. It is Chart No. 41-D. (See Page 136.) If there is even one characteristic, attribute or property of even one human being which could have come into existence only by the creative power of God, then that one human being constitutes proof that God does exist. Notice, I am talking about one human being. There is something in this world into which I have peculiar insight. I am an empirical fact. I exist, and there are things that I know about myself that nobody else knows. There *is* at least one characteristic attribute or property of at least one human being which could have come into existence only by the creative power of God. Therefore, that one human being constitutes proof, when the evidence is recognized and reasoned about properly, that God does exist.

In regard to this argument, I want you to note now on Chart No. 41-E (See Page 137) that the argument is valid. Professor Flew will not question that. Thus, it is clear that if the two

[TBW AFF.]

EACH HUMAN BEING IS PROOF THAT GOD DOES EXIST

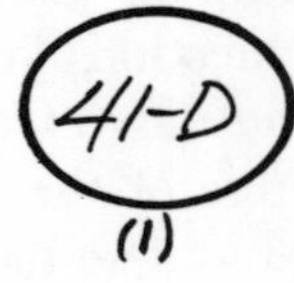

1. IF THERE IS EVEN ONE CHARACTERISTIC, ATTRIBUTE OR PROPERTY OF EVEN ONE HUMAN BEING WHICH COULD HAVE COME INTO EXISTENCE ONLY BY THE CREATIVE POWER OF GOD, THEN THAT ONE HUMAN BEING CONSTITUTES PROOF THAT GOD DOES EXIST.

2. THERE IS AT LEAST ONE CHARACTERISTIC, ATTRIBUTE OR PROPERTY OF AT LEAST ONE HUMAN BEING WHICH COULD HAVE COME INTO EXISTENCE ONLY BY THE CREATIVE POWER OF GOD.

3. THEREFORE, THAT ONE HUMAN BEING CONSTITUTES PROOF (WHEN THE EVIDENCE IS RECOGNIZED AND REASONED ABOUT PROPERLY) THAT GOD DOES EXIST.

[HUMAN BEING = PROOF, CONT'D.]

CONT'D
41-E
(2)

* IN REGARD TO THE ARGUMENT OF THE PRECEDING CHART, IT MUST BE NOTED THAT:

1. THE ARGUMENT IS VALID.
2. THUS, IF THE TWO PREMISES ARE TRUE, THE CONCLUSION MUST BE TRUE.
3. THE FIRST PREMISE QUITE OBVIOUSLY IS TRUE.
4. -SO- THE ONLY POINT WHICH CAN BE AT ISSUE IS THE QUESTION: IS THE SECOND PREMISE TRUE?

* LET US NOW PROCEED TO SHOW THAT THE SECOND PREMISE IS TRUE.

* HAVING DONE THAT, WE WILL HAVE PROVED THAT GOD DOES EXIST.

premises are *true,* the conclusion must be true. That is what you mean by a valid argument. You mean: if the *premises* are true, the conclusion must be true. The first premise is quite obviously true so the only point which can be at issue is the question, "Is the second premise true?" And we now proceed to show that it is.

Now let us notice in hart No. 41-Z. (See Page 140.) This argument is involved in symbols, and, though these symbols may seem strange to you, I assure you there is no real problem. I had intended to have it written out in simple ordinary English words but I do not have it. But I will read it so that you can understand it just as well. In the first premise, you will notice that we have an argument which involves nine premises and a conclusion at point number ten. The first premise where you see C and that little wedge or v looking thing with a circle around it which means you have strong disjunction, which means that it is either one case or the other. The C ⓥ E means: either human beings owe their ultimate origin to *creation,* or human beings owe their ultimate origin to *evolution.* Those are the *only* possibilities and therefore I have indicated that it is strong disjunction.

In the second premise we have C and a little thing that looks like a horseshoe which is the implication sign—C ⊃ G. Now that is read in this way. If human beings owe their ultimate origin to *creation,* then *God* exists. This is obvious since creation can occur only by the hand of God.

The third point, E. If E is true, that is, if human beings owe their ultimate origin to *evolution,* then that evolution must have occurred by one of these two ways—either by some human being being *born* of some ape (or some other *non-human* thing) or of being *transformed* from an ape (or some other *non-human* thing into a human being). In other words, you have this situation. In the first case you have the physical union of two apes, and I will say that, without repeating over and over, "that or some other non-human thing." Let us just use *apes* for the sake of illustration. Here are two apes, in their physical union. The result of the union is *not* an *ape* but a *human being.* And, the other case is that here is an ape but he is *transformed* into a *human being.* Now, I am saying if evolution is true, then these are the *only* possibilities. I remind Dr. Flew of his task of pointing out some other possibility.

Now in point four we note that, according to Dr. Flew, it is false that any human being was ever born of an ape. Dr. Flew has already admitted that no human now living was born of an ape, thus denying that any human that ever lived on the earth was born of an ape. So, he has admitted a very crucial point in this issue.

In point 5 we have the point that T is false. That means that no human being has ever been *transformed* from being an ape. Nothing has ever been an ape living on the earth and then turned into a human being. Dr. Flew has admitted in the questions which he answered that such has never occurred with a human being now living and it has never occurred with any human being that has ever lived in the past. I am using Dr. Flew's admissions in my case.

Further, by conjunction, we wrote in point 6, not B *and* not T. That premise means that no human being was ever born of an ape and no human being was ever transformed from an ape. Now we need to make that move so that we can make the next one, number 7, which by DeMorgan's theorem we see that the disjunction of these two premises (5,6) is false. That means it is false to say that human beings owe their origin either to being *born* of an ape or to being *transformed* from an ape. Now, since we have now falsified the consequent, look back up in point number 3, we have now falsified the consequent of that compound proposition. It then follows, in point 8, that the antecedent is falsified. Every proposition which implies a false proposition is false itself. Now that is what this premise means. Since evolution implies the false proposition that man owes his origin either to being born of an ape or of being transformed from an ape, since that premise itself is false, then evolution is false. And since evolution is false, going back up to premise number 1, you find that this is strong disjunction, if one of them is false the other must be true. Since I have shown that evolution is false, then creation must be true and since we see in the second premise that if creation is true then God must exist. Therefore I can draw the conclusion from premises 2 and 9, by what we call modus ponens, "Therefore, God does exist."

COSMO. ARG.

[THE ARGUMENT PUT IN SYMBOLIC TERMS— CONT'D.]

TBW'S PROPOSITION: "I KNOW THAT GOD DOES EXIST"

41-Z (3)

* THE FOLLOWING ARGUMENT PROVES THAT PROPOSITION:

1. C ⓥ E. ONLY POSSIBILITIES.
2. $C \supset G$. OBVIOUS, SINCE THERE CAN BE NO CREATION WITHOUT GOD.
3. $E \supset (B \vee T)$. IF EVOLUTION IS TRUE, THEN THESE ARE ONLY POSSIBILITIES.
4. $\sim B$. HUMANS ARE NOT BORN OF APES.
5. $\sim T$. APES ARE NOT TRANSFORMED INTO HUMANS
6. $\sim B \cdot \sim T$ 4, 5, CONJ.
7. $\sim (B \vee T)$ 6, DE M.
8. $\sim E$ 3, 7, M.T.
9. C 1, 8, D.S.
10. G 2, 9, M.P.

* PROOF OF THE EXISTENCE OF GOD IS "RIGHT BEFORE THE EYES" OF EACH AND EVERY HUMAN BEING.

My friends, you have seen an affirmative argument. The argument is valid. All of the premises are true, some crucial ones admitted by Dr. Flew. It is therefore a sound argument. It therefore demands the truth of the conclusion that God does eixst. I wish I had 30 minutes to review for you the ten questions, which I gave to Dr. Flew—some of which have not been answered. Again, we have three questions for which there is *no answer at all!* Dr. Flew is very strong in pointing out in his writings that when men cannot face up to questions, when they must involve themselves in the denial of major undisputed facts, they are involved in a false position. Thus, it is clear that his failure to answer at least 6 questions in the first 2 nights indicates that we ought to be rather suspicious of his procedure in dealing with questions.

But now let us notice, and I will not have time to go into all of them, but I will try to show you the great significance of the answers and non-answers which he has given to these questions. Question No. 1: Answer true or false: "It is possible for God to be infinite in some of his attributes and finite in others." For example, he can be infinite in love but finite in justice. He answers, "True." Well, Dr. Flew you and I are talking about two different *Gods!*

QUESTIONS FOR DR. FLEW, WEDNESDAY NIGHT, SEPTEMBER 22, 1976

1. ☐ True ☐ False
   It is possible for God to be infinite in some of His attributes and finite in others; for example, He can be infinite in love but finite in justice.
2. What would be involved in God's being infinite in love?
3. What would be involved in God's being infinite in justice?
4. ☐ True ☐ False
   It is not possible that the justice of God could entail *any* punishment for sin.
5. ☐ True ☐ False
   It is possible that this infinite justice of God might entail at least one minute of punishment when this life is over.

6. I know what the punishment for sin should be by: (check appropriate boxes)
   - ☐ by intuition;
   - ☐ by deduction from the concept of God;
   - ☐ by deduction from the concept of sin;
   - ☐ by deduction from some empirical fact;
   - ☐ from the combination of the concept of God and some empirical fact;
   - ☐ from something else (please explain) ____

7. ☐ True ☐ False
   All men have done at least some things they know they ought not to have done.
8. ☐ True ☐ False
   Philosophy offers nothing by way of salvation from this feeling of guilt which results from knowing that one has done what he ought not to have done.
9. List below at (1) the attribute of God which contradicts with the attribute of God which you list at (2):
   (1) ____________________ Versus (2) ____________________
10. To obtain and maintain the status of a philosopher one must (please check all appropriate boxes):
    - ☐ Sound as if he does not really mean what he says;
    - ☐ Sound as if he doesn't really care whether anyone believes what he says or not;
    - ☐ Hold that no one has any moral obligation to believe what he says;
    - ☐ Hold that no one has any real moral obligation to be rational;
    - ☐ Not demand of others that they be rational;
    - ☐ Not be lovingly and genuinely concerned about the spiritual and moral welfare of people;
    - ☐ Refrain from making any appeal (with feeling) for people to follow any certain course of action;
    - ☐ Hold that he is one who has no obligation to pay any attention to what he is doing.

FLEW'S FIRST NEGATIVE

(Wednesday Night)

Dr. Warren may be assured that I am sobering up from God intoxication. I shall be writing considerably less, if anything, in this area in the future. I shall be concentrating largely on social matters—except of course for trying to reply to things that people write against the things I have written in the religious area: either to say: "No I don't think they have got it right," or to say: "Well, yes, I think you have got it right."

Second thing: Dr. Warren is also right in observing that I do find it somewhat difficult in this particular case to decide whether to say "atheist" or "agnostic." I have tried to give my reasons for deciding, with some difficulty, that it should be "atheist" rather than "agnostic." But he is absolutely right that this is a thing which I have had difficulty with. I think the situation is, for reasons I have given, one in which there is bound to be some difficulty; though I believe the answer that I have offered is the right one.

Now for two more substantial points. Let us take the one that came up last first because that will be the more clearly in people's minds. This is the business about human and non-human. The reason I find difficulty with Dr. Warren's elaborate and certainly valid argument here is this: that all these arguments take it that "human" is a precise term; that is to say that in all cases, if you knew all the facts and could see what is going on, then you could have no reasonable doubt in saying either definitely human or definitely non-human. And making this assumption himself, Dr. Warren then takes it that an adherent of evolutionary theory makes the same assumption. He then triumphantly draws, from a combination of evolutionary theory and this assumption which evolutionary theorists deny, conclusions that are incompatible with that theory.

Of course his argument here is entirely valid. The trouble about it is that it does not show that there is a contradiction in the evolutionary theory. It only shows that there is a contradiction between evolutionary theory and Dr. Warren's view of human beings; and in particular, his idea that the term human is in this way a precise term. That is to say that there is a contradiction: not in evolutionary theory itself; but between evolutionary theory and that view of the nature of the term "human" which Dr. Warren and others who deny evolutionary theory all share. So, I will not go into the details of these arguments, which I am sure are perfectly valid. The trouble with them is simply that they attribute to the evolutionary theorists something that evolutionary theory denies, and then triumphantly derive the conclusion that there is indeed an inconsistency between evolutionary theory and this claim which the evolutionists deny.

The other thing which I would like to take issue with briefly is the matter of freedom and guarantees. Okay, let it be allowed that God could know what free human beings, both in this life and in a life to come, would do and not do and that this is entirely consistent with their being free human beings. I believe that this is indeed so. But the consequence of this seems to me to be that we have got to say that God created certain creatures, the majority indeed of his creation as I understand the traditional view, in the full knowledge that these would sin and would be numbered among the damned. It makes the whole idea of this life as a sort of proving ground gratuitous.

If you could know—and I agree that you could know this if you were God—that this creature would behave in this way and that creature would behave in that way, then there is surely no need to have the proving ground; and, above all, no needs to have the gigantic wastage involved in these proceedings.

I hope that deals with the main points just raised. Let us now go on to something else. It is often suggested that an atheist naturalist cannot explain how the universe came into existence or how it comes to have whatever fundamental characteristics, whatever fundamental laws, it may be found in fact to have. The suggestion made then goes on to conclude: either that theism, the hypothesis that the universe was made and arranged by God, must be true because it can provide the missing explanations; or/and that an explanation in these theists' terms will in principle explain everything. It is also thought and urged as if this were a truism—that science only tells us *how,* never why. Thereafter it is usually concluded that there must in consequence be, as it were, a vacant slot for a religious system providing explanations of what science cannot explain. Dr. Warren, of course, would want to say alternatively or additionally that in the very special case of the origin of species the scientists have got it wrong, and that the true explanation how, in this particular case, is provided not by evolutionary biology but by Biblical Christianity.

I think it might help to get a clearer view of all these matters if I spent a bit of time on some fundamental principles about explanation. My first and very radical point is that we cannot take it as guaranteed that there always is an explanation, much less that there always is an explanation of any particular desired kind. Of course we usually and rightfully believe that there is, and all our past success in the search provides the best possible ground for confidence that there will be; at least in those areas where we have in fact had such success in the past. But there is nothing contradictory in the suggestion that there just is not any explanation at all. Still less is there anything contradictory in the suggestion that there just is not any explanation of some particular preferred kind. An explanation is always an answer to a question, and the question to which it is in answer may make an assumption which is not in fact correct. I may come back to this first rather radical point later. But in any case it should be more clearly understood, and more clearly seen to be true as we go along.

Second point. Consider this supposed truism. "Science can only tell us *how*, never *why*." Certainly the word "why" has here to be construed in a special way. It has to be. For if it is construed as most natural scientists would in their working hours construe it, then the supposed truism "Science can only tell us *how*, never *why*," is not a truism but a manifest falsism. To avoid that it has to be construed as referring to an explanation in terms of motives, purposes and intentions. The intended contrast is between an account of mechanisms; and an account of what went on in human or quasi-human terms—an account, that is, referring to the motives, purposes and intentions of a human or quasi-human agent. But now, if that interpretation is correct—and I believe it is in fact both sympathetic and correct—then there are two things to be said. One is that it is not true, at any rate it is not true if the human sciences are allowed to rate as sciences, that "Science can only tell us *how*, and never *why*." Anthropology, psychology, even psychoanalysis, are forever telling us what people are about; why—in terms of motives, purposes and intentions—we do some of the queer things that we do do.

The other point under this second head is that to ask for an explanation why, in this interpretation just explained presupposes that whatever you are asking this question about was in fact done for a reason, and done by some personal or quasi-personal being. You clearly can not insist on getting an explanation of this kind except where this basic assumption applies. Now, this second point of mine about "Science only tells us how never why," shows in one particular case what I was saying under the first. Read namely, that to provide an explanation is to answer a question. It also shows that you can only provide such an answer where assumptions of the question are correct. Now in the case of the universe as a whole, and of features in the universe which are not the work of men, you can only ask why, in this interpretation of "why," if you are already prepared to assume that it was indeed all the work of some personal or quasi-personal being. What you can not do is what people often do do. You can not argue: from your insistence that there must be answers to such questions; to the conclusion that there is such a being.

The third point I want to make about explanation is that it is in principle impossible to explain everything. Suppose that you are thinking of explaining why the paint over the gas cooker goes brown and dirty before the rest of the paint in the same room. Then your explanation of this will be in terms of chemical principles; something or other in the gas or the gas fumes combine with this or that in the paint. You thus explain what you are asked to explain in terms of chemical regularities, which are not themselves at this stage explained.

Let us distinguish between the explainers, the elements which do the explaining; and the explained, what is explained. Of couse you can go on from this first question to ask for an explanation of those regularities which were the explainers in the first explanation. These explainers are now explained by reference to laws not of chemistry but of physics. So in this case what was previously an element in the explanation now becomes the thing to be explained.

The point of this example is that it becomes obvious that,

however long this sort of chain of explanations can be made, and often it can be made very long indeed, still every link in it will leave something which at that stage is not itself explained. So, clearly, it is impossible for everything in such a series to be explained. Of course you can on occasion reasonably fault someone for not pursuing the series of explanations as far as he could or should pursue it. But you can not fault him for ending with principles which are explainers not themselves explained.

This same fundamental point obtains even when at some stage chains of two different kinds of explanation are linked together. Thus, we may ask why a person does one of those queer things that people sometimes do. And we may eventually reach some conclusion, some adequate explanation of this queer conduct, an explanation referring to the fundamental desires, drives and so on of the person, and no doubt referring to the circumstances in which he did this. But once one has got to these fundamental drives and desires then presumably explanation in terms of motives, purposes and intention must stop. Just because these are his fundamental desires there is no further we can go on these lines. But of course at that point you can go on to ask a different sort of question. You can ask why, in another sense of "why," he has the desires and fundamental drives and what not that he does have. The answer to this will presumably be in terms of physiology; not in terms of motives, purposes and intentions but in terms of physiology.

Or, again we may having reached the end of a series of explanations of the facts of the universe by arriving at certain fundamental laws of matter we may start again to ask why. Suppose now: that it is the case that there is an answer to such questions at that stage; and that the universe is indeed a divine creation; and that God did have purposes in making it, and in subjecting it to the fundamental laws which it has. Okay? Okay: the same principle still holds. Sooner or later some facts, this time about the existence of God and about God's basic nature, will have to be taken as ultimate; explainers which cannot themselves be explained.

The moral I want to draw from all this is that the theist may reasonably reproach the atheist for failing to explain anything which can and should be explained; a failure which he will account for by reference to the atheist's blindness to the existence and nature of God. But what the theist must not do is to chide the atheist for failing to explain everything. For in the nature of the case there must be in every system of thought, theist as well as atheist, both things explained and ultimate principles which explain but are are not themselves explained. In the theist world these ultimate explainers are, I take it, the brute fact that God does indeed exist and that he does indeed have such and such a nature. In my atheist naturalism the ultimate explainers of whatever can be explained are the brute fact of the existence of the universe itself and the further fact that it is its nature to have these and these fundamental characteristics.

"Whatever has he been doing all that for?" you may ask. I have been doing all that partly because I think it throws a lot of light on the nature of explanation and the sort of questions one can and cannot sensibly ask and sensibly demand an answer for. But I have been doing it mainly in order to try to bring out how at the end of the day things look to an atheist naturalist. He sees the universe as itself ultimate and its fundamental regularities as being the fundamental principles in terms of which other things can be explained, though these fundamental principles cannot themselves be explained. He looks at it indeed as presumably the theist looks at things. But the theist sees the fundamental principles which cannot themselves be explained as different principles.

WARREN'S SECOND AFFIRMATIVE

(Wednesday Night)

Dr. Flew, Gentlemen Moderators, Ladies and Gentlemen. I assure you that I am pleased to be back to reply to the speech which you have just heard.

Before I give attention to the questions which he answered, that I just started at the end of my last speech, I must say that while Dr. Flew was supposed to be in the *affirmative,* he spent all of his time in the *negative,* and tonight, that he is supposed to be in the *negative,* he spends all but about two minutes of his time in the *affirmative.* While I do not know exactly the customs in England, Dr. Flew, I assure you that is very peculiar for those of us in Tennessee and Texas.

Now, I want to begin again with *Question No. 1.* The question was, "True or false. It is possible for God to be infinite in some of his attributes and finite in others." For example, he can be infinite in love but finite in justice. He answered, "True." I suggested a moment ago that Dr. Flew and I then are talking about different Gods. The God I am defending in this debate is infinite in *all* of his attributes. I know there are all kinds of things that men refer to when they use the word "God," but I am not talking about a God who is infinite in love but not infinite in justice. Now you can understand that since an atheist really has only one argument, all the other things he may say are peripheral. He really has only one argument—which Dr. Flew has not really made. I wish he would even yet really "buck up" to it and make it. The one argument you have, Dr. Flew, is that of "evil." Thus, he cannot then admit—without giving up—that God is infinite in *justice* because that would mean that God would be right in punishing men who are guilty of *sin!* So, he says, "Oh, yes, God can be infinite in *love,* but he cannot be infinite in *justice.*"

Question No. 2. "What would be involved in God's being infinite in love?" What is Dr. Flew's answer? He is as silent as the stars. Not one single word did he say about it. What indeed is involved, Dr. Flew? I challenge you to answer that question. What is involved in God's being infinite in love? What if it were in contradistinction to what you have said about His being finite in *justice?* What would be involved in God's being infinite in *justice?* What if He were infinite in justice, then what would He do? What would be involved in such?

Question No. 4. "True or false. It is not possible that the justice of God would entail any punishment for sin." And, lo and behold, to my utter consternation, he says it is false. In other words, he is admitting that God *can* consistently punish—when his whole argument seems to be that if God *does* punish, such would prove He is not a God of *love*.

But that is not all of it. Let us note the next one. *Question No. 5.* "True or false. It is possible that this infinite justice of God might entail at least one minute of punishment when this life is over." He answered "true." Now note, it might entail at least one minute of punishment and not be out of harmony—the basic concept of God would not be self-contradictory. What about two minutes, Dr. Flew? What about three minutes, four minutes, an hour, a day, a year, a month, a hundred years, a million years? Where do you stocp? Would a billion years be long enough? Could God punish a man a billion years and still be just and loving? You can see that he has given up tonight, just as he has on each night. He has shown his inability to answer these questions in harmony with the atheistic position and the implications which follow from it. He himself is on record as saying when a man cannot do that, then it is clear that he holds a false position.

Question No. 6. I know what the punishment for sin should be by: (1) intuition (2) deduction from the concept of God, (3) deduction from the concept of sin, (4) deduction from some empirical fact, (5) the combination of the concept of God and some empirical fact or (6) something else." Which one of those do you suppose he answers? Not a single one! Note please that I had a box which said "something else." If the other boxes did not give his answer he could have checked this one. But he did not. My friends, when men have the truth, they do not handle questions in this fashion.

Question No. 7. "True or false. All men have done at least some things which they know they ought not to have done." Dr. Flew has been on *both* sides of the question as to whether morality is *subjective* or *objective!* He confesses that there is a real objective wrong, but then he winds up arguing in such a way as to imply that it simply depends upon a function of the human mind. He has contended that before there were human beings there was no value in the world and, therefore, given that answer, value can be nothing more than a function of the human mind. Nothing more than *likes* or *dislikes*—such as, you do not like spinach, you do like ice cream. You do not like adultery, you do not like murder, but you do like kindness. It is nothing but a matter of your own *opinion!* Now that is what he is doing with this crucial matter. Now in this question no. 7, he admits that all men know they have done things they ought not to have done. In connection with the work of the Nazis and the charges against them and their condemnation, he has admitted by implication that there is a higher law which transcends the provincial and the transient. That means it transcends what each *individual* thinks. It even transcends what a whole *nation* thinks. It even transcends what a whole *group* of nations thinks. There is a higher law above mere human law, which can be only the law of God. And yet he here admits that all men know that they have done something they *ought not to have done!* That, in effect, is another admission of defeat. He has made such over and over and over in this discussion.

Question No. 8. "Philosophy offers nothing by way of salvation from this feeling of guilt which results from knowing that one has done what he ought not to have done." He answers, "True." After answering that everybody knows he has done something which he ought *not* to have done—and therefore that everybody has guilt feelings—he says, "Philosophy is the only thing I have to offer, but philosophy does not have any answer to the problem." How much more clearly could one give up? Just try to think about how you could give up (admit defeat) any more completely than has this learned man from our fellow-country which we all love and admire.

Question No. 9. "List below at 1 the attribute of God which contradicts the attribute of God which you list at 2." Under number 1 he lists *justice* and *goodness.* Then, in number 2, he lists *sustaining hell.* He does so because he holds that God is *finite* in *justice.* That is *not* the God we are defending! That is not the God of Christian theism. The supreme personal Being, creator of the world, transcendent of the world, infinite in all attributes. Dr. Flew is talking about somebody else's God. Dr. Flew, come up here and talk about the God we are talking about in this debate and *then* answer that question, "Which two of the attributes or characteristics of God contradict one another?" When you recognize that God is not only infinite in *love* but also infinite in *justice*, then you will see that there is no contradiction in the matter of the sustaining of hell.

I want to look at his speech. At the most, he gave about two minutes, if I timed him correctly, to replying to my speech and spent the rest of the time in doing what would have been closer to what he ought to have done the first two evenings than anything he actually did. He said that he is really having trouble. He confesses that he is having trouble deciding whether he should be an atheist or an agnostic. I pointed out to you that in his discussion with Dr. Plantinga in California—he really came down strong on it as I recall—he contended that any *agnostic* is simply not willing to face up to the facts: "If you are with atheists, you sort of *lean* in that direction. If you are with *theists*, you *lean* in that direction," Dr. Flew asserted of agnostics. He indicated that agnostics are somewhat cowardly and that they ought to come on and recognize that the evidence demands that they can *know* that God does not exist. But now notice this significant matter, Dr. Flew you signed an *atheistic* proposition! Now, if later on you would like to discuss with somebody and sign an agnostic proposition, that would be perfectly alright with me, but in *this* proposition, in *this* debate, you signed an *atheistic* proposition! You did not say that no one can know whether God exists. You said "I, Antony G. N. Flew, *know* that God does not exist." In "flirting" with the agnostic position, Dr. Flew admits defeat in this present debate!

Now notice this my friends, we have had quite a bit to say about the Nazis and their treatment of the Jews. I do not believe there is a man living but what has an abhorrence for what happened there. Perhaps someone says, "All that you are appealing to is emotion." No, I am not. I am appealing to *facts*. Every argument I am making in this debate appeals to *facts*, empirical facts. Now here is the fact that these people put little children into box cars coated with quicklime so that they would not only die but die agonizingly over a period of days. Dr. Flew has admitted that they were guilty of objective moral wrong. But now note how he responds to my argument on the Nazis—to which he gave about a snap of the finger of recognition—he said, "The reason why I need give no more attention is because you can not really draw a clear line between the human and the non-human." Now, friends, that is one thing you have to believe to be an atheist. If so, then, it turns out that the Nazis were right. If you can not tell the difference between a human and a non-human, what was wrong with what they did? Dr. Flew, you cannot prove then that the people they executed in those horrible, terrible ways were really human, can you? You do not really know the difference between a human and a non-human. The truth of the matter is that Dr. Flew, like the philosopher David Hume (whom Dr. Flew seems to admire), does not really believe his own doctrine. He does not really believe that you can not tell the difference between a human and a non-human. He believes, as do you and I, that those Nazis were guilty of monstrous, heinous crimes because they were guilty of murdering and torturing little children—human beings!

That brings us again to the law of excluded middle. Why this man will, on the one hand, *admit* the law of excluded middle and, on the other hand, turn right around and *deny* it, I am beyond the ability to explain. He admitted last evening—after quite a bit of sparring for two evenings—that the law of excluded middle is true, that *every* precisely stated proposition is either *true* or *false!* Now then, *this* proposition—that every object either has the property of being human or it does not—is a precisely stated proposition! That proposition is either true or false. Every object in this world either *is* human or it is *not* human. The fact that somebody may have some difficulty, in some particular case, in deciding whether a given object is a dog or a cat does not refute this truth. Even if I can not decide I do know one thing: I know that this one right here (pointing) is either a dog or it is not a dog and I know that that one (pointing) is either a cat or it is not a cat. Dr. Flew, you know that every object in this world is either human or non-human and all that you have had to say about that is absolutely worthless.

Now then let me have my chart (41-Z) (See Page 154) again with the diagram of my argument on the board. I have pointed

[COSMO. ARG.]

[THE ARGUMENT PUT IN SYMBOLIC TERMS— CONT'D.]

TBW'S PROPOSITION: "I KNOW THAT GOD DOES EXIST". (41-Z) (3)

* THE FOLLOWING ARGUMENT PROVES THAT PROPOSITION:

1. $C \circledv E$. ONLY POSSIBILITIES.
2. $C \supset G$. OBVIOUS, SINCE THERE CAN BE NO CREATION WITHOUT GOD.
3. $E \supset (B \vee T)$. IF EVOLUTION IS TRUE, THEN THESE ARE ONLY POSSIBILITIES.
4. $\sim B$. HUMANS ARE NOT BORN OF APES.
5. $\sim T$. APES ARE NOT TRANSFORMED INTO HUMANS
6. $\sim B \cdot \sim T$ 4, 5, CONJ.
7. $\sim (B \vee T)$ 6, DE M.
8. $\sim E$ 3, 7, M.T.
9. C 1, 8, D.S.
10. G 2, 9, M.P.

* PROOF OF THE EXISTENCE OF GOD IS "RIGHT BEFORE THE EYES" OF EACH AND EVERY HUMAN BEING.

out to you that this argument is a valid argument. Dr. Flew admits it. Now to admit that an argument is valid is to admit that if the premises are true then the conclusion must be true. He tried to rid himself of this argument by his reference to the difficulty of deciding what is human and what is not. I have shown that he was not successful in that effort. Not only that, but he chooses to ignore the fact—as I have pointed out repeatedly—that on the first night he admitted that no human being has ever evolved from any ape or any other non-human being. He admits—in quite crucial admissions—that no human being has been *born* of an ape and that no human being has ever been transformed from an ape. That is the only two conceivable ways it could have happened. Therefore, it is clear that no human being on this earth owes his ultimate origin to evolution but rather he must owe it to God. Note that the argument makes clear that human beings owe their origin to either creation or evolution. It is my conviction that in this great land of ours, state universities, by and large, are not really giving our young people a "fair shot" at the real information on this matter: creation or evolution. And they cannot prove evolution. This man, as good as they have to represent them, has admitted what is crucial to the whole argument and thus has given up completely! There is not one argument for evolution that he can show is sound. He has already admitted the crucial premises 2, 4, and 5 (of my argument 41-Z) and he admits the argument is *valid.* It therefore follows that the argument is a *sound* argument. Therefore, it follows that we are here by creation and, therefore, that we are here by the power of Almighty God and, therefore, that God exists. Now, Dr. Flew, that is an *argument* that has been presented to you, and you must deal with it if you are to fulfill your responsibility as a *negative* speaker.

Now before I respond to the other matters in his speech which are basically about *explanation,* I want to ask Dr. Flew to answer these questions on explanation. Please jot them down, Dr. Flew. In fact, I will leave this sheet right here for you, and you can answer them when you come. You can just come here and follow from this sheet. First, "True or false. Any explanation of the existence of phenomenon must be a scientific hypothesis." Second, "All explanations of facts are of the type of scientific hypothesis." Third, "A rational explanation and a scientific explanation are exactly equivalent." Fourth, "A non-scientific explanation does not explain anything."

I want to give my second argument, the design argument. I want to see Chart No. 42-J. (See Page 157.) Dr. Flew has already admitted, in Question No. 9 of the second night (regarding the Mars probe), that if we could find a message carved on a rock on Mars—by this Viking device—which had a picture of a king and his coat of arms and a message expressing gratitude by the people for the wonderful work he had done, that this would constitute proof that *intelligent life* was on Mars! Now this is an *admission* by Dr. Flew that the basic thrust of the argument from empirical fact to knowledge of the existence of something that you have not observed is a valid procedure! Note the significance of that. This means that he has in fact recognized the validity of the basic thrust of natural theology. All of this palaver about "explanation" is simply beside the point. He needs to come up as the negative speaker and recognize what he has already admitted in regard to these matters.

Note that in his effort last evening—when he introduced before it had ever been introduced as an affirmative argument in this debate, when he should have been giving *affirmative* arguments he gave a *negative* argument in reply to the design argument—he said that after all we can take care of all these matter such as the eye and the respiratory system, the cardiovascular system, the endocrine gland system in the human body because these things *grow* but things like automobiles are *made*. Dr. Flew seems to have forgotten that he has already admitted that no human being came by *transformation* and that no human being came by *birth* from an ape or any other non-human being; therefore, it is clear that human beings could have originated *only* by miraculous power. So, you see, the first human pair (Adam and Eve) were made or created by Almighty God. They were made and the law, the power of reproduction, was put into their bodies and every one of us who has lived from then until now owes his existence to that power of reproduction put in the human body. The atheist has absolutely no way he can explain that which makes any sense whatever.

Now let us note in an argument that I have introduced very

[INTELLIGENT LIFE ON MARS?]

42-J (2)

2. WHAT IF WE FOUND ON MARS—

In honor of King John XXVI of Mars, who with such great valor put down the uprising of wicked men who would have murdered or enslaved us, who so generously assisted in the development of medical science, and who helped us to see that the one true God really lives.

3. SHOULD WE CONCLUDE—
(check all correct answers)

- ☐ THAT AT LEAST AT SOME TIME INTELLIGENT LIFE HAD BEEN ON MARS.
- ☐ THAT THE CARVING OF THE FACE AND THE MESSAGE WAS THE RESULT OF THE PURELY ACCIDENTAL (CHANCE) ACTION OF THE ROCKS AND DIRT ON MARS.
- ☐ THAT IT IS IMPOSSIBLE TO COME TO KNOWLEDGE OF THE EXISTENCE OF INTELLIGENT BEINGS WITHOUT ACTUALLY OBSERVING THEM.

briefly, and I want you to have Chart No. 42-A(1) (See Page 159) on the screen, in which we see the passage of air along side the passage of blood in the alveoli in our lungs. In the lungs we have a gaseous interchange between oxygen and carbon dioxide. The reason why you see this interchange, if you will notice on the screen, is going from the oxygen in the air to the oxygen in the blood, is because of a greater tension of pressure in the particles of oxygen in the air passage than in the oxygen particles in the blood. The reason the carbon dioxide passes through the wall of the blood into the air passage is because of the opposite of that, a greater pressure of the carbon dioxide particles in the blood than there is in the air. We cannot live longer than five minutes without this interchange. Physicians tell us that if you have been in the situation in which your brain has been deprived of this process for more than five minutes, you are considered dead. Now then, evolution requires, so evolutionists tell us, long periods of time (millions of years) for these complex changes to occur. Dr. Flew, you have the obligation of explaining how this occurred in a five-minute period. How did it *evolve* in that period of time?

I am going to give it in a formulated, precise logical way. Here is the first premise. If the gaseous interchanges, that is of oxygen and carbon dioxide, in the respiratory system of a human being possess such properties or involve such things as to make clear that such interchanges were not brought into being by any part of or the totality of dead matter, then the respiratory system of the human being in which these interchanges occur must have been brought into being by the Creator who transcends the universe, that is *God*. The second premise—the gaseous interchanges in the respiratory system of a human being do possess such properties as to make clear that such interchanges were not brought into being by any part or the totality of dead matter. Therefore, the respiratory system of the human being must have been brought into being by the power of God Almighty. I am leaving the sheet there for you, Dr. Flew.

[USE WITH 41-D]

[RESPIRATORY SYSTEM— CONT'D]

✿ THE MARVELOUS INTERCHANGE OF OXYGEN (IN AIR) AND CARBON DIOXIDE (IN BLOOD):

AIR → OXYGEN ↓ ↑ →

BLOOD CARBON DIOXIDE

1. WITHOUT THIS AMAZING INTERCHANGE, NO HUMAN BEING COULD LIVE MORE THAN A FEW MOMENTS.
2. YET, THE ATHEISTIC POSITION DEPENDS UPON ITS EVOLVING OVER A PERIOD OF TIME AS LONG, PERHAPS, AS A MILLION YEARS
3. EVOLUTION COULD NOT HAVE OCCURRED—
4. —SO— ATHEISM IS FALSE!

*cf. CHART 41-D

FLEW'S SECOND NEGATIVE

(Wednesday Night)

First, the fact that I have had difficulty in deciding something does not mean that I have not decided it. It just means that I say that I have had difficulty in making this decision; for reasons I have tried to give before.

Second, the fact that it is possible to have cases in which the human shades into the non-human, the clearly human at one end of the scale, of development, but clearly non-human at the other end of the scale does not in any way involve that there are not many, many, many cases in which there is not the slightest difficulty about saying either that something is human or that it is not. It is not the case that, if you believe that there was a continuous development from the higher animals to man, you are committed to saying that you can not tell that Mrs. Wilkinson next door is human. All that you are saying is: that there could be cases shading off from the unambiguously human end of the scale to an unambiguously non-human end of the scale and that in the past such cases actually did exist.

Third, about infinite in justice and infinite in love. The reason why I do not offer any account of what these phrases mean is that they are not phrases that I have any inclination to use. If I did have an inclination to use them, I would endeavor to try to give some meaning to them. On the other hand it does seem to me clear that those who do use them must intend, whatever else they intend that the being thus described should be at least minimally just, at least minimally loving. Whatever else they mean they must mean at least that. This being so, I take it that there is some possibility of arguing about infinity in justice and infinity in love, drawing some conclusions from what people say about these even if you are far from clear about the whole of what people mean in these cases.

Next, about: "If one says that some punishment might be justi-His attributes and finite in others. For example: "Can He be infinite in love but finite in justice?" Well, of course, it may very well be that the term "God," as Dr. Warren and others define it, specifies these two requirements together, while they also believe that there is a Being who has both these characteristics together.

Nevertheless, the reason why I answer that, it seems to me possible for God to be infinite in some of his attributes and finite in others—for example he can be infinite in love and finite in justice—is that though I have the difficulty already explained about what "infinite" in these characteristics means, I take it that both are intended to imply at least minimal lovingness and at least minimal justice. It seems to me that would be perfectly consistent for someone to assert that their concept of God involves some combination of these characteristics which Dr. Warren's does not.

Next, about: If one says that some punishment might be justified, there is really no stopping point between a minute and eternity." Well, if the difference between a minute and infinity is as unimportant as all that, why are people so mad keen that the hated sinners should be punished for all eternity? Why, if there really is no substantial and significant difference between a small degree of something and an unlimited degree? If you are wanting to say, "Oh well if you have allowed a minute then there is no stopping place; it is just as good to allow eternity." Then okay, okay, "What is eternity between friends?" If this difference really does not matter, could not Dr. Warren and his God settle for a minute?

No, of course they could not. Because he agrees that there is an enormous difference. So, what, with a—perhaps uncharacteristic degree of vehemence, I am trying to bring out here is that differences of degree can be enormously important. Indeed almost all the humanly important differences are differences of degree. Once you have seen this you can not go on saying: "Well, the difference between age and youth, sanity and insanity, riches and poverty, of free society and one in which, as in Imperial Germany, everything that is not forbidden is compulsory, are differences of degree. So they do not matter—you have allowed that there should be some real laws against doing some things so there is no stopping point before you allow that there should be laws forbidding absolutely everything you can think of."

The serious point is that differences of degree can matter. By allowing that some modest punishment, some punishment commensurate with the offense, might be appropriate you are not thereby conceding: "Oh, well, then everything might be alright; it is just a difference of degree." This really will not do at all.

Next, the Argument to Design again. What I have not just admitted but asserted in saying that one can reasonably and rightfully argue from the presence of an automobile, and from our knowledge of the world, that this is an artifact, that this must have been designed and put together somewhere. What I have allowed here is simply that we can learn, we do learn, in the experience of our lives that certain sorts of cunning things are in fact made by people. They do not just happen or drop from the sky. Automobiles do not drop from the sky, neither do watches, and so on. We have also learned from our experience of the world that there are some other remarkable things, even more remarkable perhaps, that at least to ordinary observation, just growed and were not designed or made.

Next, a series of further homework questions. "Any explanation of the existence of a phenomenon must be a scientific hypothesis." Hum: there surely are quite a lot of explanations which people would not dignify with the name of science. For instance: when Kojak offers an explanation as to what the hoods were doing, would one call that a scientific explanation? Presumably not. So it would appear that this statement is false.

"All explanations of facts are of the type of scientific hypothesis?" I suppose so. But "of the type of," that is a rather extensible notion.

"A 'rational explanation' and a 'scientific explanation' are not exactly equivalent?" Surely not. No, one can offer explanations of points of logic and so on which people would not call scientific.

A non-scientific explanation does not explain anything? Supposing I explained why my daughter was cross. A scientific explanation? Surely not. And yet it could well be the reason why she was hopping mad.

"If a proposition is logically necessary then it is a purely formal one, and this does not explain anything." Well, a logically necessary truth can be at least part of a system of explanation that explains some factual matter. It can also be part of the truth which explains, I suppose some matter in geometry and the like.

Let us have a look at the ones I was set before. By the way, I think I should say that the reason why I have not been exercising my right under the terms of the debate to ask questions in return is not indolence or anything like that. It is just that it does not seem to me that in this sort of area one can ask any very helpful questions. The questions which one can ask will not get the discussion moving, because to get the discussion moving one requires more context, more explanation of what people are about than can be offered in this sort of multiple choice examination. But on this occasion I will try to go through all of these: either to answer them; or to explain what reasons led me not to answer.

"It is not possible that the justice of God could entail any punishment." Why I said that was false is that it was certainly not clear to me that there could not be just punishments. I am hesitant about this one. The reason for hesitation is that it seems to me so difficult to see how God could be in an appropriate position to be the punisher. No doubt it would be possible for a person justly to deserve some punishment. But as God will have been an accessory before and during the facts in the behavior of His creatures, it does not seem to me that it would really be proper to speak of Him doing the punishment justly. So, after hesitation, I put down "false."

"It is possible the infinite justice of God might entail at least one minute of punishment when this life is over?" Same background to that as to the one before I think I have already made what is the cruical point, that really we are not going to get very far towards justifying what needs to be justified by providing a hesitant justification for some moderate punishment. Would anyone say that, just because they thought it was entirely proper for the federal government to prescribe certain punishments for murder, therefore it would be entirely alright to have a federal law under which people were tortured indefinitely as long as they could be kept alive? You would not go: from saying it is proper to have some system of punishments, to saying that there is no stopping place between some and absolutely anything.

"I know what the punishment for sin should be": various options here. Well of course, it is very difficult for me except by showing sympathy and great good will to give any answers about the punishment for sin. "Sin," as I well know, is defined in terms of God's will. So naturally what I am thinking about when someone talks about sin, though I know this, is something else which appears to be an aspect of most cases to which people who use the notion of sin would apply this notion; namely, that most though not all sins are also moral offenses. So, when I try to answer a question about punishment for sin I am thinking of the moral offenses which might be thought by some to be at the same time sins.

"All men have done at least some things they know they ought not to have done." I do not have any difficulty with that one. Yes, indeed, you do not have to be one of the two presidential candidates to be aware of having yourself done things that you ought not to have done. However, some people are also aware that it is entirely possible and consistent to say that other people have done things which they ought not to have done; not withstanding that you can sympathize with the other people who have done these things, and not withstanding that you are very hesitant to throw the first stones, and all that: and all this while still insisting that it was wrong for the other people to have done them. That is a little intervention in your presidential election campaign with a little bit of moral philosophy. It seems to me that it was quite unnecessary to say that you do not blame, reproach or what not people for doing something you say is wrong. I think you can and should blame or reproach; but do it in a very sympathetic way.

Away from your internal affairs. Your private affairs we might even say in this context. On to what philosophy offers. Besides being paid as a philosopher, I am a human being. It is also the case that the fact that I am paid to know about philosophy and to do philosophy does not involve that I am paid to know about philosophy and to know nothing else, or to do nothing else. So I may very well answer questions that Dr. Warren put to me here not, so to speak, with my philosophical hat on but with another hat on. Well, philosophy offers nothing by way of salvation from this feeling of guilt which results from knowing that one has done what he ought not to have done.

I put this one down as true for two reasons. One is that it does not seem to me that philosophy constitutes any sort of program for salvation anyway. I also, I must say, had a little hesitation about this, do not like in this context to talk about a feeling of guilt. Surely the point, and I am sure this is Dr. Warren's point, is that his religion offers salvation from the actual guilt not from the feeling of guilt. Someone may have a feeling of guilt, which is not justified. They may also have guilt, be guilty, without feeling guilty. Surely what we are arguing about, or what we should want to argue about in this sort of context, is actual guilt, actual salvation, and so on. Well, I think I have done all my homework, or else given an explanation about why I have not felt able to do it. So I may go back later to this business of incongruously being affirmative when I should be negative, and negative when I should be affirmative. I take Dr. Warren's point about that, I think he is probably right. Nevertheless, I do not know what there is to be done about it; other than to try as and when I can to meet the points which he raises; and to try as and when I can to say other useful and relevant things. This is what I have been trying to do all the time as best I can.

WARREN'S THIRD AFFIRMATIVE

(Wednesday Night)

Dr. Flew, Gentlemen Moderators, Ladies and Gentlemen. I confess to you that I weary of the whole matter of getting Dr. Flew to pay attention to the arguments which I present. I have presented, in as precise logical form as could be presented, an *argument* which shows that by *his admission* that every *premise* involved in the argument concerning creation or evolution is *true* and that the *argument* is *valid.* Therefore, the argument demands that the conclusion be true. I further gave you an argument in regard to a specific characteristic of an individual human being making clear that it was absolutely impossible for such to be the case according to a purely materialistic, naturalistic or evolutionary explanation. I showed that it demanded a miraculous explanation and therefore God. Dr. Flew has paid no attention at all to that. I suppose he will pay attention to it in his following 19½ minute speech and then I shall have opportunity to reply to it only in a 1½ minute rejoinder. The thing he should have done was to have replied to it in these two speeches which preceded.

My plan for this particular speech is to go through the things which he has said to which I have not given attention and then to introduce a *third argument* which will be presented in precise logical fashion. I will at least entertain some faint hope that he will pay attention to the logic of this argument.

Dr. Flew has had considerable to say about "explanation" and this involves us in the so-called scientific method. The scientific method involves the envisioning of a line which separates the area below it from the area above it—the area *below,* of facts, empirical facts, the world in which we live which we may experience with our senses. (We make certain observations, *problems* come to our minds.), and the area *above,* of theory (solutions). We have certain solutions, or possible solutions, to come into our minds and this brings us above the line, which is the realm of theory. We postulate various hypotheses, and we then conclude that, a certain one of these is the most plausible of all the possible solutions which we have decided upon. Then by deductive logic we make a prediction of what will occur if indeed our hypothesis is true and then we try either to verify or to falsify that hypothesis by coming back down *below* the line into the realm of the empirical. What the scientist is involved in doing is trying to find explanations that can be either verified or falsified. But this is *not* the only way of explaining things, as Dr. Flew in effect admitted a few moments ago in the answering of the questions which I gave him. It is an *explanation* to give a *sound argument.* To give a sound argument is to give an argument which is valid, the premises of which are true. Now you may have a valid argument which has false premises and even a false conclusion but if you have a sound argument you have both a *valid argument* and *true premises* and this *guarantees* the *truth* of the *conclusion.*

Now what have I done in this discussion in my affirmative by way of *explanation?* I have shown that—granted Dr. Flew's own admissions—the materialistic, naturalistic, atheistic viewpoint cannot provide an explanation for what we ourselves experience. The naturalistic, materialistic, atheistic position cannot provide an explanation even for the existence of each one of us. I have shown that by *argument.* I have shown it by *his own admissions.* But he has paid practically no attention to it. I even went further to show in specific detail that man could not live longer than five minutes without his respiratory system functioning as it does and—showing what is involved in it—that oxygen and carbon dioxide must pass through the capillary wall. Dr. Flew, how long did it take for that to develop? This lets us all see the simple impossibility of its having evolved, as Dr. Flew's materialistic explanation would imply it would occur.

I submit to you that this is an explanation which carries us beyond this physical universe. In the previous questions—about which Dr. Flew has complained somewhat—he has admitted that you can reason from an empirical fact to the state of affairs of the class of things which is transcendent of this universe! He himself concludes that it is an empty class but notice carefully that he has admitted the basic thrust of the theistic argument while he gives all of this "explanation" about *explanation*; while he pays no attention to the affirmative argument.

As to his "different degrees of difference in hell" and his talk about God being *finite* in *justice* while He is *infinite* in *love*—saying that this is an entirely satisfactory explanation—I submit to you that it is not satisfactory. I reiterate: he is talking about a different God from the one I am talking about. I am talking about the *infinite* God. It is not merely that you might envision some person who is infinite in one attribute and finite in another but we are talking about the infinite God. To show that God does *not* exist, you must find some logical contradiction, as this seems to be your basic approach, between the concepts of that God. I have already charged that you cannot do so, that you cannot take the concept of God alone and take one attribute of God and to weigh it against another attribute of God and show that they contradict one another. That as a matter of fact that you, along with all other atheists, will refer to some empirical fact or something that God does—such as punishment. But now you are concluding that God is finite in justice, whereas the truth of the matter is He is infinite in justice. You may show that there is some conflict between a God who is infinite in *justice* as well as infinite in *love,* but that you have have not done. As a matter of fact, you have not even addressed yourself to the matter.

Let me suggest, Dr. Flew, in all concern for you as a person, that we can know what *sin* deserves in only two ways. Not by looking at rocks, not merely by intuition, not merely by some deduction from some concept or from some empirical fact, but only (1) by what it costs to get man out of it—the death of the Son of God—and (2) the punishment that must be meted out for those who live andd die in it (sin). But Dr. Flew projects himself, not only outside the *physical universe,* but outside of *God* as well, looks down upon the universe and God and judges God to be unfit and unworthy, "monstrous," even "satanic" (as he put it last evening) and I submit to you that he has no springboard on which to stand to make such a judgment.

He admits that *philosophy* does not have anything to offer to resolve guilt, so there is nothing more I need to say there. That is simply an admission of fact, and you have admitted, Dr. Flew, *real guilt,* not merely a *feeling* of guilt! You have admitted that *all men know* that they have done what they know they ought not to do. You said you had difficulty in deciding whether you should be an *atheist* or an *agnostic,* but Dr. Flew, what we are interested in is not merely the fact that you have had difficulty but whether or not you have decided which one you are going to be! You signed the proposition in this debate that you were going to be an *atheist.* I suggest that at least until you come straight out and say "I have now decided that I will reject my position of atheism and will become an agnostic," that you try to stay with atheism.

He again brings up the point that a car has a *maker* while the eye and the ear and the respiratory system merely grow. But, my friends, I have shown, by clear precise logical argument, that the respiratory system had to be *made* by the eternal Creator of the world. I have further shown that even in the case of the car, while the car has a *maker*—given his theory—the maker of the car has no maker. You might just as well have figured that a whirlwind blew through a junk yard and blew him together absolutely by sheer chance. Dr. Flew, give some attention to the *maker* of the car. We grant the car was made, but who made the *maker* of the car? That is the problem to which you have not addressed yourself at all in this discussion.

Again, he comes to the explanation as to why we both get back to a place—he says—where we can not explain. Not so, Dr. Flew. What Dr. Flew does is start off with an *assumption* which he got from Strato of Greece—and which he calls the "stratonician presumption" which he quotes by way of saying that every —notice this carefully, I want you to get it—that "everything there is is a product of nature." Now notice what nature is. If everything there is is a product of nature, and if nature itself *is,* then nature is a product of itself. If nature is a product of itself, then at one time nature did not exist. If so, then at one time nothing existed. But, lo and behold, nature comes along and creates itself, for there is nothing there to create it—not even nature! Talk about *incoherent concepts,* talk about *lack of explanation!* This is *not* an *explanation,* it is a mere *assumption.* He *assumes* his case that matter is all that exists, and he does not give an explanation. We, as theists, do not face that kind of problem. I have reasoned from empirical fact in this world. What have I done? I have said here, *I* am an empirical fact. *You* are an empirical fact. I have given you precise logical arguments showing that from individual human beings you must reason—if you reason correctly, validly, logically, soundly—to the ultimate Creator of every human being. Now that takes care of all he had to say on "explanation." Science cannot give the ultimate answer and the "stratonician presumption" cannot do so. It assumes what it must prove, and it is self-contradictory.

I want to give another argument in the remaining time that I have. Again I want you to note, and this is certainly not done in sense of a braggadocio. It is simply doing what every affirmative speaker ought to do. And, every *negative* speaker ought to *follow* an *affirmative* speaker when he does this. We have had a complete failure on Dr. Flew's part. I appreciate the very humorous confession that he made along that line a few moments ago. Certainly, you can not help but like him a great deal the way he makes these confessions, but nevertheless that does not help his case one bit. Notice the admission that he has made regarding the moral argument. He has indicated that before there can be real, objective moral wrong, some *law* must be violated.

Dr. Flew says the reason why he has not presented any questions is because they simply do not get us very far along. Dr. Flew, I think we have just taken "big jumps" by the answers that you have given to these questions. At question number three, the first night, you said that there can be no wrong unless some *law* has been violated. The Nazis were wrong, they were guilty of real moral objective wrong in torturing and murdering those Jews, but you said it was *not* because they violated the law of *Germany; not* because they violated the law of *England; not* because they violated *American* law. Ultimately, we got him to admit that it was not even just international law. But, as Robert Jackson said, it was some higher law that transcends the provincial and the transient, which means that it transcends mere *human* law. The only way you can really show an explanation as to the justification of the conviction, punishment and *execution* of those Nazis for their murder of those children is the fact that they violated the law of *God!* Dr. Flew has, in effect, admitted it. That is why we ask these questions, Dr. Flew. That is why it is so obvious to anyone who has followed this argument that you have completely admitted defeat in this discussion.

Secondly, he admits an actual case of real objective moral wrong when he admitted the Nazis were guilty of real moral wrong in torturing and murdering these children. He thus admits a higher law, above the provincial and the transient. But, he violates the above admission when he holds that *value* did not exist before the first human being! Now Dr. Flew says that when a man holds a postion that violates major undisputed facts, then he knows he has got a false position. Well, here we have a man who is violating major undisputed facts, and he has got himself into serious self-contradiction. If value did not exist before human beings existed, then value is nothing but subjectivity—I do not care how much he does not like the word "merely" or "nothing but" in connection with subjectivity, that is what he has got to face, that is what he has got to accept when he says that value did not exist before the first human being was here. It is nothing, according to that answer, but a function of the human mind and, yet, the conscience within him (Dr. Flew) will not allow him to say that when the Nazis said, "We were right in doing it" and the British said, "They were wrong in doing it," that both of them (Nazis and British) were right at one and the same time. He *knows* the *British* were *right* in saying that the *Germans* were *wrong*. And, when he says the *British* were *right* in saying the *Germans* were *wrong*, he knows the *Germans* were *wrong* when they say they were right. But the only way he can consistently say this is to recognize the law of Almighty God.

Now I want to give this precise statement of the moral argument. (Chart No. 43-A13. (See Page 173.) First premise. If the moral codes and/or actions of any individual or society can properly be subjects of criticism [by that I mean that we can judge properly that they are guilty of real moral objective wrong as Dr. Flew himself has done in connection with the Nazis as to real moral wrong], then there must be some objective standard, that is, some higher law which transcends the provincial and the transient which is other than the particular moral code and which has an obligatory character which can be recognized. Now all of us could do that, even my learned colleague could do it, in the case of the Nazi Germans. But you may say, "Oh, I am tired of hearing about the Nazis, the Germans must have really won in this debate," but my friends it is simply a fact on this earth that no materialistic, no atheistic system can deal with unless they are willing to say that the Nazis were simply doing what they *thought* was right and therefore they were just as right as we were. But Dr. Flew's conscience will not let him say that. He

MORAL CODES—AND GOD (1)

43-A13

1. IF THE MORAL CODE AND/OR ACTIONS OF ANY INDIVIDUAL OR SOCIETY CAN PROPERLY BE SUBJECTS OF CRITICISM (AS TO REAL MORAL WRONG), THEN THERE MUST BE SOME OBJECTIVE STANDARD (SOME "HIGHER LAW WHICH TRANSCENDS THE PROVINCIAL & TRANSIENT") WHICH IS OTHER THAN THE PARTICULAR MORAL CODE AND WHICH HAS AN OBLIGATORY CHARACTER WHICH CAN BE RECOGNIZED. (18)
2. THE MORAL CODE AND/OR ACTIONS OF ANY INDIVIDUAL OR SOCIETY CAN PROPERLY BE SUBJECTS OF CRITICISM (AS TO REAL MORAL WRONG).
3. THEREFORE, THERE MUST BE SOME OBJECTIVE STANDARD (SOME "HIGHER LAW WHICH TRANSCENDS THE PROVINCIAL & TRANSIENT") WHICH IS OTHER THAN THE PARTICULAR MORAL CODE AND WHICH HAS AN OBLIGATORY CHARACTER WHICH CAN BE RECOGNIZED.

(cont'd.)

himself recognizes a moral code that can stand in judgment of a nation, that can stand in judgment of the individuals of that nation, therefore, he admits that there is a higher law which is greater than the law of that individual or the law of combinations of nations.

Now, the second premise in this argument. The moral code and/or actions of any individual or society can properly be subject to criticism as to real moral wrong. Incidentally this is Chart 43-A13 and we would like to have it on the screen. You can see the rest of it while we read together.*

Now the conclusion. Therefore, there must be some objective standard, that is, some higher law which transcends the provincial and transient which is other than the particular moral code, that is, of a particular nation such as the Nazis under Hitler. It has to be other than that and it must have an obligatory character which can be recognized.

Now let us look at Chart 43-A10. (See Page 175.) Alright, now we look at Chart No. 43-A10. It has been in the debate earlier, but because it involves such great admissions from the answers to questions by Dr. Flew, and because it shows how this argument works exactly, I want to bring it up again. Notice over on the left of the chart you will see that the law of England is *authoritative*, in this arrow pointing down to the people of England. The individual members of England are under the law of England. Now we in America are not amenable to English law. Only people who are in Great Britian or who are citizens of Great Britian are the subjects of that law. Notice the arrow pointing from the law of England toward Germany. I have it X'd out. It is *not* authoritative over *Germany*. Now notice the law of Germany, it is authoritative over the people of Germany. But note that the law of *Germany* is *not* authoritative over *England*. What the Nazis passed had nothing whatever to do with either Dr. Flew or with me during World War II and the days just preceding, but nevertheless the British as well as we Americans charged the Nazis with crimes, not merely of violating the *German* law (their very defense was that they had not violated but that they were obeying, that it was their moral duty and obliga-

*The projector operator already had the chart on the screen.

[MORAL LAW — ARG.]

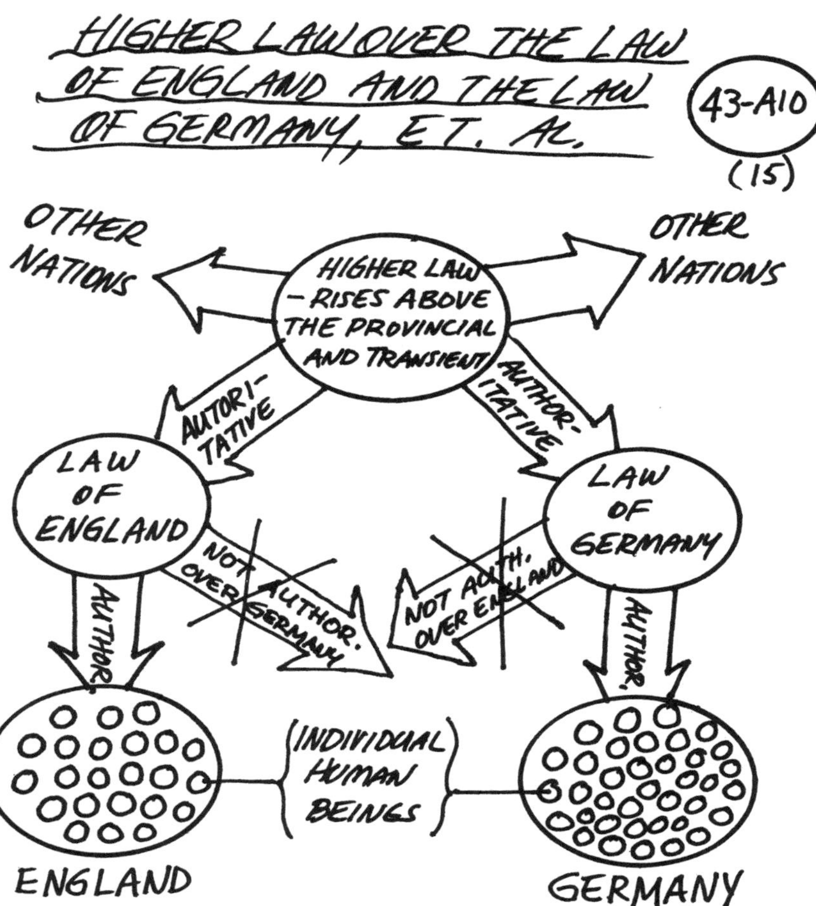
HIGHER LAW OVER THE LAW OF ENGLAND AND THE LAW OF GERMANY, ET. AL.
43-A10
(15)
OTHER NATIONS
OTHER NATIONS
HIGHER LAW — RISES ABOVE THE PROVINCIAL AND TRANSIENT
AUTORI-TATIVE
AUTHOR-ITATIVE
LAW OF ENGLAND
LAW OF GERMANY
NOT AUTHOR. OVER GERMANY
NOT AUTH. OVER ENGLAND
AUTHOR.
AUTHOR.
INDIVIDUAL HUMAN BEINGS
ENGLAND
GERMANY

tion to obey the law of their own land, they were only doing what their superiors had said). The British and the Americans joined together in condemning the Nazis—and Dr. Flew joins with me in saying that they did rightly in doing so. He answered one question to say that the judges did not have the right to come together and say, "Let us formulate, in effect, a *new* international law and say that we *cannot punish* them." As a matter of fact, international law does not really deal with these matters. There was a recognition of a higher law which transcends the transient and the provincial. It transcends the area of Germany: "You people cannot justify yourselves for having slaughtered, murdered these Jewish men, women and children; six million of them in the most agonizing and horrible ways, by saying that you obeyed the law of Germany." Dr. Flew agrees to that, but how *can* he consistently agree to it? Only because if you will look up there (on the chart), there is a *higher law* which rises above it, a higher law which is authoritative over not only the law of England but also over the law of Germany.

Let us look quickly, as our time closes, at Chart No. 43-A12. (See Page 177.) Notice how there was moral degeneration in the nation of Germany from (1) the time preceding the Nazis and (2) the take-over by Hitler. In Germany from 1939 to 1945, the people of Germany were under Nazi powers. They changed the laws according to Hitler's whims and fancies. It became the law of the land to really intend to exterminate the Jews. But notice there is a higher law that goes above [pointing to chart] both the law of England and the law of Germany.

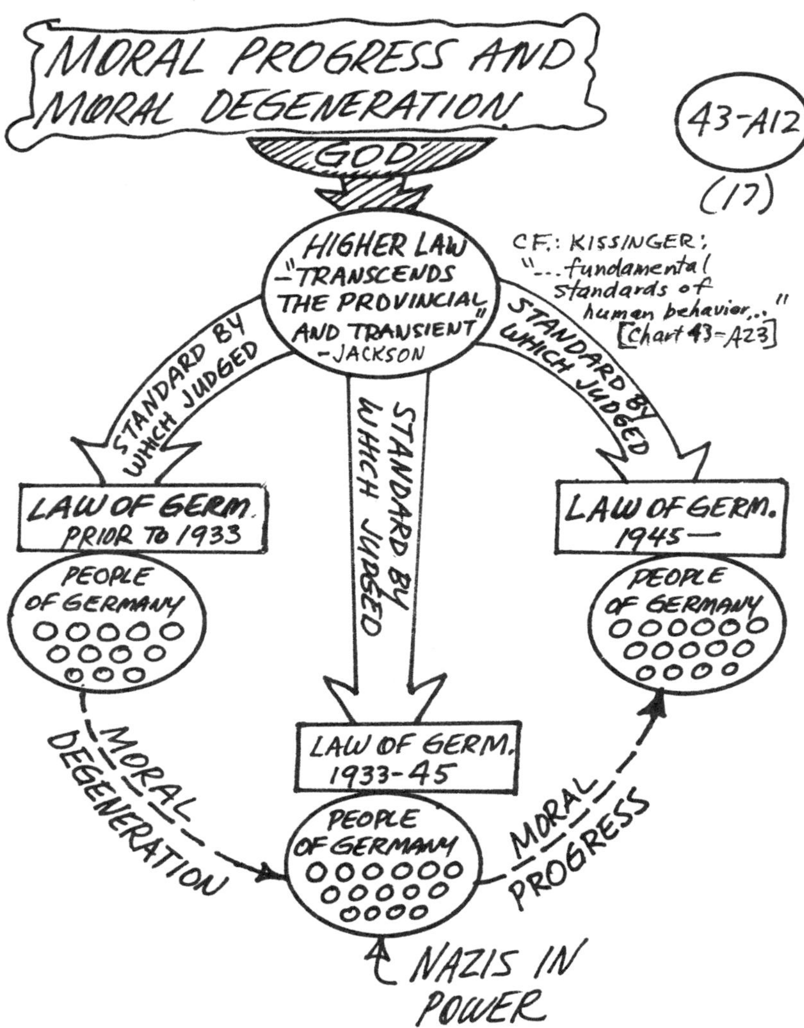
MORAL PROGRESS AND
MORAL DEGENERATION
43-A12
(17)
GOD
HIGHER LAW
–"TRANSCENDS
THE PROVINCIAL
AND TRANSIENT"
–JACKSON
CF.: KISSINGER:
"...fundamental
standards of
human behavior,..."
[Chart 43-A23]
STANDARD BY
WHICH JUDGED
STANDARD BY
WHICH JUDGED
STANDARD BY
WHICH JUDGED
LAW OF GERM.
PRIOR TO 1933
LAW OF GERM.
1945—
PEOPLE
OF GERMANY
PEOPLE
OF GERMANY
LAW OF GERM.
1933-45
PEOPLE
OF GERMANY
MORAL
DEGENERATION
MORAL
PROGRESS
NAZIS IN
POWER

FLEW'S THIRD NEGATIVE

(Wednesday Night)

My preacher father used to have a favorite warning: "Cause not a brother to stumble." Well, I am afraid I may have been guilty of that fault, because it seems to me that Dr. Warren himself, now when he is supposed to be taking the affirmative line is doing what he rightly accused me of doing when I was supposed to be taking the affirmative line, namely, the opposite. I suppose the conclusion I ought to draw from this is that it is high time I reformed, in hopes that Dr. Warren would then no longer be by me caused to stumble. But I do have difficulty in seeing anything more I can usefully say, at any rate at this stage, about the points that he was raising.

There is one thing which I can helpfully develop. That is that there is an artificiality about our whole debate here. But this is no one's fault. Any confrontation between any spokesman for an atheist naturalism (shall I say that "atheist" again just to satisfy the public?) any confrontation between any spokesman for an atheist naturalism and any spokesman for any system of belief about some transcendent reality, would have to be artificial in the same way as this one is. Although this is quite unavoidable, I think that for that very reason we do need to see what this artificiality is. We need then to allow for it in our thinking about such questions.

The artificiality which I have in mind arises from the fact that this confrontation—"the debate of the century"—like that other confrontation which you will all very likely be watching in the TV repeat later this week, is and has to be between spokesmen for two but only two opposing parties. Now in the other, the presidential case, this two party structure is not only necessary and unavoidable, it is quite unmisleading. After all in that case there are effectively only two parties in the race. Indeed, sometimes and to some people it may seem as if this time there is only one and that it is all over but the voting. But our case here tonight is different. For, however it may seem to us here in this hall, both Dr. Warren and I are speaking for positions which confront innumerable alternatives.

It may be that for any individual person only one, or at most only two or three or four of these innumerable alternatives constitutes what William James would have called "a live option." Still Dr. Warren and I do confront, and everyone here confronts, innumerable theoretically possible alternative belief systems. If not on this present occasion then at least some other time, he and I both have to vindicate our chosen positions: not only against the particular alternatives each presented by the other; but also against all the other alternatives which have been and might be proposed. It is, I think, important that we should all recognize that there are these innumerable possible rivals not represented on this platform. Few of course, if any, of these can at this time represent for many of us psychologically live options. The possibility of being converted to most of these alternatives is not, that is, a live possibility which might be realized in the immediate foreseeable future. Most indeed of the theoretically possible alternatives have not in fact been formulated and maintained by anyone. It is, nevertheless, essential if we are to see this four night confrontation in Denton, Texas, in proper perspective to realize that there are all these other rivals off stage.

This is a point which, it seems to me, Dr. Warren was noticeably failing to recognize when he took it that if he could, or if he can, show that the theory of evolution by natural selection is false, then he is home and dry; not merely having thereby established creation by something or other but really having established creation by the particular God for whom he is acting as a spokesman.

The best way to suggest this wider and deeper perspective that I think we should all remember, and the best way to show that and why it is a background which we all need to keep in mind, is to consider a very famous old argument. This is the argument called Pascal's Wager. Certainly it was not invented by Blaise Pascal, who was a French Jansenist Roman Catholic mathematician living in the 1600's. It was certainly imported into France from Spain where it had earlier been employed by Moslems: a point which, as we shall see, Pascal ought to have remembered.

Be all that as it may, everyone calls this argument Pascal's Wager and I am going to consider it in his version. Pascal began by presenting the human predicament as a gambling situation.

There are, as he truly observed, many rival life styles, many world outlooks, all soliciting our personal commitments. However, he went on, and this is of course much more disputatious, reason can decide nothing here. I do not think it is by any means certain that Pascal himself was saying this second thing in his own person. Maybe he was only allowing it to an opponent, as they say, for the sake of the argument. It is in fact quite an interesting question whether he was or not. For a denial of what he was thus allowing later became a defined doctrine of the Roman Catholic Church by decree of the First Vatican Council; though many Catholics now rather wish that it had not, and even seem to have forgotten since the Second Vatican Council, that in 1870-1 it did.

Pascal starts by observing that there are many different life styles supported by many systems of belief about the transcendent. All these are soliciting our personal commitment. Stage two is to insist, if only for the sake of the argument, that reason can decide nothing here. No evidence can make any of these alternatives even more probable than any of the others. So, Pascal concludes, we have a betting situation. Now, what are the stakes, and how shall we place our bets? Giving no reasons to warrant this limitation, Pascal proceeds as if there were only two betting options in this gambling situation. Option A is Roman Catholicism. Bet on this; and, if you turn out to be right you will enjoy an eternity of bliss. Bet on this; and, if you turn out to have been wrong, what have you lost? Option B is an atheist naturalism. Bet on this and, even if you turn out to have been right, what have you had? At best an agreeable four score years and ten. Bet on this and, if you turn out to have been wrong, then from then to eternity you will be suffering the agonies which, in Dr. Warren's view, constitute a manifestation of the Creator's justice.

Obviously, if the betting situation is as Pascal describes it and if in particular there are only the two options which he allows, then it must be madly imprudent to do anything but bet on the Roman Catholic option, and Pascal here thoughtfully allows for those who still find it hard to persuade themselves: "Take holy water, hear masses said and you will come to believe."

Having presented this famous old argument, let me draw

some lessons. First, notice what sort of argument it is. Pascal is not offering evidence to show that Roman Catholicism is true. He is not, that is to say, offering what we might label "evidencing reasons," reasons as evidence. He has already insisted, if only for the sake of the argument, that there are not or cannot be reasons of this kind in this most important of all cases. What Pascal is offering is motivating reasons, reasons as motives. The desired conclusion is that in your own interests, you must persuade yourselves to believe Roman Catholicism; and this in spite of the lack of evidencing reasons. Anything else would be madly imprudent.

The second thing to notice is that Pascal has no business at all to limit the betting options to two. Certainly, as William James observed, in the circles in which Pascal moved no one would ever have seriously considered conversion to Islam, although, as William James curiously failed to observe, some people at that time and place did become Protestants. But, of course, no fact of this sort about which if any of these options are or are not psychologically live for this or that person or group is either here or there. If Pascal's wager argument is to work as an argument, then we have got to find some reason consistent with his initial assumptions or concessions, which will justify his limitation of the options to two. That we cannot do. For if, as he allows, there really is no good evidencing reason for dismissing any self-consistent alternative system then we shall have to admit among the runners Islam, various brands of Protestantism and indeed infinitely many others. For, discounting for the moment all but the hell-threatening options, that still leaves us with infinitely many theoretically possible options. For for every way of life you can think of, you can construct a system which promises heaven for all and only these who pursue that lifestyle; and for all the rest what the winners will no doubt see as the just punishment of eternal torment.

Granted Pascal's own allowed assumption that there can be no adequate evidencing reason for or against any self-consistent system, then for every such system you could also construct another in which all and only those who would under the first system be rewarded by the joys of heaven will instead suffer the torments of hell; and all those who would in that first system suffer the torments of hell will instead enjoy eternal bliss—a bliss of which perhaps one element would be the contemplation of the "justice" of the punishments of those who are on the second system the losers.

Where has all this got us? Well, first we have got a fundamental distinction between two sorts of reasons and in particular, two sorts of reasons for believing. One sort, the only proper sort in my view, is evidencing reasons, reasons for holding a belief to be true. The other sort is motivating reasons, reasons for trying to persuade ourselves that some belief is true; whether or not it actually is. Second, we now know, if we did not know before, both what Pascal's wager argument is and why it is not, even on his own assumptions, a good argument. Third, and this is by far the most important, this is really what I am after, we have begun I hope to see why anyone who takes any position about some possible transcendent reality behind and above the everyday world of common sense and behind and above the hidden structures revealed by science, must be seen as confronting innumerable self-consistent alternative theoretical possibilities.

Here in this hall tonight you see a spokesman for an atheist—repeat, atheist—naturalism confronting a spokesman for the Church of Christ. But neither of us and none of you must forget that all these other theoretically possible alternatives are in the running. Some of them have had millions of adherents. Others have never even been thought of, and have never won any adherence. In practice we all reject all but one of these systems. We are all atheists in terms of almost all understandings of the word "God." But one of these innumerable alternative systems is, for better or for worse, in a special position in relation to all the others. That special one is the one for which I stand.

I am, of course, in being confronted by innumerable alternatives, in exactly the same boat as Dr. Warren and everybody else. Where I and my lot do differ from all the others is that we reject the whole idea of any transcendent reality behind or above the universe. We start and stop with what is common to all men of all religions and of none. That is to say we start and stop with the universe itself, with the everyday world of common sense and common experience and with those hidden mechanisms of that world which are progressively revealed by the advance of science. We reject all transcendent supernatural systems; not because we have examined, or could have examined, each in turn;

but because it does not seem to us that there is any good evidencing reason to postulate anything at all behind or beyond this natural universe. And, for the reasons I gave earlier on, this is a perfectly possible position. It does of course leave the existence of the universe and the fundamental principles of the universe unexplained, every system, including every conceivable rival system, must contain fundamental principles which it has to leave unexplained.

Having got a little time left over after having not been doing the negative, I can run through some of the things I noted down about Dr. Warren's last not I think frightfully positive positive affirmation. First, then about the law, positive or moral. One of the fundamental things one needs to distinguish here is: on the one hand systems of positive law, with human authorities prescribing punishments, penalties and so on, prescribing things to do and the notion of a moral law which can be distinguished in many ways but the most obvious thing about a moral law is that the moral law can legitimately be appealed to to criticize the content of any system of positive law and it does not have a structure of enforcement by rewards and punishments and hence it is perfectly possible and can be perfectly consistent to say that those people arraigned by the court at Nuremberg were indeed guilty of offenses under the moral law but perhaps there was not any system of positive law including the alleged system under which they were in fact condemned and punished which did make what they did illegal before they did it.

Second, about how if you do not believe that values were laid down or are in someway endorsed by God you have got to say that they are *merely* the desires of individuals or groups. May I perhaps remind people again of the account I gave of one particular sort of value: namely, going market price. Now that clearly is not something that is determined at the whim of any individual or group. Yet equally, clearly the going market price of a Volkswagen would be a senseless notion, even if there were any Volkswagens around, if there were not any consumers and sellers of Volkswagens. So you can not just assume that because something is in some way a function of human desires therefore it is just a matter of people's whims and can be arbitrarily determined by any individual or group. Well, I have got some more for tomorrow.

WARREN'S REJOINDER

(Wednesday Night)

Dr. Flew, Gentleman Moderators, Ladies and Gentlemen. In this brief rejoinder I should like to raise a question to Dr. Flew, and I shall have to do so very hurriedly. On one occasion he admits there is real moral objective wrong, and I have asked him again and again if so, which law is violated? He has admitted that *some law* must be violated for there to be real *objective* moral wrong as distinguished from mere *subjective* wrong. Now, when it is *subjective* wrong, that means merely that *human beings* have decided upon it. It is purely a function of the human mind. It is a state of opinion—of either approval or disapproval. But to say that something is *objectively* wrong—really morally objective wrong—entails the violation of the law higher than that which is merely provincial or transient. In fact, if we humans are only *matter in motion,* then there is no real wrong at all. The ultimate "creator" of man is only rocks and dirt.

I submit the question: *Who is being rational in this debate?* Certainly not Dr. Flew, because it is *I* who has presented these arguments in precise logical fashion while *he* has *failed* to do so with a single argument. Further, he has spent his time in the negative in paying little or no attention to those affirmative arguments.

Now Dr. Flew comes back to an "explanation" in which he says that, as a matter of fact, we both must wind up with *no explanation.* I admit that *he* does so, because he can go back to nothing else than rocks and dirt. It is a sort of "God" that he goes to, because it is his position that rocks and dirt are the ultimate "creator" of all there is. But we theists actually do have an *explanation!* We get back to *the God* who explains everything because the God in whom we believe is living, personal and thinking.

I myself will try to have a bit more tomorrow night.

WARREN'S FOURTH AFFIRMATIVE

(Thursday Night)

Thank you, Gary. Dr. Flew, Gentlemen Moderators, Ladies and Gentlemen. I assure you that it is indeed a matter of great pleasure to me to be before you tonight, to affirm the prosposition which has been read in your hearing. Before I continue with the presentation of affirmative arguments, I would like to pay just a little attention to some of the things said by Dr. Flew in his closing negative last evening. Since he had nearly a 20-minute speech in that negative, and I had only a minute and a half rejoinder, it was impossible for me to deal with everything that he said. One thing I want to make clear is: he seemed to recognize (1) that he had *not* done what he *should* have when he was in the *affirmative* and (2) that he had *not* done as he *should* have in the *negative*. He then sought to get me into "the same bed," as it were, with him, asserting that I had not been functioning in the affirmative, that I had gotten over into the negative. But I want to point out that it is the responsibility of the affirmative speaker not only to give precise affirmative argumentation as I did. (those of you who were here last night know that I did so), but it is also the responsibility of the affirmative speaker to *reply* to what the *negative* speaker says. And so, in replying to what he was saying, I was *not* forsaking my role as an affirmative speaker.

Dr. Flew suggested last evening, that the market value of a Volkswagen might shed some light on the matter of moral value. He said that since the market value of a Volkswagen is not necessarily the price that I *want* to pay, then it is not the value that I simply *invent*. On the other hand, he continued, if there were no humans around, the car would have no market value at all. But I have a question for Dr. Flew along that line: if the Volkswagen is worth $500.00 at one place and $1,000.00 at another place, how is the *actual* or *real* value of the car to be decided? Or, does it have any *real* value? Now, if your illustration is worth anything at all, it will have to have some real value, or else you will have to say that no human being has any real value, and you will have joined the Nazis in a thorough-going way to say that the Jewish people did not have any real value (only a market value that might fluctuate up and down and therefore would be worth nothing under the regime of the Nazis). Dr. Flew, you ought to think those illustrations through before you give them.

Now on the question of matter. Dr. Flew claims that the difference between him and me is that we only stop at different places in lacking explanation. One time, he seemed to indicate that he did not really hold to the eternality of matter, but Dr. Flew you can not do that—not and be an *atheist!* You have got to come on with it and admit that you have got to hold to the eternality of matter. But, let us see something about that. A thing that he writes about and has really hinted at in this discussion is what he terms the "stratonician presumption." Now this is merely an assumption. It *begs the question,* as I have already explained in quite some detail. It is really ridiculous and incoherent for it says that everything there is is a product of nature; thus, nature is a product of itself and therefore the stratonician presumption is entirely meaningless. It is not even an explanation, because of its incoherency. It does not explain matter. It does not explain its origin. It does not explain its existence today. It is simply that he begs the question by starting with it. Dr. Flew, get on with your job of proving the eternality of matter for it is absolutely necessary to your case.

But we theists have an explanation! We are not in the same "hole" with you on that matter at all. God Almighty is an *explanation* for the world. It is an explanation for humankind which you have admitted tacitly that you have no explanation for. God is the explanation which needs no explanation. He is in fact the self-existent being who accounts for the world and for mankind. I should like to note this—in connection with his points on matter—and refer to the Second Law of Thermodynamics from physics, and I have it formulated in a syllogistic form.

Now it seems that Dr. Flew in this debate has given very little credence to precise logical argumentation. This is in sharp contrast to what he does when he writes and opposes other men. He chides other men when they do not write logically. He jumps on them, as it were, with both feet! He demands that they be rational and insists that to be rational means that you draw only such conclusions as are warranted by the evidence. I have quoted from Dr. Max Black of Cornell University, a world renowned logician who said in quoting Josiah Stamp in his book,

Critical Thinking, that four hundred pages of crowded fact and argument may deceive the very elect but when reduced to a three line syllogism, it will lay bare the bones of the argument so the fallacious reasoning may be easily seen. That is why *theists* are not afraid to lay their doctrine on the line and say "Here it is" in precise logical argumentation while *atheists* will say "Ah, but here is a *suggestion* and there is a *suggestion,* and we do not really need this kind of logical argumentation." But I am going to give it to you whether Dr. Flew thinks we need it or not, because I think you can see, in the light of his own contention which I have read from his works, that to be irrational is to refuse to face up to the implications of your own doctrine; it is to refuse to face up to the implication of your basic premises and draw that conclusion.

Now, notice carefully this reasoning. *First premise.* If the Second Law of Thermodynamics is meaningful only in a finite system and if it is meaningful in the world, then the world is a finite system. *Second premise.* The Second Law of Thermodynamics is meaningful only in a finite system and it is meaningful in the world. *Conclusion.* Therefore, the world is a finite system (and is not eternal). Now, to know that this conclusion is not true (in order to meet the point that I have made here), Dr. Flew will have to *know*—not merely to *guess,* not merely to say "it seems strange to me" or "it has some sort of a curious aspect," —he must know that the Second Law of Thermodynamics is *false!* Now, Dr. Flew, I suggest that you give your attention to that in the matter what you have argued in the question of matter.

Dr. Flew's position demands that matter is eternal. If not, then at one time nothing existed because, you see, he maintains that nothing but matter exists. Now if nothing but matter exists, then, if at one time matter did not exist, that would mean that once nothing existed. But if it ever were the case that nothing existed, then nothing would exist *now.* But since it is clear that something *does* exist now, it is just as clear that Dr. Flew is wrong, as it seems he usually is—and I say this kindly, I even say it lovingly—on almost everything he has said in this discussion.

He talked about "Pascal's wager." My moderator, Dr. Bales, passed me a note last night when Dr. Flew began on Pascal and said "Congratulations, Tom, for such a wonderful argument which you made on Pascal," facetiously indicating that Dr. Flew, in making an argument on Pascal, was following me as the affirmative speaker when, of course, I had said *nothing* about it. But there is nothing new about this argument. We study about this in our classes every year. Many of my students are here, and I am sure that they knew exactly what was coming and that was very little. Why did Dr. Flew introduce "Pascal's wager"? Not because *I* introduced the matter as an affirmative speaker. I did not. I think Dr. Flew simply brought along an article from the *Rationalist Annual* and read it, or at least he read something that is very close to what is in that journal. He seemed to be using it in something of an effort to counter my argument which had been set out on Chart No. 41-Z (See Page 190), I believe it is, in which I showed that every human being owes his ultimate origin either to *creation* or to *evolution*. I then showed that this was strong disjunction, because it constitutes the *only* alternatives. I then showed that if it is by creation, then God exists. I then showed that if evolution is true then it was either by being born of some ape or some other non-human being or being transformed from an ape. But Dr. Flew has clearly *admitted* the error of *both* of those: no one has ever been *born* of an ape and no one has been *transformed from* an ape. Therefore, by conjunction I pointed out that it is false both that one is born of an ape and that one is transformed from an ape for we have by DeMorgan's theorem, after that conjunction, it is false that either by birth or by transformation—which means that you have, then, the *falsity* of the *consequent* of that third premise: E implies either B or T. Now when you have a form of that kind it means that you have also falsified the *antecedent* of that premise, which means that if you have the case that if evolution is true, then it is either by birth or by transformation. But if it is false that it is either by birth or by transformation, then evolution is false. I have hammered this matter, pleaded, begged, conjoled and done everything I know to do to get him to notice this matter and he has

COSMO. ARG.

[THE ARGUMENT PUT IN SYMBOLIC TERMS— CONT'D.]

TBW'S PROPOSITION: "I KNOW THAT GOD DOES EXIST"

41-Z (3)

* THE FOLLOWING ARGUMENT PROVES THAT PROPOSITION:

1. C Ⓥ E. ONLY POSSIBILITIES.
2. $C \supset G$. OBVIOUS, SINCE THERE CAN BE NO CREATION WITHOUT GOD.
3. $E \supset (B \vee T)$. IF EVOLUTION IS TRUE, THEN THESE ARE ONLY POSSIBILITIES.
4. $\sim B$. HUMANS ARE NOT BORN OF APES.
5. $\sim T$. APES ARE NOT TRANSFORMED INTO HUMANS
6. $\sim B \cdot \sim T$ 4, 5, CONJ.
7. $\sim (B \vee T)$ 6, DE M.
8. $\sim E$ 3, 7, M.T.
9. C 1, 8, D.S.
10. G 2, 9, M.P.

* PROOF OF THE EXISTENCE OF GOD IS "RIGHT BEFORE THE EYES" OF EACH AND EVERY HUMAN BEING.

paid absolutely no attention to it. By these *concessions* he has *clearly admitted* that human beings are *not* here by *evolution* and that the alternative is *creation* and since creation can occur only by God, then God exists!

But, now notice, he is trying here to use "Pascal's wager" as he gets into the matter of trying to show that there are many options. But there are *not* many options! There is either God or there is not God. This is not a matter of simply looking out here and saying "Well, there is the God envisioned by Hartshorne, another God envisioned by Brightman, or the God envisioned by Whitehead, or the God envisioned by the Hindus" and so forth and so on. As was made clear by one speaker who said, "Choose you this day whom you will serve, whether the Gods on the other side of the river or the Gods of the Amorites in whose land you now dwell, but as for me and my house we will serve Jehovah." It is either God or no God. There are many things that are *called* "God" but there is simply the eternal God.

In the matter of eternal punishment—Dr. Flew's treatment of the matter is to try to prove some kind of inner incompatibility in the concept of God. This is what he is after. I pointed out that he cannot do it by simply taking the concept of God, but he has got to try to use some empirical fact—or some maxim—and therefore he is saying that if indeed there is eternal punishment, there is incompatibility in the concept of God, and God does not exist. He has not really formulated a precise argument. I am going a little further than he did, in somewhat making his argument for him. I wish he would make it precisely so we could see perhaps even better what he means.

But now note this reply. His effort fails. I admit that the question of evil might be considered to be relevant to the question of the existence of God, but remember: the existence of real or objective moral evil *proves* God. It does not *disprove* God. It proves God because it demands the objective moral standard which actually is God. God is the ultimate good. Again and again and again, every night in the questions and in his speeches, Dr. Flew has wavered back and forth between the subjective view of morality and the objective view of morality. He has done so again in his answers to the questions tonight which I shall get to in the second speech.

But the eternal punishment of the wicked is not evil. The only intrinsic evil is sin, violation of the will of God. God's punishment of the wicked is not evil. Dr. Flew has made no effort whatever to *prove* that *eternal punishment* is *evil!* He slides over this responsibility of his in the light of his particular argument. In fact, there is no way he *can* prove it. He admitted that if God did exist and were even finitely just, that it would be just for God to punish a wicked man for at least one minute after this life was over. Now notice carefully, last night in a question he admitted that it would be just for the God who is infinite—infinite in *justice*—to punish a man for one minute. In making this admission, Dr. Flew set forth a response which indicated that he apparently misunderstood and clearly misrepresented my position to this audience. In attempting to explain my response to the audience, he charged me with holding there is *no difference* between punishment of one minute duration and one billion years. Dr. Flew, I am sure you did not do it intentionally but that is as far from my position as anything possibly could be imagined. The truth is, my argument was not even related to such a contention.

My point was this, and let us look at Chart No. 27-A16 (See Page 193) and following that Chart 27-A17. (See Page 194.) Now, again, I want to give this argument, and I want you to notice carefully that is formulated precisely. The argument is valid and the premises are true, and the conclusion therefore must follow. It must be true. It is an amazing thing to me that we are involved here in a philosophic discussion with men who are now contending that they are under no responsibility to present precise logical argument. This will surely be a shock to the philosophical world when it becomes well known among our colleagues in the philosophical association.

Number one. Here is the first statement in this argument in reply to Dr. Flew on eternal punishment. If Dr. Flew grants that God, who is infinite in justice, can justly punish a wicked man for *some* length of time, say X, after this life is over, then Dr. Flew grants that God, who is infinite in justice, can justly punish a

FLEW ADMITS DEFEAT IN REGARD TO ETERNAL PUNISHMENT (27-A16)

1. IF FLEW GRANTS THAT GOD (WHO IS INFINITE IN JUSTICE) CAN JUSTLY PUNISH A WICKED MAN FOR SOME LENGTH OF TIME, SAY X, AFTER THIS LIFE IS OVER, THEN FLEW GRANTS THAT GOD (WHO IS INFINITE IN JUSTICE) CAN JUSTLY PUNISH A WICKED MAN FOR THAT LENGTH OF TIME PLUS ONE MINUTE (I.E. LENGTH OF TIME X PLUS ONE MINUTE).

2. FLEW GRANTS (QUESTION #5, WED. NIGHT) THAT GOD (WHO IS INFINITE IN JUSTICE) CAN JUSTLY PUNISH A WICKED MAN FOR SOME GIVEN LENGTH OF TIME [SPECIFICALLY, ONE MINUTE] AFTER THIS LIFE IS OVER.

3. THEREFORE, FLEW GRANTS THAT GOD (WHO IS INFINITE IN JUSTICE) CAN JUSTLY PUNISH A WICKED MAN FOR THAT LENGTH OF TIME PLUS ONE MINUTE (I.E. LENGTH OF TIME X PLUS ONE MINUTE).

[FLEW ADMITS DEFEAT, CONT'D.]

* THIS JUST ANOTHER WAY OF DESCRIBING INFINITY—OR—ETERNITY. 27-A17

THIS CONSTITUTES AN ADMISSION ON FLEW'S PART THAT GOD (WHO IS INFINITE IN JUSTICE) CAN ETERNALLY PUNISH A WICKED MAN AND STILL BE JUST IN DOING SO!!!

wicked man for that length of time plus one minute, that is, length of time X plus one minute." Now, I want you to catch the significance of that.

The second statement is, "Dr. Flew grants, under question number 5 last evening, that God [who in the question was described as being infinite in justice] can justly punish a wicked man for some given length of time; specifically, one minute after this life is over." Therefore, here is the conclusion, "Dr. Flew grants that God, who is infinite in justice, can justly punish a wicked man for that length of time plus one minute, that is, the length of time X plus one minute." Notice friends what has occurred. This is just another way of describing infinity or eternity. It is in fact another way of saying that the God of infinite justice can with justice punish a wicked man eternally. Now, Dr. Flew, if anybody ever gave up on a point which he himself had introduced into a discussion, I suggest *kindly*, I suggest *gently*, yet I suggest *firmly*, that *you* have done it. This constitutes an *admission* on Dr. Flew's part that God, who is infinite in justice, can *eternally punish* a wicked man and still be *just* in doing so! Now, I ask you to be on guard against his coming up here and saying "Well, this is a *curious* matter. We ought to have gone about it this way, or we ought to have gone about it this way." But any man who wants to function as a *rational* thinker, a man who wants to function as a rational philosopher—rather than as an existentialist—will take up this argument and will deal with it point by point. He will show either one of two things—either that the *argument* is *invalid* or that one of the *premises* is *false*. Otherwise, that conclusion follows and it is sustained and this man, this *atheist*, has admitted that it is *just* for an *infinite God* to punish a man eternally. And, it is the *only* "argument" that he has had in the whole debate. It is the only argument that any atheist has against Theism, namely that there is some sort of contradiction between the eternal God and some sort of problem or suffering or wrong.

In Revelation chapter 20, verse 10, the Bible says "and where also the beasts and the false prophets are . . ." That would indicate, at some moment of time, where they *are*, and then it says ". . . and they shall be tormented day and night for ever and ever." Now, friends—putting it back in our terms, that is, of the philosophical jargon that we philosophers use as we "throw dust in the air and then wonder why nobody can see anything"—it is X and then X plus one and then X plus 2 and so on and on until X plus n, that is, on through infinity.

Chart No. 41-D (See Page 197.)

Now, I want to introduce again the argument to which I referred a moment ago. *First Premise.* "If there is even one characteristic, attribute or property of even one human being"—I am one human being. I have special insight into myself you have special insight into yourself—"which could have come into existence only by the creative power of God, then that one human being constitutes proof that God does exist." *Second Premise.* "There is at least one characteristic, attribute or property of at least one human being which could have come into existence only by the creative powers of God." *The conclusion.* "Therefore, that one human being constitutes proof, when the evidence is recognized and reasoned about properly, that God does exist." Friends, that argument is valid. The premises are true. Therefore the *conclusion must be true!*

Now, let us look at this 41-Z again. (See Page 198.) Dr. Flew, I ask you in all kindness to recognize your responsibility. You have already *admitted* the *validity* of this *argument.* I ask you now, since you have admitted that validity, to point out which of the *premises* on this argument is false. If you cannot do that, you will have admitted that the theistic case is sustained. I have said that if there is strong disjunction between creation and evolution, there are no other possibilities.

Just here I am talking about human beings alive here on this earth, I am talking about myself as an individual. I owe my ultimate origin either to the creative miraculous act of God or else to evolution—from some ape or some other form of *non-human* life. Now it is shown that if it is by *creation,* then *God* exists. If it is by *evolution,* then it is by *birth* or *transformation.* Dr. Flew has admitted in the fourth case that it is not by birth from some non-human. He has admitted, in the fifth case, that it is not by transformation from an ape, etc. Nobody has ever been born of an ape. Nobody has ever *changed* from an ape into a human. Therefore, it is in the conjunction of those two you have not B and not T and then by DeMorgan's theorem you have, it is false

[TBW AFF.]

EACH HUMAN BEING IS PROOF THAT GOD DOES EXIST

(1)

1. IF THERE IS EVEN ONE CHARACTERISTIC, ATTRIBUTE OR PROPERTY OF EVEN ONE HUMAN BEING WHICH COULD HAVE COME INTO EXISTENCE ONLY BY THE CREATIVE POWER OF GOD, THEN THAT ONE HUMAN BEING CONSTITUTES PROOF THAT GOD DOES EXIST.

2. THERE IS AT LEAST ONE CHARACTERISTIC, ATTRIBUTE OR PROPERTY OF AT LEAST ONE HUMAN BEING WHICH COULD HAVE COME INTO EXISTENCE ONLY BY THE CREATIVE POWER OF GOD.

3. THEREFORE, THAT ONE HUMAN BEING CONSTITUTES PROOF (WHEN THE EVIDENCE IS RECOGNIZED AND REASONED ABOUT PROPERLY) THAT GOD DOES EXIST.

COSMO. ARG.

[THE ARGUMENT PUT IN SYMBOLIC TERMS— CONT'D.]

TBW'S PROPOSITION: "I KNOW THAT GOD DOES EXIST"

41-Z (3)

* THE FOLLOWING ARGUMENT PROVES THAT PROPOSITION:

1. $C \circledvee E$. ONLY POSSIBILITIES.
2. $C \supset G$. OBVIOUS, SINCE THERE CAN BE NO CREATION WITHOUT GOD.
3. $E \supset (B \vee T)$. IF EVOLUTION IS TRUE, THEN THESE ARE ONLY POSSIBILITIES.
4. $\sim B$. HUMANS ARE NOT BORN OF APES.
5. $\sim T$. APES ARE NOT TRANSFORMED INTO HUMANS
6. $\sim B \cdot \sim T$ 4, 5, CONJ.
7. $\sim (B \vee T)$ 6, DE M.
8. $\sim E$ 3, 7, M.T.
9. C 1, 8, D.S.
10. G 2, 9, M.P.

* PROOF OF THE EXISTENCE OF GOD IS "RIGHT BEFORE THE EYES" OF EACH AND EVERY HUMAN BEING.

that this disjunction, either B or T, either by birth or transformation. Therefore, evolution is false because, when you go back up to point three, you have the falsification of the consequent, which means then that the antecedent, that is, the E (what comes before the if . . . then), must also be falsified and therefore not *evolution* but *creation!*

FLEW'S FOURTH NEGATIVE

(Thursday Night)

You may notice that, as sort of a tribute to the influence of the Texan ethos, I thought I might wear my brightest shirt and tie this evening. But to turn to the subject. First, about market value. I hope that I did not confuse people about this. Of course I do not think that moral value is in all respects like market value. One terribly important dissimilarity is precisely that market value does vary very freely with a place and time. The reason I introduced that illustration was to try to bring out something about saying that values are in some sense, and I tried to explain in what sense I meant, a function of human desires; and hence that there could not be any sort of value in a world that was totally uninhabited. What I was trying to show was that to say this is not the same thing as saying, nor does it warrant one going on immediately to say, that all talk about morality is a matter of the expression of the preferences of the individual speaking of this group or that. I wanted to show how it is possible for something to be a matter of some sort of value and for the particular value in question to be independent of the desires of any particular person or group.

Second, about the eternity of matter. Certainly I myself am inclined to believe that the universe was without beginning and will be without end. Indeed, I know no good reasons for disputing either of these suggestions. But I do not think either of them —in particular the one that Dr. Warren is the more concerned with, the one about the beginning—is something that an Atheist Naturalist is by his atheist naturalism committed to defending. He will probably want to defend it for other reasons. The reason he is not committed to defending this is that there is nothing actually contradictory in the suggestion that indeed the universe might have had a beginning and that there might have been absolutely nothing before that. I do not believe that this was so. But I do not see anything contradictory in this suggestion.

Third, back again to eternal punishment. Perhaps this would be a good occasion to say that I have seen a lot of members of the Church of Christ in the last few days. The disparity between their goodness and forthcomingness as people concerned with other people, and the alleged conduct of the God whom they admire as supremely just is perfectly extraordinary. I am very glad indeed that they in fact live as they do and do not model themselves upon the being whom they describe as perfectly just.

This makes a good occasion for answering Dr. Warren's second question this evening which I notice I omitted to answer. The question was: "By what standard do you judge that it is evil that anyone should be punished in eternal hell?" I think the best answer for that is: "By the sort of everyday standards of human decency and compassion and concern which I am sure that all the members of the Church of Christ cherish; by reference to the sort of good neighborliness and concern for people which they try to show in their ordinary lives. It is by those standards that I judge the conduct ascribed to their God by Dr. Warren and I fear by many of those Church of Christ members. I describe it as the rather rude things I do describe it as by just those standards.

Fourth, about evolution and creation. Oh, dear me! Certainly I do not believe that Darwin's theory of evolution by natural selection is going to be disproved. But suppose that it were. This would not in fact begin to establish the sorts of things which it seems to me that Dr. Warren thinks would be established. After all, the theory of evolution is a theory about what goes on and what has gone on within the universe. It would be perfectly consistent with a rejection of belief in his God to say that there have been jumps in the development of things within the universe, and that either these are just inexplicable, that they just happened, or perhaps that—more engagingly—they were the work of several powerful spirits within the universe. None of this begins to get us to a Creator of the whole thing with the various characteristics postulated by Dr. Warren.

It is not that I believe that the theory of evolution is in any serious danger of being shown to be untrue. But I think it is just worth pointing out that even if it were, then what would be at stake is not quite what Dr. Warren thinks is at stake. It might well be that proof of the theory of evolution would disprove Dr. Warren's religion. But I do not think a disproof of the theory of evolution would establish the whole works.

I suppose this would be a good moment to say something about the respiratory system. I am not at all sure that anyone has got more than the roughest of rough outlines of the evolution of the respiratory system. But then, you know you can have very good reasons for believing the general theory of evolution without having at this stage a full account of the whole course of the whole process. A full account of the whole course of the whole process is just not going to be had for a very long time indeed. What is surely sufficient to make the theory of evolution by natural selection immensely plausible is: that it can be made to fit a large area; that where it is tested it is not disconfirmed; and that continual progress is made in filling in some of the gaps.

Now I think we had better get back to objective value and higher laws. Once again, let me start by saying that I am in this matter genuinely agnostic about a lot of issues. That is to say, I do not believe that the work of the moral philosophers has been completed. All I can offer here is some things that seem to me to be clearly true, and I can offer the reasons for saying them. I can not give a complete story. Later we will no doubt find from my answers to Dr. Warren's Question One of this evening that I do not claim to be able to give a complete moral philosophy.

Here are some of the things that seem to me to be relevant and also to be true. First, value—including moral value—is some sort of function of human preferences and human wants. Just about all that I think one can mean by this claim, what and just about all that it implies, is that in an uninhabited universe nothing could be said to be valuable or valueless. To use the same illustration for the third time, it would be as absurd to speak of moral value with respect to such a universe as it would be to ask for the market value or market price of anything in it.

Second, to say that something ought or not to be done, that something is or is not good or evil, is nevertheless not the same as, nor does it by itself imply, that any particular individual likes or dislikes that something, or stands to gain or lose by it. Some new stuff here. When in Plato's *Republic,* the cynic Thrasymachus said: "By the word 'justice,' we mean nothing else but the advantage of the stronger," what he was saying did not simply happen to be wrong. Thrasymachus, in saying this, was fundamentally, totally, diametrically wrong, and hence rather usefully wrong. Suppose that we say in our cynical and debunking moments, that when our political opponents—notoriously corrupt and hypocritical characters—say that they are concerned to establish a just society, a "socially just society," what they really mean is they hope to get or to retain well-paying government jobs in welfare agencies. If we ever say this sort of thing, then of course it is quite wrong to construe our statment as an account of what the word "justice" means on their detested lips. What the word "justice" means on their lips is presumably much the same as whatever the word "justice" means on our lips. This is one of those cases where hypocrisy is the tribute which vice pays to virtue. Of course justice does not mean anything of the such. What our opponents would say if they were not being such a lot of obvious hypocrites, is that there is a fat job in Washington in it for me and I am pretending in order to fool the suckers to be concerned about justice ("social" justice).

More positively, the whole point of an appeal to justice is that it should be an appeal from any and all particular or group interests, to a standard by which adjudications can be made between such possibly, and indeed usually, conflicting individual or group interests. Thrasymachus was thus totally, fundamentally, diametrically and instructively wrong in trying to define the word "justice" in terms of any particular set of interests whatever.

Third, morality and, if you like, the moral law, is of its very nature a higher law than any system of positive law. By "positive law" is meant the law of any particular country, or custom with the force of law, or international law: a system laid down by men, with punishments attached, and so on. All such systems of positive law are in principle reviewable and judgable by reference to, if you like, a higher law, if you do not like, by reference to morality. What does this mean? It means that it always makes sense to ask: "Yes, it is United States law, Texas law, British law, even international law, but is it right, is it just, ought it to be as it is? Ought U. S., Texas, British or international law to be as it is?" That is what I mean by saying moral law is a higher law.

Where are we? The first point was to show what is meant by saying that value is some sort of function of human desires, needs and such. The second point was to bring out that and in what sense moral and other sorts of value can, nevertheless, be objective and independent of people's passing wants, of particular group interests, and so on. The third point was to show that and in what sense moral assessment is essentially an appeal to a higher law. These three—shall we flatteringly call them insights?—all prepare the way for the most relevant fourth point. Nothing said under the first three heads says or implies anything about God. That this is so, indicates that the objectivity and the overridingness of morality is in no way dependent upon, nor does it owe its authority to, the will of any superb Being. The most—and it could in practice be a most important most—the most which any such superb Being could do here is something utterly different. It could throw its power behind whatever is moral, or for that matter it could throw it behind whatever is immoral; and it could reward or punish those who acted or failed to act on whatever principles it decided to support.

The fourth insight, to which all the first three have been building up, is derived once again from that famous old challenge in Plato's dialogue *Euthyphro*. Are the things which are just just because God endorses them, or does God endorse the things which are just because they are just? In order not to be distracted by any claims that since the word God is in part defined in terms of justice and goodness, and that therefore any Being if incorrectly described as God must be good and just, let us reformulate that question is referring only to an omnipotent Being. "Are the things that are just just because some omnipotent Being endorses them? Or does some omnipotent Being endorse them, if he does, because they are just?"

Anyone who chooses the first of these two alternatives thereby abandons morality in favor of the worship of naked power. For by making this choice he in effect defines the word "justice" in terms of the sheer will of any being that happens to be omnipotent. The word "justice" so defined no longer refers to any standard which is objective in the sense explained, or overriding in the sense explained. And the respondent in question, the person who answers like this, by defining the word "justice" in this way, makes it very clear that he is in favor of anything whatsoever which his particular Mr. Big chooses to support.

But anyone who chooses the second alternative becomes by that choice committed to recognizing both that the standards of justice are indeed in the sense given objective, and that they are not definable in terms of the will of any individual or group—not even in terms of the will of an all-powerful Being. By that second choice he becomes committed to saying that the conduct attributed to an all-powerful Being can be assessed by reference to those objective standards. Under that assessment that Being may not even achieve a passing grade. Those are four things which, for the reasons given, and I reckon can relevantly and reasonably be said to be known about morality in this context. But there are a great many questions about the general principles and the theory of morality to which I do not know the answer. Trying to find the answers is what moral philosophy is about.

(Timekeeper—About a minute and a half) Thanks.

What can I usefully do in that other minute? Yes, there is one small point we might as well get straight. This refers to the first of the questions in my multiple choice test. If it is the case that real objective moral value is comparable to market value, then it is the case that it is possible that real objective moral value can change. It is the case that the torturing and murdering of the Jews by the Nazis could probably come to be considered to be morally right. Well, I did that one false. I ought before doing it false to have crossed out that "to be considered to be." After all it is not in dispute between Dr. Warren and myself but people might very well mistakenly change their views about what was moral or not. Clearly the crux, and the point that he wanted to ask me, was whether it would actually in fact cease to be immoral and become moral. He was not wanting to ask me whether people might change their minds. Of course, they might change their minds. People might become mistaken about this or they might get right about it.

WARREN'S FIFTH AFFIRMATIVE

(Thursday Night)

Dr. Flew, Gentlemen Moderators, Ladies and Gentlemen. Since there was not just a great deal to reply to in the speech to which you just listened, I am going to depart from my usual format of replying first to those matters to the presenting of a further affirmative argument. And I want to refer to a statement that Dr. Flew has made on a number of occasions in regard to various things about the human body as though we are against material things that we human beings design and make, such as automobiles, watches and so forth. Dr. Flew has said a car is *made* but an eye *grows*. Well, he certainly will have no conflict with me on that matter, but what Dr. Flew seems to have forgotten is that he has already admitted something that is fatal to his whole contention along this line. He has already admitted that no human being owes his ultimate origin to transformation from an ape or any other non-human being, that no human being ever came into being by being born of an ape or some other non-human being, and, therefore, he has admitted that what little he said about evolution a moment ago did not touch the issue of what has been before us in this debate, top, side, edge, or bottom. Therefore, it is clear from what he himself has admitted that human beings could have originated only in some way other than by the physical law of reproduction which we know in the union of the human male sperm and the human female ovum. He has admitted that is not the case. Further, he has refused to notice, in the face of our repetition of the matter, that while *we* admit that the car is *made, he* says nothing at all about the *maker* of the car. Remember: he has tacitly admitted that the maker of the car could have been here in no way other than by creation; and therefore, his point that the car is *made* but eyes and respiratory systems *grow* simply falls by the wayside.

Let us look at Chart 42-I (See Page 208) and follow that with 42-J. (See Page 209.) Now in Chart No. 42-I we have the drawn picture of a rock, presumably on Mars. You remember the great excitement that went through the world when someone thought perhaps he had seen the single letter B on a rock. I am sure that every atheist, every evolutionist in the

INTELLIGENT LIFE ON MARS—& OTHER PLANETS?

(42-I (1))

1. WHAT IF WE FOUND ON MARS—

A ROCK WITH THE LETTER "B" CLEARLY CARVED INTO IT?

*WHAT SHOULD WE CONCLUDE?— (CHECK CORRECT ANSWERS):

- ☐ THAT AT LEAST ONE INTELLIGENT BEING HAD AT SOME TIME BEEN ON MARS?
- ☐ THAT THE "B" WAS DUE TO THE ACCIDENTAL RESULTS OF THE ACTION OF DIRT, ROCKS, WIND, ETC. (I.E. NON-INTELLIGENT PHYSICAL FORCES)?
- ☐ SOMETHING ELSE. ______________
  EXPLAIN

[INTELLIGENT LIFE ON MARS?]

42-J (2)

2. WHAT IF WE FOUND ON MARS —

In honor of King John XXVI of Mars, who with such great valor put down the uprising of wicked men who would have murdered or enslaved us, who so generously assisted in the development of medical science, and who helped us to see that the one true God really lives.

3. SHOULD WE CONCLUDE —
(check all correct answers)

- ☐ THAT AT LEAST AT SOME TIME INTELLIGENT LIFE HAD BEEN ON MARS.
- ☐ THAT THE CARVING OF THE FACE AND THE MESSAGE WAS THE RESULT OF THE PURELY ACCIDENTAL (CHANCE) ACTION OF THE ROCKS AND DIRT ON MARS.
- ☐ THAT IT IS IMPOSSIBLE TO COME TO KNOWLEDGE OF THE EXISTENCE OF INTELLIGENT BEINGS WITHOUT ACTUALLY OBSERVING THEM.

world was ready to pronounce "Here you see absolute conclusive proof" (of intelligent life on Mars), so that everyone who would deny it must immediately classify himself as non-scientific, non-philosophic and certainly on the level of an ignoramus to hold that this would not prove that there was intelligent life on Mars.

But, we go a little further. They had to admit they did not find the B. They had to admit that it no doubt was from just some physical phenomenon by chance, so I proposed a hypothesis. On Chart No. 42-J, I have asked him "What if we found on Mars a carving in a rock?" Here is a very smooth place carved in a rock and on the rock is the head of a king carved with his coat of arms and this message "In honor of King John XXVI of Mars who with such great valor put down the uprising of wicked men who would have murdered or enslaved us, who so generously assisted in the development of medical science and who helped us to see that the one true God really lives." Now, Dr. Flew *admitted* that this would force us to conclude that we could have *knowledge* of intelligent life on Mars which we had *never observed!* I pointed out to you that this indicates that he admits the *basic thrust* of the argument of natural theology, that is, from empirical fact within the universe to something that we cannot see. Now, he admitted that of something within the universe—of course Mars is within the universe—but he has further admitted that by the combination of the concept of God with what he alleges to be evil we may reason and therefore conclude that we have *knowledge* concerning the number of members in the class of things which is transcendent of the universe. Therefore you see, he has admitted both that we may gain knowledge of something we have not observed by proper reasoning from what we have observed, not only reasoning to knowledge of what is *in* this universe but also to what *transcends* the universe! Now, friends, if ever anybody has made an admission concerning the validity of natural theology, Dr. Flew has done so.

I made an argument earlier, we did not get to say a great deal about it, but I want to say more about it and introduce some new material as well. I want to introduce the human body. I am an individual empirical fact. I exist. I know there are some philosophers who deny that, but they do not really believe it.

Philosophers say a lot of things they do not really believe. Philosophers sometimes say we can not really know the external world is there (exists), but they always get off the railroad track when a train is coming, and you can not get them to jump off of a bluff down to the rocks that are 100 feet below.

Now notice carefully that the human system constitutes a single system. I am a single person. You may not think much of me but, as a matter of fact, I am a marvelous complex system. I am made up of sub-systems. I am a single system made up of sub-systems, and each of these sub-systems has functions. Now, let us look at some of these. I am no expert at these matters but I have checked these matters with men who are, so what I am giving you is not just something that I have sort of tossed off here.

There is the system which we know as the skin. It provides protection, support, heat regulation, absorption, excretion, stimuli reception. You can not live very long without your skin. There would be no possibility that "ancestors" of humans could live through some long millions of years while skin was evolving. And, all of these systems had to be here at the same time. What good would your skin have been if you did not have a *digestive system* or a *respiratory system*, or a *cardiovascular system*? Or what good would your respiratory system have been without your *skin*, and so forth.

And, how on earth did whatever it was that Dr. Flew thinks was out there before there were human beings—even though he has now admitted it could not have come that way—how did they *reproduce* themselves before this very complex reproductive system that we find in the human male and female came along? Dr. Flew, I would like to see you struggle with that just a bit and explain to us how they reproduced themselves before that "evolved."

There is the skeletal system, which provides support, protection, posture, motion, locomotion, manufacture of blood corpuscles by bone marrow, transmission of sound waves (ear bones). There is the *muscular system*: locomotion, movement of body parts such as stomach, intestines, heart, and so forth. You can not live without these matters. *Digestive* system: ingestion, digestion, absorption of food, the elimination of waste. *The circulatory system:* transportation of foods, waste, oxygen, heat, carbon dioxide, endocrine hormones, and so forth. *The respiratory system*: supplies oxygen, eliminates carbon dioxide and other wastes. The *excretory system* secretes and eliminates waste materials. *Nervous and sensory system*: receives stimuli, transmits and interprets impulses for purposes—notice that, *purposes!* You can not really describe the human body without saying "Well, this is for that purpose"—correlation, movement, locomotion, behavior, secretion, centers of sight, hearing, taste, smell, equilibrium, and so on. *The endocrine or ductless gland system*: conduction of hormones for correlating and regulating body processes. Friends, you cannot live long without a proper regulation of insulin, a hormone which comes from our pancreas gland. If you have too much of it, you will not have any blood sugar. You will not have any sugar in your blood and you can not function. You will even pass out and finally die. If you do not have enough of it you can not utilize the sugar that is there. You would not have time for this to have evolved over a long period of time.

You see what I am talking about here is not merely something that is "curious" or interesting or say "Well that seems to be very complex." What I am talking about here is something which is necessary to life. Dr. Flew, you need to address yourself to this argument.

Now I am going to give this argument. Again it is going to be given with precisely stated propositions, in a valid way. When an argument is presented in this way, it is the common practice of philosophers to ask two questions. One: "Is the *argument* valid?" If so, then you proceed to the premises. You then ask, "Are the *premises* true?" If you do not care to be rational, then you say "Oh, well, I just do not feel that I want to accept that," or "There are some *curious* things about it that are rather obnoxious to me and so I just decide that I will not accept it," or "I will take a leap into the dark and believe this or that." That is irrationalism—existential philosophy or neo-orthodox theology—but it is *not* what my learned colleague has espoused in the past. I do not know what has happened to him in this discussion.

Chart No. 42-A3. (See Page 213.)

But at any rate, here is the argument. *Premise No. 1.* If the gaseous interchanges—that is, of oxygen and carbon dioxide—in

[TELEO]

ARGUMENT ON RESPIRATION

I. THE ARGUMENT STATED:

(42-A3)

(1)

1. IF THE GASEOUS INTERCHANGES (I.E. OF OXYGEN AND CARBON DIOXIDE) IN THE RESPIRATORY SYSTEM OF A HUMAN BEING POSSESS SUCH PROPERTIES (OR INVOLVE SUCH THINGS) AS TO MAKE CLEAR THAT SUCH INTERCHANGES WERE NOT BROUGHT INTO BEING BY ANY PART OF OR THE TOTALITY OF DEAD MATTER, THEN THE RESPIRATORY SYSTEM OF THE HUMAN BEING (IN WHICH THESE INTERCHANGES OCCUR) MUST HAVE BEEN BROUGHT INTO BEING BY A (THE) CREATOR WHO TRANSCENDS THE UNIVERSE (GOD).

2. THE GASEOUS INTERCHANGES IN THE RESP. SYSTEM OF A HUMAN BEING POSSESS SUCH PROP. (---) AS TO MAKE CLEAR THAT SUCH INTERCHANGES WERE NOT BROUGHT INTO BEING BY ANY PART OF OR THE TOTALITY OF DEAD MATTER.

3. ∴ THE RESPIRATORY SYSTEM OF THE HUMAN BEING (...) MUST HAVE BEEN BROUGHT INTO BEING BY A (THE) CREATOR WHO TRANSCENDS THE UNIVERSE (GOD).

the respiratory system of a human being possess such properties or involve such things as to make clear that such interchanges were not brought into being by any part of or the totality of dead matter, then the respiratory system of a human being in which these interchanges occur must have been brought into being by the Creator who transcends the universe, that is God. That is the only one who could have done it. All of this talk about men holding to various gods—such men as Hartshorne and Brightman and Whitehead and so forth—the gods they envision could not have done that. It demands the God, the infinite God, infinite in all attributes. *Premise No. 2.* The gaseous interchanges in the respiratory system of a human being possess such properties as to make clear that such interchanges were not brought into being by any part of or the totality of dead matter. Therefore, notice this. Conclusion: The respiratory system of the human being must have been brought into being by the creator who transcends the universe, that is God.

Now I want you to listen carefully to the explanation of this interchange of oxygen and carbon dioxide in the human respiratory system, and I want, on the screen Chart No. 42-A-1 (See Page 215), so the audience can see what I am talking about as we see the air passage laid along side the blood passage. This interchange does not occur as if you have a water hose here and the water is pouring out of it, and you hook another hose on to the end of it, so that the water is simply pouring out of one hose into another. But it is rather more like putting two hoses along side and the water in one hose is simply going through the wall of this hose into the other. My friends, you cannot live longer than 5 minutes without this interchange occurring. I am begging, I am pleading for Dr. Flew to give some attention to the fact that I am claiming that it is *impossible* for the mechanism involved to have evolved because the time factor involved simply will not allow it. Now notice this explanation. "The tension of oxygen is lower in the venous blood than in the alveolar air, but the venous blood has a higher tension of the carbon dioxide. The pulmonary capillaries and the air in the alveoli are separated by membranes which are so delicate as to be freely permeable to these gases—that is, oxygen and carbon dioxide. The differences in the relevant pressures are favorable to a rapid inward diffusion of oxygen (from

[USE WITH 41-D]

[RESPIRATORY SYSTEM— CONT'D]

✱ THE MARVELOUS INTERCHANGE OF OXYGEN (IN AIR) AND CARBON DIOXIDE (IN BLOOD):

42-A1

(1)

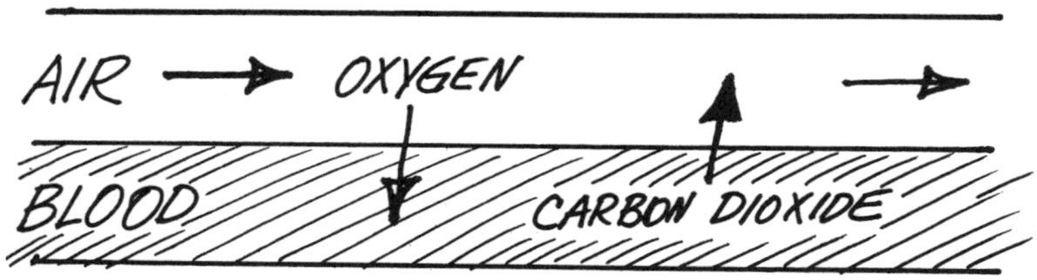

AIR → OXYGEN →

BLOOD CARBON DIOXIDE

1. WITHOUT THIS AMAZING INTERCHANGE, NO HUMAN BEING COULD LIVE MORE THAN A FEW MOMENTS.
2. YET, THE ATHEISTIC POSITION DEPENDS UPON ITS EVOLVING OVER A PERIOD OF TIME AS LONG, PERHAPS, AS A MILLION YEARS
3. EVOLUTION COULD NOT HAVE OCCURRED—
4. —SO— ATHEISM IS FALSE!

*cf. CHART 41-D

alveolar air to blood) and an outward diffusion of carbon dioxide, (from blood to the alveolar air)." Now notice, you have got to get oxygen *into* your blood and it has got to go all over your body or you will die. And you have got to get the carbon dioxide *out* of your blood and out of the air as you breathe or you will die. And, that has to occur within at most a five-minute period. I am therefore declaring it is impossible otherwise. Dr. Flew admits that if it can be shown that *purposive* action—and thus *design*—has occurred, then some intelligent being or designer exists. He has admitted that. Now I am saying that here is something which shows purposive action that could not have come by sheer accident or by sheer chance. He would have you to believe that this matter—that has to occur within this five-minute period—occurred like something like a whirlwind blowing through a junk yard and blowing a watch out on the other side of it. It simply will not work.

Note further: there is purposive action in sub-human levels of life. There is purposive action in human levels of life and there is purposive action in life transcendent of human life. Let us look at that Chart 42-A1 (See Page 215) for just a moment. I want you to look at it. Notice now—follow the pointer—here is air coming along in the air passage. The oxygen—being of greater pressure in the air passage than the oxygen particles in the blood—passes through the capillary wall into the blood and then is carried to the various parts of the body. On the other hand, the carbon dioxide in the blood has greater pressure than the carbon dioxide in the air passage; therefore, it passes through to the air. This is a well known fact. It is involved in the law of physics and the law of gases, and Dr. Flew has before him something that he simply cannot handle.

Now, I want to present something further along this line. I want you to put on the screen if you will please, Chart No. 9-GG. (See Page 217.) Here we have the drawing of the pelvic skeletal section with the thigh bones and knees and part of the lower bones of the leg, and on the left side as you look at it is the person in the drawing, his right side, you will see a bone which I have numbered No. 1. This is the *natural* thigh bone and in this thigh bone is bone marrow. The bone marrow plays a very crucial role in the manufacture of cells for the blood without which we cannot live very

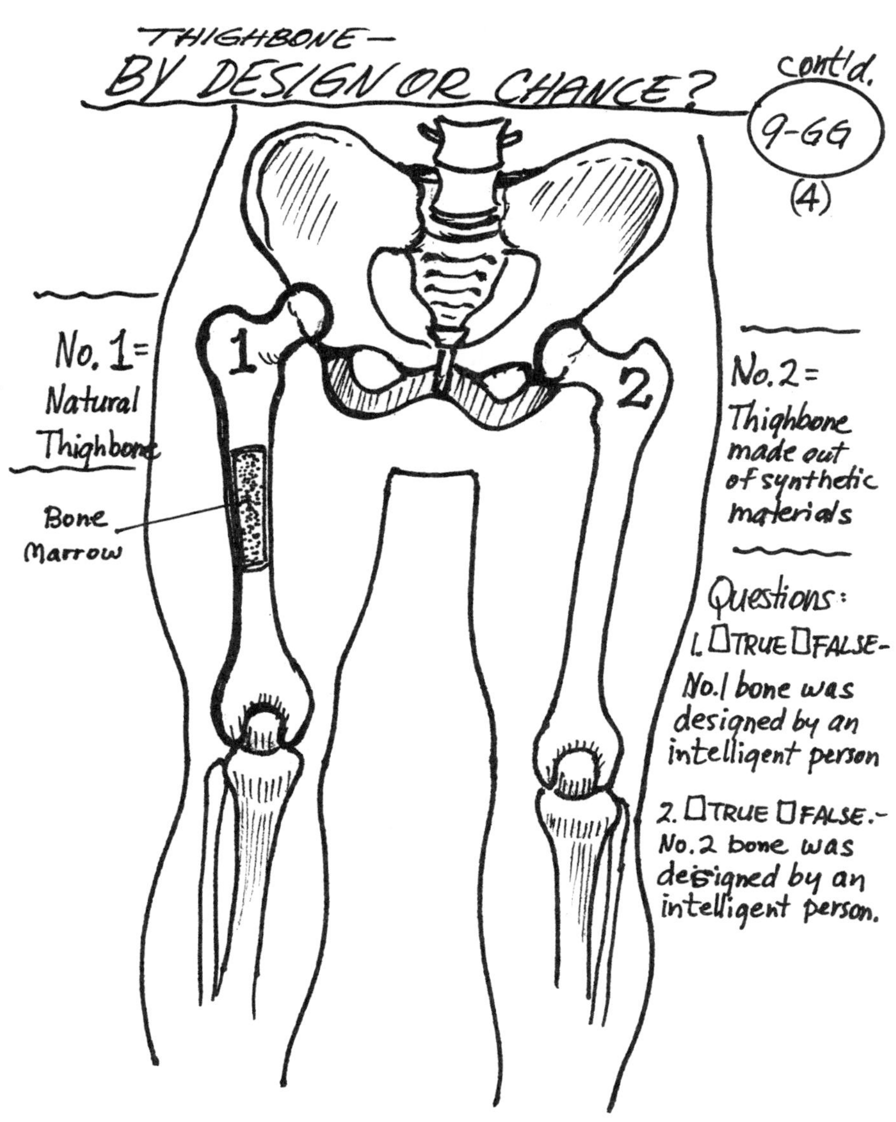
THIGHBONE—
BY DESIGN OR CHANCE?
cont'd.
9-GG
(4)
1
2
No. 1=
Natural
Thighbone
Bone
Marrow
No. 2=
Thighbone
made out
of synthetic
materials
Questions:
1. ☐TRUE ☐FALSE-
No. 1 bone was
designed by an
intelligent person
2. ☐TRUE ☐FALSE.-
No. 2 bone was
designed by an
intelligent person.

long. On the right side is a *synthetic* bone. Certainly medical scientists and orthopedic surgeons have been able to develop marvelous things along this line. Here is a man perhaps whose thigh bone has degenerated to the point that it had to be replaced, and so thigh bone number two is made of synthetic material. I am going to leave this chart here on the lectern for Dr. Flew. I want him, as he looks at it, to identify as to whether the thigh bone number two was created by design (or was designed by some intelligent person) and whether thigh bone number one was designed by some intelligent person. Of course, what he will *have* to say, to even *try* to stay in this debate, is that thigh bone number one, the real (natural) one (the one with bone marrow in it, the one that the other one is designed from, that it is copied from, the one upon which your life depends) came into being by mere chance, starting off with nothing but rocks and dirt! The "God" who brought that into being is rocks and dirt. He could not for a moment admit, he can not even contemplate the idea, that the great God of the universe designed and planned it, but he would not admit for a moment that the synthetic thigh bone was not designed by some intelligent human being.

I want now to look at Chart No. 9 HH. (See Page 219.) You see we have two skeletons. On the left, we have a *natural* human skeleton; that is, someone who is dead and all the flesh and so forth is off of his bones. On the other side, there is a synthetic human skeleton, one that is made of *synthetic* material. Dr. Flew, I am going to leave this up here (on the lectern) for you to mark or to tell us about. I want you to tell us whether the *natural* human skeleton was the result of *design* or the result of *chance* and whether the *synthetic* human skeleton was the result of *design* or the result of *chance*. Now, friends, to be an atheist, to be a materialist of the sort of which Dr. Flew is, he will have to say that the natural human skeleton just by sheer accident—no planning, no purpose, no intelligence—that it came into being even though they could not have been born or transformed from an ape. He still has not told us how it is supposed to have gotten here. But, on the other hand, he would insist as strongly as anybody that the skeleton made out of *synthetic* material was *designed* by somebody. Now, friends, the human skeleton represents a masterpiece. I am reading here a statement from a scientist. Listen to this, "The

THE AMAZING HUMAN SKELETON

cont'd.
9-HH
(5)

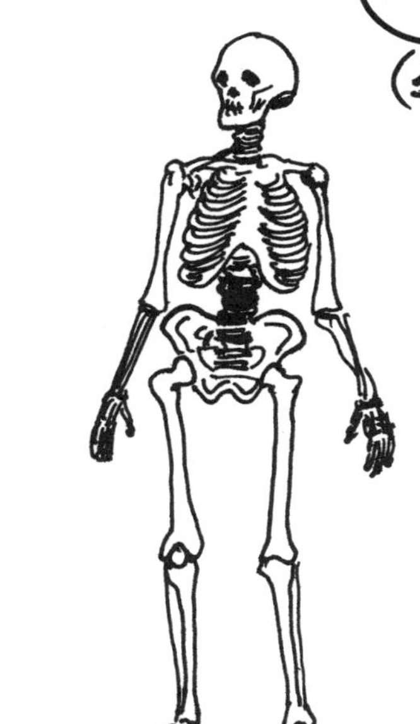

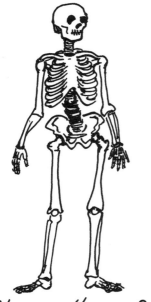

NATURAL HUMAN SKELETON

- ☐ RESULT OF DESIGN
- ☐ RESULT OF CHANCE

SYNTHETIC HUMAN SKELETON

- ☐ RESULT OF DESIGN
- ☐ RESULT OF CHANCE

(check correct answers)

WILL DR. FLEW DRAW THE CONCLUSIONS WHICH THE EVIDENCE WARRANTS?

human skeleton represents a masterpiece of engineering design with each component part tailored to a specific job. The brain is protected by the skull. . . . The spinal cord, a highly sensitive and vital nerve center, is protected by vertebra. The spine even has its own built-in shock absorber—the discs of cushioning cartilage between segments. The leg bones are hollow, in keeping with the engineering principle that a hollow column is stronger than a solid one of equal weight. On a weight-for-weight basis, bones are stronger than steel. Bone construction is comparable to reinforced concrete." That is from *Our Human Body*, Readers Digest, 1962. And in V. F. Miller, M.D., *Man and His Body,* "The human skeleton is a remarkable piece of functional architecture." You do not have *architecture* without somebody being an *architect,* and that means an intelligent being. Now, I will leave one more thing up here, "What Atheists Must Know." They must know that the human male reproductive system with all of its complexity developed by sheer chance. I started to draw a picture of it—though there would be nothing wrong with it, I thought that perhaps some of you might be offended by it—and the details of the female human reproductive system, its awesome complexity, its greatness. To imagine that this "happened" by sheer *accident* is simply incredible to anyone who is thinking rationally about this entire matter. I leave this chart also with Dr. Flew so he can try to tell us if that came by *accident* or by *design.* I leave this with him to tell us whether the human cardiovascular system, the human respiratory system, the human digestive system, the human eliminative system comes from its "creator" which is *rocks and dirt* rather than from the eternal God!

Chart No. 42-A8 (See Page 221), look at two hands. Here is a man who has one *natural* hand and one *mechanical* hand. Which one is *designed?* Are the *both designed?* Are they *both* by the *accident?* Oh, no, says Dr. Flew, the *mechanical* hand, the one made out of metal and wire and so forth, is *designed.* There had to be *intelligence* behind it. All right, thank you. I will leave that one too. It would not be possible for me to use the 20 seconds which Dr. Flew left would it?

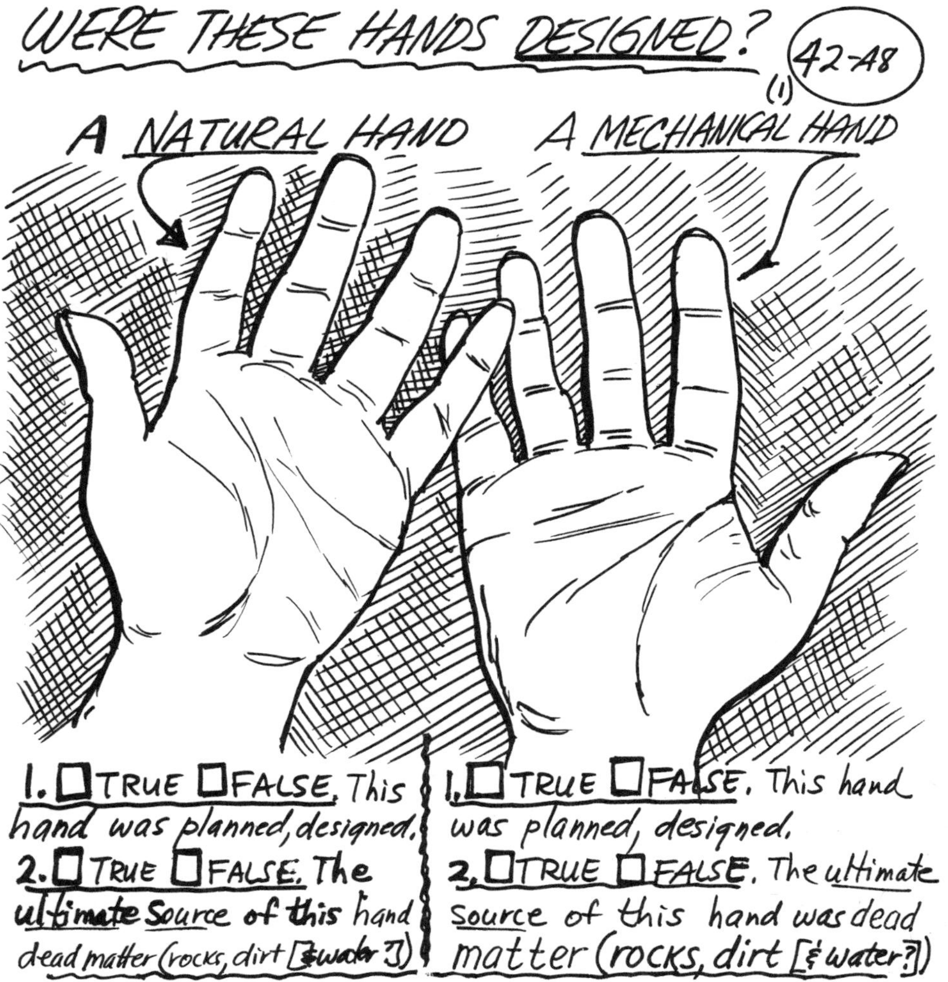
WERE THESE HANDS DESIGNED?
42-48
(1)
A NATURAL HAND
A MECHANICAL HAND
1. ☐ TRUE ☐ FALSE. This hand was planned, designed.
2. ☐ TRUE ☐ FALSE. The ultimate Source of this hand dead matter (rocks, dirt [& water?])
1. ☐ TRUE ☐ FALSE. This hand was planned, designed.
2. ☐ TRUE ☐ FALSE. The ultimate source of this hand was dead matter (rocks, dirt [& water?])

FLEW'S FIFTH NEGATIVE

(Thursday Night)

First, about the respiratory system. Here it does seem that you need a biologist and not a philosopher, someone who has at his fingertips a description of some particular discovered mechanisms. I know there are plenty of these discovered mechanisms. I have read about them but I am not able to give offhand any descriptions of some things that would have looked to Dr. Warren as if they must have been designed but where the detailed mechanisms of the way in which they presumably emerged without design has been discovered. I am sorry about that. I am just, I fear going to fail you on that point. There has got to be someone else for this monkey trial.

I will turn to the sorts of things about which I can say something useful and relevant. Point one. I have made this before but perhaps if I make it in another way it will get across. With reference to all this stuff about evolution, I want to say to Dr. Warren, in the words of the title of a best selling Student Christian Movement Press book in my own country: "Your God is Too Small." The point is that the most that any sort of argument of this sort is going to prove is a powerful intelligent Being capable of the considerable achievement of designing consciously from scratch a human organism to work on the basis of the materials available in this universe. But this is not the infinite, the unspeakable, the eternal: the Creator of all being and power and justice. "Your God is too small!" It is just not the right thing. It is not beginning to get to the point, the point expressed as I have just expressed it, with some vehemence, is a point which has often been expressed less vehemently about any Argument to Design. The thing about design, where design occurs, is that it is an application of intelligence within certain limitations. What is clever about the design is that you made a revolving crane out of match sticks. Oh, you clever thing, to make a crane out of these materials! But a being that is all powerful and omniscient can achieve its ends directly by fiat, without artifice and ingenuity. "Your God is too small!"

Besides the one just made, another point which I can make about evolution refers to the record of the rocks. One of the things that I do know about because it was one of the first things which led Darwin to think along the lines on which he did think, is the geological record. This shows more complicated, more sophisticated, more integrated organisms appearing at later stages. Now, if we are going to have a special creationist account of the origin of species what this progressive development suggests is precisely not the infinite, the unspeakable, the eternal, the omniscient. Instead it suggests a very powerful being that took a hell of a lot of time to get good at it. It made a few very simple ones at first and then a million or so years later it had another go, doing a bit better than the amoeba this time around. Yet it still managed to create only very simple organisms. Then after some millions and millions of years of geological development it created the first man. No, really it will not do, it will not do.

About the reproductive system. I am a bit surprised to find Dr. Warren talking about the human reproductive system. I know it is all a bit fashionable—the presidential debates and all that. Nevertheless the human reproductive system is not the right thing to refer to if you want to say that people could not appear without special creation. For to refer to this is to refer to the way in which we all know that human beings do appear, and this appearance reveals no artifice or special creation. Human beings appear without non-human design in a way that is all too familiar, and which we describe as the facts of life.

Now these questions that I have got before me: was the ultimate source of this hand dead matter? Yes, certainly, I do believe that living organisms evolved over an immeasuraby long period of time from non-living materials. But it is not strictly right to describe these as dead. That is very misleading: it is living from non-living, not living from dead. To say that something is dead implies that it must have been alive beforehand.

Yes, of course I can distinguish between something that growed and something that is a human artifact. And how do I make this distinction? Because I know that artifacts were designed, and have seen some of them designed and made. By contrast I do not see human beings being designed, and I have watched some of my contemporaries and my juniors growing. You may argue that somewhere at the end of the line there was some conscious design in it. But if we are just going to look at the contrast between artifacts and non-artifacts now, what I have said is surely the right thing to say.

Enough about evolution, I think. We have had a lot about arguments to design and of course quite a lot about an argument from the objectivity of value. One thing which has not been mentioned so far is religious experience. I think it needs to be. For people do often claim that they have enjoyed abundant assurance in their own lives, that they know that there is a God because they have enjoyed direct commune with this God. They have had, as many would say, experience of God.

One way to go on when you have made a claim like this would be to say that you were present at the great spectacle in North Texas which Dr. Warren imagined and described to us. You might be able to say that you had actually been there watching it all happen, whereas I, perhaps, had seen only a replay of the TV newscasts. That would be one way to go on. But it is, for pretty obvious reasons, not the way taken by those to whom I am now referring. The other way, which is the interesting one which I want to consider, is to urge that whereas we who have not enjoyed the revelatory experiences vouchsafed to the believer cannot reasonably be required to accept his claims, this believer himself is in a sure position to know. We can only deny his reports about his experience of God by calling him a liar. And this, of course, we are unwilling to do: not solely, or even mainly, because such charges are embarrassing for all concerned; but for the much better reason that we know the claimant to be a perfectly honest man.

So, what do we say to such claims to have enjoyed privately an irrefragable revelation of one particular God? Well, one thing we might and perhaps should say is that such claims would be more impressive if they referred to deities not worshipped in the circles in which the claimants actually moved. It is, I think, a noteworthy fact that visions of the Blessed Virgin Mary seem to occur in Lourdes, in a strongly Catholic area of France, rather than—I am sorry I cannot give you any truly local examples—in some of the hillier parts of Tennessee. At least until recently visions of Shiva the Destroyer occurred only in places like Benares or Mysore and not—not that is until the wave of Indian immigration after World War II—in Birmingham or Manchester. In ancient China, people had visions of dragons. In Japan, they saw demons. And of course in your own country nowadays it is flying saucers and little green men from Venus.

That is a good first point and one that should be made. But the crucial point is different and philosophical. We need to distinguish two fundamentally different senses of the word "experience" and of such phrases as "a vision of." In one sense—let us call it experience (private)—the claim to have had experience refers only to something essentially private. It is like a matter of claiming only: that it seems to me like this; or that I had an experience of a patch of color, but I am not saying there was anything out there. In the private sense of "experience" the person who has the experience does have a special authority. If that is all you are claiming then you after all are in the best position to know. But the fact that you had this sort of experience, which seemed very vivid to you but was altogether private has no significance except insofar as you have reason to believe that it was in fact caused by some corresponding being.

In the other sense of "experience," which is in fact the every day ordinary sense of "experience," a claim to have experience of something is not just a claim about how it seemed to you in the privacy of your own head. It is a claim about the contacts you have had with, the knowledge you have acquired of, the universe around us. It is in that second public sense of "experience" that people advertise that they want to hire some people with experience of computer programming. But now, in this second sense of "experience" your honest claim is not the last word, you may be mistaken in what you claim to have seen, what you claim to have experienced.

Consider for instance an example which has been very famous and very important and about which a distinguished novel was written, *The Song of Bernadette*. (There was also a movie which probably your grandparents saw when I saw it.) The story is the story which led to the establishment of the cult of the Blessed Virgin at Lourdes. Surely no one was in any doubt at all that the young peasant girl Bernadette Soubirois who said she had a vision was quite honestly telling everyone how it had seemed to her. It had been like a dream in which she dreamt of seeing and talking to the Blessed Virgin. In Bernadette's vision she looked quite remarkably like one of those representations from the neighborhood religious objects store which Bernadette will have seen in her local church! What of course was in dispute and what the machinery of the Roman Catholic Church was deployed to try to find out, was whether this private experience, about which her honest testimony was the last word, had actually in some way been caused by the surviving spirit, personality, or what have you of the Blessed Virgin Mary.

Why am I doing all this? I am doing all this because I think something ought to be said about this sort of appeal to religious experience. This is extremely common in Protestant circles in my own country, though maybe it is not a thing in the Church of Christ here. The distinction between two senses of the word "experience" is absolutely crucial for considering this sort of move. What will not do, but what is all too often done, is to try to slide from a claim about experience in the private, limited sense, a claim about which you do have a special authority, after all it is your dream, your vision or whatever, you cannot expect anyone else to have or see your dream, your vision, your hallucination or whatever, the temptation is the temptation to which people all too often succumb, to move from a claim about their experience in the private sense, a claim about which they do have a special authority, to a conclusion maintaining that you have had experience of something independent of yourself and that you have had experience in the public sense.

Maybe you have. But this further and bolder claim—the one that refers to the causes out there and to something other than your private experience—is not one which other people, or, for that matter, you yourself can or should accept against all probability on your say so alone. Not even you, however vivid it was, are justified in saying: I actually had an experience that was caused by something out there. I have been in contact with the Blessed Virgin, or whatever it may be. Even you are not entitled to do this, in defiance of other evidence as to what was going on out there and without any inquiry about what any independent evidence of what was going on out there showed. Of course it may have been terribly vivid. So may a hallucination be. Of course you are very much inclined to say that you have had not merely experience of God, in the sense of which someone having a dream of the Blessed Virgin would have had an experience of the Blessed Virgin, but experience of God, in the sense in which someone who is said to have had experience of type six computers would have had experience of type six computers if they had actually had dealings with these computers.

That has all been something which I have been presenting here mainly because nothing has been said about experience before. In any case I just do not know what to say about all this about evolution; other than what I have already said, that at best, or at worst, no disproof of evolutionary theory would begin to establish the desired conclusion about an omnipotent God. Of course it would be dreadfully embarrassing. I should be worried sick, and I would not know what to think next. But it would not do what Dr. Warren hopes it would.

There do seem to be some minutes left. So yet once again, I ought to try to bring out this point about human beings and persons and babies. The fundamental trouble about this is that Dr. Warren wants to employ—and this is entirely reasonable granting Dr. Warren's beliefs about how the world is—a notion of a human being, and of course notions referring to all other species, which are quite inconsistent with evolutionary theory. That is to say, all his notions referring to species are by him interpreted in such a way that there just are absolutely sharp lines between species with no development from one to the other. Well, that may be right or it may be wrong. But what cannot be right is to produce an argument which is supposed to contain, both an account of the evolutionary theory, and these species terms used in an anti-evolutionary way; and then conclude triumphantly that there is an inconsistency. Of course there is an inconsistency between the denial of evolutionary theory and the assertion of it. But that is not an inconsistency in evolutionary theory.

WARREN'S SIXTH AFFIRMATIVE

(Thursday Night)

Dr. Flew, Gentlemen Moderators, Ladies and Gentlemen. I am certainly pleased to appear before you for my last full speech of this discussion, and I want to say at this time that I certainly do so with high regard for Dr. Flew as a person. I wish him only well and nothing that I have said in this discussion should ever be interpreted to be any attack upon him as a person. What I am arguing constitutes an attack upon his *doctrine*. But the doctrine, I must admit, is extremely weak. It is not only weak, it is false. Let us go through his speech as rapidly as possible, so that I may then present another affirmative argument. I have the responsibility to do so in more detail than I gave it last evening.

Dr. Flew begins in his last speech by expressing the wish that he were a professional *biologist* rather than a professional *philosopher*. He based that upon the supposition that we are now involved in some sort of "monkey trial." I have noticed that evolutionists seem to think that they rid themselves of responsibility for being rational about this problem by referring to "the monkey trial." You see, when you say "the monkey trial," you no longer have to give any more information. You do not have to give any logical arguments. You do not have to give any true premises. You just say "Oh, the monkey trial—all of us *scholarly* people have already decided that, and anyone who disagrees with us is some sort of ignoramus." But I suggest that this simply is not a valid course of procedure. In the first place, to decide the *origin* of human beings is not strictly speaking a *scientific* problem. It is rather a philosophical and/or a revelational problem. There is no single discipline within the various natural sciences that would claim that it and it alone can prove the theory of evolution. I want you to imagine here a series of circles above me, each one representing some natural science such as biology, paleontology, biochemistry, physics, chemistry, astronomy, and so on. What do they do in their efforts to make some sort of effort at proving the theory of evolution? They draw alleged facts from each of these disciplines and then try to *synthesize* them. But notice—the *synthesis* of scientific information is not the function of science as such; it is rather the function of *philosophy*. So, Dr. Flew, you are just the man to do it. But he tells us he does not really know anything about it. But, you see, his whole case depends upon his knowing how to prove evolution. How can a man claim to be an atheist while recognizing that if man is here by the creative act of *God* then he cannot rightly be an atheist and then come and confess that he does not know enough about atheism to even deal with the argument which I have given you, which was based clearly upon the *impossibility* of it being true. Now, Dr. Flew, it is not *monkeys* that are on trial here, it is *atheism!* Atheism and theism. And I suggest that a reference to a so-called "monkey trial" that occurred a few years ago in Tennessee is completely irrelevant, and it does not decide the issue.

He says "Your God is too small, it proves only a God of power and intelligence." Well, thank you, Dr. Flew. At least we have come far enough for you to admit that there is one being transcendent of the universe who is powerful and intelligent. Now let us see Chart No. 22. (See Page 230.) Dr. Flew, I am going to leave this chart here for you to answer. In the first place I have a drawing, an oval, and this is labeled God. Inside of that oval I have this expression, "Supreme personal being distinct from the world and creator of the world." Over to the right of that I have *true* or *false*: "I, A.G.N. Flew, know that God of this definition does not exist." If he answers "true," thus claiming that he *knows* that the God of this definition does not exist, then he admits (in contradition to some things he has said) that this is a sufficient definition of *God* for our debate. If he answers "false," thus admitting that he does *not* know that the God of this definition exists, then he admits defeat in this debate. If he says, "No, that is not true, I do not *know* that that God does not exist," then he admits that the God who was at issue in the debate between Professor Copleston and Professor Russell—by reputation two of the world's supreme philosophers—was a God the concept of which was coherent and is at issue in this debate. At the beginning of that discussion Professor Copelston said "I suggest as a definition of God that he is the supreme personal being distinct from the world and creator of the world. Is that definition acceptable to you?" And Professor Russell said, "Yes, that definition is acceptable." Now, what I want to know, Dr. Flew, is it acceptable to *you*? If you say "Oh, no that is *not* the *God* I am talking about

THE CONCEPT "GOD" (22)

DR. FLEW, PLEASE CHECK CORRECT ANSWERS.

1. "GOD"

SUPREME PERSONAL BEING, DISTINCT FROM THE WORLD, & CREATOR OF THE WORLD

☐ TRUE ☐ FALSE. I (A.G.N. FLEW) KNOW THAT THE "GOD" OF THIS DEFINITION DOES NOT EXIST.

2. "GOD"

SUPREME PERSONAL BEING, DISTINCT FROM THE WORLD, & CREATOR OF THE WORLD—& OMNIBENEVOLENT

☐ TRUE ☐ FALSE. I (A.G.N. FLEW) KNOW THAT THE "GOD" OF THIS DEFINITION DOES NOT EXIST.

3. "GOD"

SUPREME, PERS. BEING, DISTINCT FROM THE WORLD & CREATOR OF THE WORLD—& OMNIBENEVOLENT, & OMNIPOTENT.

☐ TRUE ☐ FALSE. I (A.G.N. FLEW) KNOW THAT THE "GOD" OF THIS DEFINITION DOES NOT EXIST.

in this debate, and I would say that that God exists but I want to deny that if you add omnibenevolence to it then he does *not* exist. Or I maybe will not admit that if you add omnibenevolence to it, in the second place, then I would admit that God exists, but you will have to add the last thing—that is, *omnipotence*—and then I will deny that he exists." Or if that will not do it, Dr. Flew, add another one and they will see about it. Now, I am going to leave Chart No. 22 here and I want you to tell us whether you believe that *first* God exists or not. Or, is *that* God not at issue here?

Now let us note Chart No. 44-C. (See Page 232.) Dr. Flew, we are not talking about *everything* in the world we can *know* about *God.* I have proved that God—the supreme personal being, distinct from the world and creator of the world—exists. And, *you* came here to *deny* that, but I want to show in this chart—if you will look at it turned on its side—I have over on the left in this circle, "Man X." This man may learn about God by examining himself, as I have given you the clear proof. And what attention has Dr. Flew given to those arguments? Has he taken them up and declared the validity or invalidity? Has he considered each and every *premise,* declared them true or false and shown you why? You know, as well as I, that he has not. My arguments stand clearly unassailed. His admissions on the first night—which amounts to the argument regarding evolution—by his own admission made clear that it was impossible that man is here by evolution. Now that makes clear that we are not here by evolution and —since we are here either by evolution or creation—so we are here by virtue of the miraculous creative action of the God who is described under that first category that I gave you a moment ago: "the supreme personal being distinct from the world and creator of the world." Now, notice in the circles just above. As you follow the arrow up from "Man X" to where it says "Man X himself," and then an arrow down into that inner circle that is *dotted.* Notice that I point out that you can learn *some* attributes of God from *man himself.* I have *not* said that you can learn *everything* about God from man himself, but I *have* said that you can learn *some* things about God and you can learn *that God is.* Now, on the other hand, you have *the Bible* and you can learn that if the Bible possesses certain properties then God does exist—that it is the

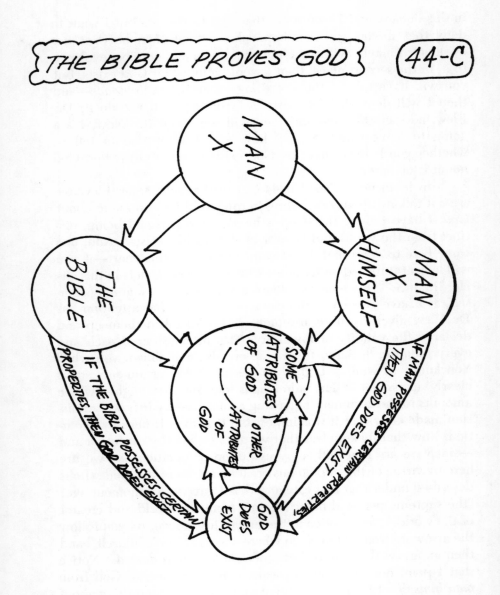

THE BIBLE PROVES GOD 44-C

MAN X

THE BIBLE

MAN X HIMSELF

SOME ATTRIBUTES OF GOD

OTHER ATTRIBUTES OF GOD

GOD DOES EXIST

IF THE BIBLE POSSESSES CERTAIN PROPERTIES, THEN GOD DOES EXIST

IF MAN POSSESSES CERTAIN PROPERTIES, THEN GOD DOES EXIST

book of God and, therefore, God does exist. Note the arrow going through the larger circle which not only includes all the attributes that you can learn from studying *man* himself but *other* attributes as well.

Now, Dr. Flew, if you would like to discuss in a similar situation for four evenings, each of us two nights in the affirmative, regarding the inspiration of the Bible, I am authorized to let you know that I would be pleased to come to England, to Reading University—or somewhere nearby—to discuss *the inspiration of the Bible* also in connection with the question of the existence of God. Now in *this* dicussion we are discussing the existence of God, but I shall be very happy to go further into the matter of the inspiration of the Bible.

Next, he comes to the matter of the record of the rocks and intimates that perhaps by the record of the rocks he is going to do something about proving evolution after he has already confessed that he does not really know about evolution. But, Dr. Flew, the so called "geologic column" does not actually exist anywhere in the world, does it? That is something that has been conjured up by various evolutionists. Rocks do not prove evolution. As a matter of fact, I wrote letters to at least 50 men who signed a so-called "Evolutionist Manifesto," asking them to send me the *sound argument*—that means a valid argument with true premises—the conclusion of which is, "Therefore, I know that man evolved from some lower or non-human form of life." Not all of them answered but *not one* of the ones that did answer, I think about 20 some odd, gave the sound argument! *Not one* of them, as a matter of fact, even gave an *argument!* Some of them rather facetiously said that they did not need to answer it, others said that they did not bother with such simplistic formulations. Isn't that nice? I wrote to a man who wrote a book on anthropology, 8 chapters of which were devoted to evolution, and said "I've read your book, I've read your chapter on evolution crowded with statements, most of which I suppose may be true, but where is your *argument* which proves evolution?" Professor Max Black—and I want to know if Dr. Flew disagrees with this (I have quoted it several times)—Dr. Max Black who is a recognized authority in logic, said that 400 pages of crowded fact and argument may deceive the very elect, but reduced to a three-line syllogism, lays bare the bones of the argument so that you can see whether the argument really proves what the speaker or writer claims that it does. That was a quotation from Josiah Stamp. Now why do you suppose that these men who are posing as authorities did not set forth a sound argument? Dr. Flew, none of those men would help you if they were here. I think there were 103 of them. If all 103 of them were here, there is not one of them who could write you a sound argument that proves that evolution is true. You need to "get on with it" as a *philosopher* and do your job of synthesizing information from science and of showing us *why* the theory of evolution is true.

Now he comes to the human reproduction system and says that he is surprised that I brought it up. "Why," he says, "human beings are *born*." Dr. Flew, would you like to shake hands with me on that? But, remember, he said that none of them (humans) are born of apes or of any other non-human thing. Now what more of an admission of utter devastating defeat could a man make? Human beings are *born*, but they are *not* born of any *non-human* thing! That means the *first pair* had to start, as the Bible says, by the creative act of God, who created the first man and the first woman. All the rest then have come into being according to the law of reproduction. Dr. Flew, I gave that argument with the expectation that you would fall into the very thing you did. You did just very nicely (in admitting that humans are *born*) as I had anticipated.

Now on the hands and the thigh bone and all of that, he has no trouble at all. He writes books and writes in journals and pleads with men to be *rational*. He writes in the *Rationalist Annual*, "be rational." That means: accept only such conclusions as that for which you have evidence. Dr. Flew, where did you ever see a *human skeleton* come into being by *sheer chance?* Where? Where did you ever know of *anybody* that did it? How did you come to *know* that anybody ever made an argument which proves that the *human skeleton* came into being by *accident?* When did you ever see a *human respiratory system*, without which we cannot live longer than five minutes, come into being by *accident*? But, you see for all of these contrivances such as microphones, cars, and so forth, he purports to tell us that there must be intelligence. There has got to be a mind that is intelligent that can think and plan and design and has the skill to make it. But you see things like these, the greatest vise in the world—the human finger and thumb—oh, that comes by *sheer accident.*

And, Dr. Flew, if it destroys you to say "dead matter," I will say "non-living matter." Non-living matter—rocks and dirt—it is still just rocks and dirt, but that is the ultimate creator according to Dr. Flew.

Of the complexity of the human being—with his soul, with his spirit, with his moral capacity, with his longing for God, with his recognition that he *ought* to act in certain ways and *not* in other ways—he has tacitly admitted that man has a conscience. There is no atheist that can get around the fact that he has a conscience. And I know that God has given him that conscience.

I want to spend a little more time in presenting what I have said already. I wanted to give a little more time to the discussion of the objectivity of moral law and what it proves but I am going to have time to say a bit more. I want this to be so clear. Here is a point that none of these men will be able to explain away. They may be able to go into their classes and somehow, by some clever statement, satisfy their students that they have explained on the one hand a recognition of *objective* moral law and on the other hand hold to *subjectivity.*

But before I get to that, let me say this. Dr. Flew spent a great deal of his time talking about religious *experience.* Did you hear *me* say anything about religious experience? Did *I* make any argument thus: someone has had a religious *experience* and, therefore, God exists? I said *nothing* at all about that! Dr. Flew I fight that view as well as you do. There are people all over this country who claim "Oh, a miracle occurred, a miracle occurred here and there." Well, let us see a miracle. "No, it happened over yonder; someone else knows how or where it happened." It is just like every evolutionist "knows" *somebody else* who knows how to prove it. Dr. Flew cannot prove it, but there is somebody over in some other university who can. But if you go over to that university, he will point you to some *other* university: "There is some learned man in Germany or Austria, or there is somebody in New Zealand or Australia, or there is somebody in California or Harvard who knows how to do it." But when you get there, they do not know how to do it. "There was somebody in the last century. Darwin did it." Well, Darwin did not think that he did. Dr. Flew sometimes argues as if he thinks Darwin gave a deductive argument, but that will not stand. No, I did not make the argument on *religious experience*, Dr. Flew. You are talking to the wrong crowd of people when you are talking about that. I suggest that you stay with—and try to answer—the *affirmative* arguments. I am at a complete loss to know why you *ignore* the arguments that I *do* make but *invent* other arguments and reply to them. It is sort of like Jones says "X is false" but Smith says "Ah, that is not right, Y is true," when there is no connection whatever between X and Y.

Now let us look at Chart No. 43-W. (See Page 237.) I will not have time to get into this very much, but we will get it before you and let it be the basic thing with which we will close in this main speech. In the Nuremberg trials the Nazis were accused of high crimes. Their defense was that we have acted within the laws of our own society. "Our society made its own laws based on our needs and desires." Did you hear anything tonight that sounded like that? Was not that the very argument that *Dr. Flew* made, that morality is based upon human needs and desires? That is the highest thing involved in it. Dr. Flew, the Nazis did that just as well as you did. Given your argument, there is not one ground upon which the world should have condemned the Nazis. And, given your argument, on people becoming senile or mad, or extremely emotionally disturbed means they are no longer human and therefore are subject to being regarded as nothing more than just meat, no more than a dog or cat or a cow. I submit to you again that he has *joined the Nazis* by his answer to that question. The Nazis said, "Our society commanded us to exterminate the Jews. It would have been wrong for us not to have obeyed. Now you try to condemn us by the law of an alien society." One of the nations was Dr. Flew's and another one was mine. But the prosecutor said in effect, "It is not simply the law of one land or one individual or even of a combination of laws of nations, but there is a higher law which rises above the provincial and the transient." Now notice, friends, if there is no higher law which rises above the provincial and the transient by which the conduct of individuals and/or societies may be correctly judged as either morally right or wrong, then it is false to say that the Nazis ac-

UNDER WHAT LAW WERE THE NAZIS PROSECUTED, CONDEMNED?

43-W

(2)

THE ACCUSED – THE NAZIS

THEIR DEFENSE

1. Our society had its own needs & desires.
2. Our society made its own laws, based on those needs and desires.
3. Our society commanded us to exterminate the Jews.
4. It would have been WRONG for us not to have obeyed.
5. Now you try to condemn us by the law of an alien society – a value system which had nothing to do with the Nazis (claimed an ex post facto law)

THE ACCUSERS – THE ALLIES

THEIR PROSECUTION

They appealed to a higher law which "rises above the provincial and transient ..." – (R.H. Jackson, Closing Address in the Nuremberg Trial.)

[see also: Chart 43-A23]

tually did *real* wrong in murdering six million Jewish men and women! Now on one occasion in this debate he has tried to intimate—"Oh, sure, there is positive law." Perhaps as held by Professor Hans Kelsen of Austria? What is right is what any nation decides is its laws. If that is true, then you can not rightly determine that you ought to punish the people of a nation if they are obeying their own law. And even if two nations get together and decide that a law ought to be passed, that is not a basis for us to execute people. But those men (the Nazis) were tried and convicted on the basis that there was a *higher law*, not that they became theologians but they were *implying* that they were recognizing that there is within man this conscience which can be only God-given and that only a law above mere human law can be the basis for which such a decision is made. And, when Dr. Flew admitted in answer to one of the questions that there was *no value* on earth until *human beings* came into existence, he was joining the Nazis in holding that moral law is nothing but pure *subjectivity*—nothing but a function of the mind. I declare to you that is one of the most monstrous, unGodly, satanic doctrines that was ever taught in all of the world. It is that kind of thinking that led to the Nazis. It is that kind of thinking that is leading to communism around the world. The very heart and soul of communism is *atheism*. Dialectical materialism means that there is nothing but matter and the dialectic means that the ongoing of the world has nothing whatever to do with the providence of God but with *thesis* and *antithesis*, which result in a *synthesis*—which simply means that there is "fighting" going on in the world, there is *negativity* in the world. There is this and that and the other opposing each other, and each situation of negativity results in a synthesis, resulting in something "higher." They are claiming that ultimately the whole world will be Communist, and I submit that Dr. Flew is helping to lay the ground work for it. Dr. Flew, I am leaving Chart No. 22 for your explanation.

FLEW'S SIXTH NEGATIVE

(Thursday Night)

I have met Dr. Warren's main arguments wearisomely often. So I shall not have any difficulty in obeying the rule about not introducing any new material. Dr. Warren has many times expressed his surprise and distress that having put my name to a proposition: "I know that there is no God," I have not provided him and you with a clearly stated argument starting from some series of premises and eventually ending: "Therefore there is no God. (Q.E.D.)" I am sorry that I have thus disappointed him and perhaps many others too. But I do not think I am going to be in trouble on this account with any federal or state regulatory agency for false advertising. For I do not think I have ever written or said anything which should have given rise to the kind of expectations which I have so obviously disappointed.

After all, let me ask a question. How often and when, when you make a claim to know something or other, do you undertake or expect to be construed as undertaking to provide a supporting demonstration of the kind which Dr. Warren so vigorously and so often challenges me to provide? Certainly when we claim to know anything, we do lay ourselves open to the challenge to provide some sort of sufficient reason to warrant that claim. But that sufficient reason can be of many kinds. And, although it may sometimes include some deductive syllogistic moves, the only case I can think of offhand in which a syllogism is the be-all and end-all of the whole business is that of a proposition in pure mathematics. Clearly that is not the appropriate model in the present case. What I have, as you will know, tried to provide is, not the deductive scheme which Dr. Warren wants, but what I think is the appropriate sort of sufficient reason to warrant in this special case the bold claim: "I know." Maybe—I now think not—this appropriate sort of sufficient reason is only enough to warrant the weaker claim: "I do not actually know, but I cannot help acting just as if I did." But surely this is the appropriate sort of reason notwithstanding that it is not the quasi geometrical sort of reason which I think Dr. Warren wished and expected?

Let us review once more what my supporting rationale is. The first step is a matter of method. It consists in arguing that the right starting point is what I have indeed elsewhere called the Stratonician Presumption, or The Presumption of Atheism. I actually did not bring out these phrases from my books into this debate before maybe out of that famous British reserve. But since Dr. Warren used them last night I had better explain what I employ them to mean. My point is that all questions about the truth of Dr. Warren's system and all questions about the truth of any of the innumerable rival accounts of powers and purposes behind and above the universe should start with the presumption of atheism. The presumption of atheism, like the presumption of innocence in the British Common Law, concerns the burden of proof. It is not an assumption that something is the case, it is a thesis about the burden of proof. It is the claim that, if we are rationally to proceed above and behind the universe to some story about the supernatural and the transcendent, then we need to have some positive good reason to believe in this story. If we are going to go behind and beyond what is common to all sensible people of any religion or of none, then we need some good reason for making whatever bold conjectures it is proposed that we should make.

And it is, as I argued last night, important that we should all, in considering any particular supernaturalistic and transcendental system, bear in mind that this particular system has innumerable rivals. Remembering those early Christians denounced as atheists by their orthodox pagan contemporaries, we must recognize that everyone here is an atheist in respect to at least all but one of such rival religious systems. So I start, for the reasons given, from a presumption of atheism. This basic framework dictates a certain orderly and progressive procedure. It requires that we start from the familiar and the undisputatious, and proceed towards the less familiar and the more disputatious. Following the good David Hume, I sometimes call this presumption Stratonician. And, though this is technically new material, I do not think anyone will object if I explain that Stratonician is the somewhat overstuffed adjective of Strato. Strato of Lampsacus was next but one in succession to Aristotle as the President of the Lyceum. Aristotle founded this, the second university, with money provided by this former pupil, Alexander the Great of Macedon. He founded a new institution and made himself President of that new institution, after and because he had been passed over in the competition to succeed Plato as President of the first university. That was technically new material. But it is not really a point of argument. It just seems that, if we are going to say Stratonician, you might like to know why.

Strato of Lampsacus took it, as I do, that the universe itself is the ultimate explainer. It and its laws must be the explainers in terms of which everything else which can be explained is explained. Right—perhaps at this point I should say right on. The presumption of atheism is only an initial posture, a procedural director. So what next? Well, the next thing is to consider suggested moves beyond and behind what is common to all sensible people of any religion or of none. Such suggested moves must themselves proceed on two successive stages. Stage one is the explanation and internal examination of the proposed system. Stage two is the search for reasons for thinking that the system proposed is a true representation of how things are. Now, stage one in examining any Christian scheme must again proceed in two successive stages. Stage one of these two stages of stage one centers on the challenge of evil. Where the particular variety of Christianity that one is considering includes a doctrine of hell, then the first suggestion is that this is flat inconsistent with the infinite goodness and infinite justice also attributed to the proposed God.

Of course, there is more to be said in response to this suggestion though I do not think it has been said in these last four nights. There is more to be said. For it certainly will not do to simply insist that the hell-sustaining arrangements described must be just because the God who sustains them just is just; perhaps even just by definition. That will not do for precisely what is in question is whether a being behaving in the way described can also and consistently be said to be just. Nor will it do to say, as has been said, that the critic has no business to judge God. For there really is no difference in this respect between me and Dr. Warren. To praise God as just is just as much to judge God as to say that a Being behaving as described would be monstrously unjust. I do not stop grading at the point when, after a series of flunks I award an A and congratulate the author on his fine work. Both the A's and the flunks are grading—judging, if you like.

The alternative stage one of stage one is the right move when the version of Christianity is one rather less harsh than that of Dr. Warren's. This alternative consists in the suggestion that the infinite goodness and infinite power of God are together incompatible not with one another but with the familiar facts of an often cruel and wicked world. Again, of course, there is a lot more to be said. Indeed, in my first slot on Monday night, I began to sharpen one of the instruments which any such Christian has to employ in the attempt to meet this formidable objection. That necessary tool is the distinction between logical and factual impossibility. It is, after all, no use arguing in this context that the universe being as it is it would be as a mere matter of contingent fact impossible to have certain good things without certain bad things. For, after all, the God whose credit is being maintained is supposed to be both omnipotent and good and such a being clearly could and would have arranged the facts and the laws of the universe differently. What our somewhat less harsh Christian has to argue confronted by this rather different challenge is that all the admitted evils are the logically necessary preconditions of other and more than countervailing goods. It would, for instance be self-contradictory to speak: either of a world in which there was forgiveness, without there being injuries to be forgiven; or if a world in which there was repentance, without misdeeds to repent of.

Certainly that is the right sort of point to make. Having made that you might try—an uphill task I would have thought, but you might try—to argue: both that all the actual evils of the universe are in fact exploited in this way as occasions for goods which logically presuppose these evils; and that—and it is important to note this second point—these higher order goods are abundantly worth the price. You have, that is, to argue that it is much better to have had both the logically higher order goods and the evils which these goods logically presuppose than to have had neither. You might, I suppose—reverting to the first alternative under stage one.of this stage one—even try to argue that the eternal torment of the great majority of the damned is all made worthwhile by, and is perhaps somehow, even if rather indirectly, a logical precondition of, the delights of the saved. You might, I suppose, try to do this. But it would be an ungrateful task, and the attempt to do anything of this sort would present a rather unlovely spectacle. I think here of what was in my day the unprinted and in the spoken version then unprintable, motto of the Royal Air Force: "Damn you Jack, I am fireproof."

Stage two of stage one of the systematic examination of any proposed system of transcendental belief raises the question of testability. In the good old days of Elijah the Prophet such systems seemed to have been so construed that it was possible to make valid inferences to their consequences within the universe. In those days such testable consequences could be tested as the system of Baal we are told, was tested; and tested to destruction. But these good old days seem to be over. Nowadays we are rebuked if we suggest any such straightforward test. Often we are rebuked with some knowing reference to the Devil tempting Jesus in the wilderness.

Fair enough, no doubt. But this security against the tests that might show a contention to be wrong is bought at a price. If a proposed system has no testable consequences within the universe then, by the same token it says nothing about the universe; and, I would have thought, it must be in some sense irrelevant to the universe about which it says nothing. Certainly we ought not I think be impressed by a challenge to disprove a system—presumably as Elijah disproved the system of Baal—when that system is one which has been so safeguarded that it carries no consequences which are in any way testable.

So much for the two stages of stage one. Now, stage two. Stage two is to offer and examine reasons for thinking that the system in question constitutes a true count of what it purports to describe. Now, in the last three evenings three sorts of reasons have been offered by Dr. Warren. I myself offered another couple of sorts which for the want of anything better to do I thought might be worth mentioning. One was the argument about religious experience, which I am glad to agree with Dr. Warren is altogether unsound. The other was Pascal's wager, which is both unsound and altogether improper—improper because the kind of reason offered is not evidencing but motivating. I expounded these two other sorts of arguments partly to provide occasions for making relevant and worthwhile distinctions. The three sorts of arguments offered by Dr. Warren have been: the argument from the objectivity of value; the argument from, I suppose to say to, special creation; and the argument to design. Since I have said something again already this evening about the argument from the objectivity of value, and I have also this evening said something—with perhaps an un-British degree of vehemence—about the argument to special creation, I shall make my last remarks about the Argument to Design.

Under this heading earlier on I deployed a version, a version tuned up by me of Hume's critique. The crux of that critique, you will recall, was to notice that there are two peculiarities of the case of the universe as a whole which make it inept to apply to this case the sort of argument from experience which takes us from automobiles in Denton, Texas, to manufacturers in Detroit, Michigan. One of these two crucial peculiarities is that the putative cause is by definition unique. The other is that the putative effect is likewise by definition unique. The uniqueness of the putative cause makes it illegitimate to draw any conclusions—revelation apart—about how such a putative cause might reasonably be expected to behave. The uniqueness of both the putative cause and the putative effect together rule out all possibility of argument from experience. We have not had and we could not have had experience of other universes and other causes of universes. So much for the Argument to Design.

Approaching this critique of the Argument to Design from a rather different direction, I have also tried to show that it is no fault in atheist naturalism that it leaves unexplained the existence of the universe and the fact that the universe has whatever fundamental regularities it does have. Every system of explanation must leave some explainers unexplained. And this point is neither met nor changed by describing God as a self-existent Being. To say it is or He is a self-existent being as far as I can see, is to say that this notion is for you an explainer that is not itself to be explained: that it is improper to ask who or what made God. By all means say that. But do not think that you have explained the existence and nature of God by saying: "Oh, God is a self-existent Being and therefore you must not ask what caused God." By saying that God is a self-existent Being all that you have said is that there is not any explanation of the existence of God and could not be. Maybe that is so. But it does not make any difference to the situation as between the atheists, who necessarily leave some things unexplained, and the theists who allegedly do not. They differ here because the things they leave unexplained are different things not because one scandalously leaves certain things unexplained while the other has got everything wrapped up.

By all means, Dr. Warren, have the extra few minutes—few seconds I have got if you need.

WARREN'S REJOINDER

(Thursday Night)

I am afraid, Dr. Flew, you went one second over, so you do not have any to give back.

In this minute and a half I want to just give a summation of what has occurred in the discussion. For two evenings Dr. Flew was in the affirmative. I just want to remind you that there was not one single precisely stated argument made. Surely everyone can see by this time that while there are many things we can know, for instance, I know that I have three children, I do *not* have to set out a syllogism in order to know that I have three children. But there are many things that I *do* have to set out in a syllogism. I have to *reason* about it *correctly* or we simply could not *know* it. You cannot know, as you read a 500 page book, what it teaches without *reasoning* about it *correctly,* and I think really, that *Dr. Flew* knows that as well as I do.

Further, he did not reply to the many negative arguments which I made when I was in the negative. He not only did not give affirmative arguments, he did not really reply to very much of what I had to say when I presented negative argument after negative argument showing that in order for him to actually establish his case as an atheist, in order for him to really *know* whether the proposition is true "I know that God does not exist," he would have to *know* such as that matter is eternal, that matter has always existed, that matter is the only thing that ever existed, that matter is all that exists now, that life has come from matter, and all of that. He paid no attention to that. Now, when I was in the affirmative, I gave precisely stated propositions. I do not believe that there is a philosopher in the world that would not agree that that is the basic way to go about it—unless it is Dr. Flew.

APPENDIX

In this appendix are photographic reproductions of the questions asked, according to agreement prior to the debate, of Dr. Flew by Dr. Warren. Since Dr. Flew submitted no written questions to Dr. Warren (although he had the privilege of doing so), all of the questions themselves are the work of Dr. Warren. The responses to the questions (including both answers and lack of answers to particular questions) are the work of Dr. Flew. These responses are easily recognized since they (including the X's used to indicate whether the statement was true or false) were handwritten by Dr. Flew. All of the rest of the handwriting is that of Dr. Warren (and is easily recognized by the fact that it is all inside of *brackets*). All of Dr. Warren's writing on the Question Sheet is nothing more than suggestions which he (Dr. Warren) used to remind himself of what he intended to say in commenting on Dr. Flew's response to the various questions.

The publisher feels that these questions and answers are a vital part of the debate. Thus, they are reproduced here for the benefit of the reader.

QUESTIONS FOR DR. FLEW, MONDAY NIGHT, SEPTEMBER 20, 1976

1. ☒ True ☐ False — Value did not exist before the first human being.

[Value = subj., a function of the human mind]

2. ☒ True ☐ False — In murdering six million Jewish men, women, and children the Nazis were guilty of real (objective) moral wrong.

[(1) Contradicts #1; (2) Admits objective standard]

3. In torturing and/or murdering six million Jews, the Nazis were guilty of violating (check all appropriate boxes):

☐ Law of Germany

☐ Law of England

☐ Law of U.S.A

☐ Law of God

☐ Some other law (explain): International (Nuremberg Trials) Moral [that was the basis of a higher law? —]

☐ No law at all

4. Of the following statements, check the box in front of each true statement. (If a statement is false, leave the box blank.)

☐ A woman was on earth before any human baby;

☐ A human baby was on earth before any woman.

[DIDN'T ANS.— THUS SAYS BOTH FALSE]

5. It is at least possible that a sound argument (i.e., one the conclusion of which must be true) may involve deduction from some observation (i.e., empirical fact) to (check all appropriate boxes of the following):

☒ The non-existence of some alleged existent event, state of affairs, or set of things within the universe;

☒ The existence of some alleged existent event, state of affairs, or set of things within the universe;

☒ The non-existence of some alleged existent event, state of affairs, or set of things transcendent of the universe;

☐ The existence of some alleged existent event, state of affairs, or set of things transcendent of the universe.

6. Of the following statements check the box in front of each correct answer. (If the statement is false leave the box blank.)

☐ At least one human being now living on earth formerly was an ape (or some other non-human being) and that ape was transformed into that human being;

☐ At least one human being who lived in the past (but who is now dead) was at one time an ape (or some other non-human being) and that ape was transformed into that human being.

[So— Both False]

[SO— no non-human being transformed into human being]

QUESTIONS FOR DR. FLEW, MONDAY NIGHT, SEPTEMBER 20, 1976 (Continued)

7. Of the following statements check the box in front of each correct answer.

☐ At least one human being now living on earth was begotten of a male ape (or some other non-human male) and born of a female ape (or some other non-human female);

☐ At least one human being who lived in the past (but who is now dead) was begotten by a male ape (or some other non-human male) and born of a female ape (or some other non-human female).

[SO—no human being born of non-hum.

8. ☐ True ☒ False Each one of us has a real (objective) moral obligation to become an atheist, so that if he does not become such he becomes guilty of real (objective) moral wrong. [SO—What IS the point to this debate]

9. ☐ True ☐ False Real objective evil does exist.

[DID NOT ANSWER]

10. From the concept of God and the actual existence of subjective evil one can soundly deduce the non-existence of God.

☒ True ☐ False

[chart 22-B; 22-C; 22-A chart 22.] [22-T; 22-U]

[he thus claims that mere individual opinion (disapproval) can properly be the basis of disproving the existence of God.]

Evil: 27-A1, 27-A2

Falsification—19-F; 19-G; 19-H; 19-I; 19-J; 19-K; 19-L.

QUESTIONS FOR DR. FLEW, TUES. NIGHT, SEPT. 21, 1976

1. What would have to occur (or to have occurred) to convince you that your proposition is false? [DID NOT ANS.

2. What would have to occur (or to have occurred) to convince you that my proposition is true? [DID NOT AN.

3. ☐ True ☒ False The following statement is a precisely stated proposition: either a woman was first on earth before any human baby, or a human baby was first on earth before any woman.

4. What known biological law explains the development of the respiratory system? [DID NOT ANS

5. If you met a man with one mechanical hand and one natural hand would you know (please check):

Yes ☐ That the mechanical hand was designed by an intelligent being?

No ☐ That the natural hand was ultimately designed by an intelligent being?

6. ☒ True ☐ False If the Nazis had captured you and your regiment and had given you the choice of joining them in their efforts to exterminate people, you would have had the objective moral obligation to die rather than join them in the murder of men, women, and children.

[ADMITS HIGHER LAW THAN SURVIVAL]

7. ☒ True ☐ False Every precisely stated proposition is either true or false.

[ADMIT LAW ... EXCL M...

8. ☐ True ☒ False The Judges at Nuremberg would have been justified in concluding that, since the Nazis were obeying the law of their own land, the Nazis were not guilty of real (objective) moral wrong in torturing and/or murdering six million Jewish men, women, and children.

[ADMITS THE JUDGES WERE UNDER A LAW HIGHER THAN INTERNATIONAL LAW!]

9. ☒ True ☐ False If the Mars probe discovered a rock with a king's head carved on it, and with a message of gratitude to the king, then men on earth could know that at some time an intelligent being had been on Mars.

[ADMITS COMING TO KNOWLEDGE WITHOUT OBSERVATION]

10. Maximal greatness" is (please check all appropriate boxes): [DID NOT ANSWER

☐ A coherent term; ☐ dead matter; ☐ Living matter;

☐ Non-human living matter; ☐ Human living matter;

☐ Something else? (please explain)..........

QUESTIONS FOR DR. FLEW - WEDNESDAY NIGHT, SEPTEMBER 22, 1976

1. YES ☒ TRUE ☐ FALSE

It is possible for God to be infinite in some of His attributes and finite in others; for example, He can be infinite in love but finite in justice. [We're talking about different Gods.]

2. What would be involved in God's being infinite in love? [NO ANS.]

3. What would be involved in God's being infinite in justice? [NO ANS.]

4. ☐ TRUE ☒ FALSE

It is not possible that the justice of God could entail any punishment for sin. [Great admission - the amount, then, is up to Flew - not God.]

5. ☒ TRUE ☐ FALSE

It is possible that this infinite justice of God might entail at least one minute of punishment when this life is over. — [2 min, 3 min, 1 Hr, 1 Day, 1 yr, 1 million.]

6. I know what the punishment for sin should be by: (check appropriate boxes) [NO ANS.]

☐ by intuition;

☐ by deduction from the concept of God;

☐ by deduction from the concept of sin;

☐ by deduction from some empirical fact;

☐ from the combination of the concept of God and some empirical fact;

☐ from something else (please explain) ______________________

____

7. ☒ TRUE ☐ FALSE [RECOG. OBJ. MORAL STD. —]

All men have done at least some things they know they ought not to have done. [TO WHOM ARE WE ACCOUNTABLE?]

8. ☒ TRUE ☐ FALSE

Philosophy offers nothing by way of salvation from this feeling of guilt which results from knowing that one has done what he ought not to have done.

—[SO - PHIL. HAS NO WAY OF DEALING WITH IT - BUT SINCE HAS ADMITTED A HIGHER LAW - HE HAS MAN WITH SIN & NO WAY TO DEAL.]

QUESTIONS FOR DR. FLEW, WED. NIGHT, SEPT. 22, 1976 (Continued)

9. List below at (1) the attribute of God which contradicts with the attribute of God which you list at (2):

(1) Justice & Goodness Versus (2) Sustaining Hell

10. To obtain and maintain the status of a philosopher one must (please check all appropriate boxes):

- ☐ Sound as if he does not really mean what he says;
- ☐ Sound as if he doesn't really care whether anyone beli , es what he says or not;
- ☐ Hold that no one has any moral obligation to believe what he says;
- ☐ Hold that no one has any real moral obligation to be rational;
- ☐ Not demand of others that they be rational;
- ☐ Not be lovingly and genuinely concerned about the spiritual and moral welfare of people;
- ☐ Refrain from making any appeal (with feeling) for people to follow any certain course of action;
- ☐ Hold that he is one who has no obligation to pay any attention to what he is doing.

None of these are required

QUESTIONS FOR DR. FLEW, THURS. NIGHT, SEPT. 23, 1976

1. ☐ True ☒ False [Reject other Question]

If it is the case that real objective moral value is comparable to market value, then it is the case that it is possible that real objective moral value can change--i.e. it is the case that the torturing and murdering of the Jews by the Nazis could properly come ~~[illegible]~~ to be morally right.

2. By what standard do you judge that it is evil that anyone should be punished in eternal hell?

good neighbourliness and concern [~~DID NOT ANS.~~ (Ans. in 1st Speech)]

3. ☐ True ☒ False [Good Admission]

The fact that there are 10,000 false gods proves that therefore there is not the one true God.

4. ☐ True ☐ False It depends how it is interpreted, but anything like a thorough treatment might refer to both to facts and to conceptual issues

Your proposition (I know that God does not exist) can be verified by empirical fact.

5. ☐ True ☐ False

Your proposition (I know that God does not exist) can be falsified by empirical fact. [DID NOT ANS.]

6. Real (objective) moral law does not exist unless (check all appropriate boxes):

☒ Man is under obligation to obey the law; [BUT WHICH LAW?]

☐ It is enforced; Certainly not

☐ Some one or some thing enforces it. [THUS—NO ENFORCER—THUS—NO LAW]

7. Where does real (objective) moral law exist (check all appropriate boxes):

☐ In matter? [PHIL. ASK SUCH QUESTIONS.] [?]

☐ In man's mind?

☐ In the nature of God?

☐ Elsewhere? If so, please explain. I don't think that this is the sort of thing that exists in at all. These are the wrong questions about such a [illegible]

8. Who enforces moral law?

☐ God?

☐ Man? [His real answer]

☐ Matter?

Moral law as such is precisely not as such a system of enforced positive law, though of course items in it may in fact be enforced by systems of positive law and by other social pressures

QUESTIONS FOR DR. FLEW, THURS. NIGHT, SEPT. 23, 1976

9. What makes an act morally right or wrong? (please check all appropriate boxes).

- [ ] Disapproval by one's own conscience?
- [ ] Disapproval by a minority of people in one's own society (city)?
- [ ] Disapproval by a minority of people in one's own society (nation)?
- [ ] Disapproval by a majority of people in one's own society (city)?
- [ ] Disapproval by a majority of people in one's own society (nation)?
- [ ] Violation of the laws of a nation other than one's own?
- [ ] Violation of no law at all?
- [ ] Failure to provide for one's needs?
- [ ] Failure to provide for one's desires?
- [ ] Failure to provide for one's needs and desires?
- [ ] Some other possibility? Please explain. The first ten answers are clearly all wrong, since something can in fact be morally obligatory even when none of these things apply. I cannot give an adequate and complete answer, and I do not know anyone who can. What I can do is to give plenty of examples of what is clearly right or clearly wrong, and also to specify some necessary conditions: such as that nothing can be moral unless it somehow tends to make for human welfare; and that the principles must apply equally to all those in similar situations

[Flew answers]